BACK
TO
BACH

From Mozart
to Moog:
A Listener's
Guide

ABOUT THE AUTHOR

Trained in Melbourne on the piano and cello, as well as in music theory and composition under the watchful eye of his Bach loving, German speaking mother, Michell was not sufficiently talented to contemplate a professional career. Instead, he backpacked around India and then returned to Melbourne to study architecture. But architecture did not satisfy, so he relocated to London to pursue his growing fascination with the archaeology and art of South Asia at the School of Oriental African Studies, receiving his PhD there in 1974. Since then, he spent time in India each year, accompanying visitors and carrying out research projects, notably at the ruined imperial city of Hampi Vijayanagara. In 2020 Michell returned to his original passion by assuming the role of musical sleuth, tracking the pervasive influence of Johann Sebastian Bach.

BACK TO BACH

From Mozart to Moog: A Listener's Guide

George Michell

UNICORN

Dedicated to my mother,

*for whom Bach was
a constant source of
strength and solace*

CONTENTS

PREFACE

Johann Sebastian Bach died in 1750. Ever since that time, countless musicians have turned to him for instruction and inspiration. In this book, I describe more than 300 of these Back to Bach journeys, spanning the years from Bach's day to ours. Researching and writing this book also captures my own Back to Bach journey, even if this begins improbably in a synagogue. "Why can't they play the St Matthew Passion?" my mother would whisper as we sat through one of the High Holidays during my early years in Melbourne. When I reminded her that a Jewish service was hardly the place for Bach's portrayal of the last days of Jesus, she would snap, "I know that, but the music's better!" And so, each Good Friday, she would drag me and my brother to the local Anglican church to sit through one of Bach's Passions, following the performance from a miniature score inscribed "Leipzig, 25 March 1932". The date recorded my mother's pilgrimage to St Thomas's, Bach's own church in central Germany, as she journeyed from her hometown in Transylvania to Berlin to study piano pedagogy. Importing her reverence for Bach to Australia, where she and my father migrated after fleeing Romania in 1939, she instilled in me a lifelong commitment to his music. I began with struggles over the preludes and fugues on the piano and continued with the solo cello suites, which led me to the back desk of the cello section of the Australian Youth Orchestra during the 1960s. Although lagging behind more able, younger cellists, I made headway with harmony, counterpoint and composition, equipping myself with the rudiments that underscored my later musicological investigations.

Not sufficiently gifted to contemplate a professional music career, I studied architecture – a relatively safe option in those days for anyone unsure about what direction to follow. At the end of 1965, I joined a student exchange trip to India, where I became entranced with Asian religion, art and architecture. In 1968, I relocated to London, where I eventually obtained a PhD in Indian archaeology at the School of Oriental and African Studies. From thence, my explorations brought me to the spectacular medieval city of Vijayanagara in the Deccan, better known today as Hampi. During the 1980s and 1990s I headed a team that mapped these ruins, in collaboration with my partner and colleague, the American archaeologist John M. Fritz. While conducting my India projects and authoring books on these and related subjects, I continued my mother's tradition by attending a Bach Passion each Good Friday in one of the churches in London, where I had made my home. When the Covid pandemic interrupted my travels to India, there was opportunity for another activity, and so began my return to Bach.

At first, I considered writing on the composer's music and life, and updated myself on the latest research thanks to the *Bach-Werke-Verzeichnis: Kleine Ausgabe* (1998), the definitive thematic catalogue of everything that Bach had written, and Christoph Wolff's magisterial *Johann Sebastian Bach: The Learned Musician* (2001) and *Bach's Musical Universe: The Composer and His Work* (2020). It didn't take long for me to realise that Bach scholarship constitutes a long established and credentialled academic industry beyond any contribution I could offer. However, as I read and listened ever more widely, I came to understand there was no comprehensive, accessible survey of Bach's influence on later composers and performers. Admittedly, there were the four volumes of *Bach und die Nachwelt* (1997–2002), which exhaustively documented the reception of Bach's music from 1750 to 2000, but the chapters were in German academese, with no promise of an English translation. There were also useful but brief summaries of Bach's place in music history in the "Death and Resurrection" chapter of Albert Schweitzer's pioneering *J.S. Bach* (1923), the "Reception and Revival" article in the *Oxford Composer Companions J.S. Bach*, edited by Malcolm Boyd (1999), and Nicholas Kenyon's "Bach from 1750 to 2010" section in *The Faber Pocket Guide to Bach* (2011). There was also Paul Elie's take on Bach in the twentieth century in *Reinventing Bach* (2013). But these accounts did not amount to a satisfactory, complete picture, prompting me to adopt the role of musicological sleuth, tracking the responses of musicians after Bach who felt compelled and inspired to respond to his art.

Thanks to the music library in University of London's Senate House, the mostly well-documented articles in Wikipedia, and the never-ending choice of musical treasures available on YouTube, I discovered a seemingly limitless number of Back to Bach journeys. What follows in these chapters is only a selection of these journeys, yet it amply confirms Olivier Messiaen's proposition that "Bach's music reaches all times, all places".[1]

While the many transmissions, transcriptions and transformations of Bach's ideas over the last 275 years called for an historical organisation, to limit myself to this approach would have left out the creative ways in which composers have responded to individual pieces, creating in effect an "afterlife" for these works. For this reason, I have combined the two approaches by interleaving chronological surveys with listings that focus on works that have exercised the greatest "magnetism", notably the Toccata and

Fugue in D Minor, and Passacaglia, both for the organ, Solo Violin Chaconne, *The Well-tempered Clavier*, Brandenburg Concertos, Air on the G String from the Orchestral Suites, the St Matthew and St John Passions, Goldberg Variations, and, finally, *Art of Fugue* with the B-A-C-H "signature". While readers will have to forgive me if I have passed over their favourite Bach aria, chorale, concerto or cello suite, I hope my selection is sufficiently wide-ranging to demonstrate the vast extent of Bach's reach.

With the book as a guide, readers are encouraged to delve into this musical banquet, discovering pieces both familiar and unfamiliar, exploring the Bach connections that lead in so many directions. Readers can browse through the chapters on music history to learn about Bach's impact on their favourite composer or music ensemble, then scan through the Afterlives listings to find how a particular Bach work came to be reinterpreted and reinvented. Because of the many online music sites and music and video streaming services, they will have no difficulty in accessing all the pieces I describe, often in multiple interpretations, sometimes recorded in live videos or assisted by moving music scores. Exciting discoveries await.

At the outset, I must confess that the "Back to Bach" title is not my own. It dates to the 1920s and 1930s, when it was used somewhat disparagingly for the neoclassical music of Arthur Honegger, Francis Poulenc and Darius Milhaud.[2] I have co-opted it here, as it applies so well to the journeys of so many other figures. My chapters begin with Bach's own journey as a junior musician, endeavouring to make his art worthy for "God alone the glory",[3] when he trekked from central Germany to Lübeck on the Baltic Sea to learn from the greatest organist of his day. His own journey ended at the age of sixty-five when, seated at his work bench in the shadow of St Thomas's, he contemplated all the permutations of fugal writing until blindness intervened.

The chapters that follow describe the numerous ways later composers have excerpted, distorted or reinvented the contrapuntal logic, rhythmic momentum, and emotive persuasion that are hallmarks of Bach's art. It was these qualities that thrilled Mozart in Vienna when he first scrutinised *The Well-tempered Clavier*; some 200 years later, they excited Jimi Hendrix in London as he hijacked the ostinato theme of the Passacaglia to launch one of his famous riffs. Other composers set off on different journeys: fugues written on the B-A-C-H musical signature; sets of twenty-four preludes in the major and minor keys on all twelve notes of the octave; concertos that mimic the obsessive figurations of Bach's toccatas; translations of the best-known works into the artificial tones of the Moog synthesiser; and so on. Such journeys are only possible because Bach's music is infinitely adaptable. It is also irresistible: like gravity, it draws listeners inward to explore the architectural structure and mathematical perfection; at the same time, it flows outward to envelop them with excitement, beauty and comfort.

With all the ways Bach is improvised, arranged, excerpted, reinvented, processed and juxtaposed with different musical traditions and artforms, his music continues to resonate, inspiring composers, creators and performers and delighting listeners. Bach, who himself combined so many influences, genres and sources, remains one of the most generative of presences. Judging from today's profusion of concerts, recordings, videos, podcasts, theatrical productions and even choreographic realisations, his aura glows brighter than ever.

ACKNOWLEDGEMENTS

Completing this book occupied many exacting but exciting periods of research. They encompassed some five years and spanned three continents: a flat in Covent Garden, little more than fifteen minutes from the University of London's music library at Senate House; a tropical balcony a few steps from the Arabian sea in Goa, India, where I spent serene months away from London's gloomy winter; and rented accommodations in an inner suburb of Melbourne, my home town where I first attempted Bach on the piano and then the cello. In these and other locales I benefitted from exchanges with Bach-loving friends, who listened to my discoveries, made useful suggestions and scrutinised my preliminary writings. They include Alain Adam, Joy Blech, Elizabeth Briggs, Flavia Campili, Judith Chernaik, Meg Conkey, Oliver Denis, Elizabeth Drake, Jonathan Elford, Ross Feller, Tristram Holland, Barry Jones, Norman MacSween, Paul Michell, Deanna Petherbridge, Christopher Purvis, Eleanor Sims, George Szmukler, Clare Willington and Jo Wodak. Music director and radio broadcaster Chris de Souza read an earlier version of the text and generously offered appreciative comments, while my Berlin-born, chamber-music partner Eia Asen checked the German texts.

For editorial direction and expert advice, I am indebted to George Grella in New York and David Adamson in Melbourne, who introduced me to the rudiments of writing about music and in their different ways helped me find ways of communicating my responses. In London, Iain Burns expressed instant enthusiasm for the project and made every effort to seek a publisher, as did Heather Holden Brown and Kyle ap Simon. In the end, it was my dear friend Alison Cathie, herself a former publisher, who assumed the role of literary agent, steering me towards the Unicorn Group, where I benefitted from Lord Ian Strathcarron and his expert team who have produced this splendid book.

To all these individuals I offer grateful thanks, but above all I must acknowledge John M. Fritz, my professional and personal life partner for over some forty years. Without his unswerving support I could never have embarked upon this ambitious project and pursued it through London's pandemic lockdown and in the years since. It is a great sadness that he could not be at my side as I progressed towards this final publication.

1.

BEGINNING WITH BACH

FROM ARNSTADT & WEIMAR
TO CÖTHEN & LEIPZIG

Born is Eisenach in Thuringia on 21 March 1685 into the long-established Bach dynasty of professional music-makers in central Germany, Johann Sebastian was from his earliest years immersed in music, and likely to follow his father, brothers, uncles and cousins into the orchestra of an aristocratic patron or the organ loft of a church. What could not have been anticipated during his lifetime is that the more than 1,000 pieces of music he provided for local princes and dukes, church councillors and congregations, and even for newly emerging, middle-class audiences, would transcend time and place.

STUDENT AT ST MICHAEL'S IN LÜNEBURG, 1700–02

After training with his elder brother Johann Christoph, Bach spends two years as a teenage scholar at St Michael's in Lüneburg in north Germany. The choral library of the school is supplied with a rich collection of seventeenth-century German, Italian and French church music, which Bach avails himself of. About 50 kilometres from Lüneburg is Hamburg, home of Johann Adam Reincken, one of the last representatives of the great organ tradition of northern Europe. Bach makes frequent visits to hear him play; possibly he also attends music dramas staged in Hamburg's opera house.

LACKEY MUSICIAN IN WEIMAR, 1703

As an eighteen-year-old "lackey", Bach is engaged to play violin in the court orchestra of the Duke of Saxe-Weimar. Its leader is the virtuoso Johann Paul von Westhoff, who befriends Bach, instructing him in all the tricks of the violin, which Bach later employs in his own compositions for the instrument. After six months, Bach is invited to examine the organ in Arnstadt and is offered employment.

ORGANIST AT ARNSTADT & MÜHLHAUSEN, 1703–08

In the New Church in Arnstadt and then in St Blasius in Mühlhausen, both in Thuringia in central Germany, Bach cements his reputation as an outstanding organist. Yet his playing disturbs the church authorities in Arnstadt, who complain about the "many curious variations and …. strange tones".[4] In December 1705, Bach travels more than 400 kilometres to Lübeck on the Baltic coast, reportedly by foot, to meet Dieterich Buxtehude. As a virtuoso organist, celebrated composer and sought-after teacher, Buxtehude is just the type of successful, independent musician that the junior Bach may have longed to emulate. On his arrival, Bach is welcomed by the master, who invites him to participate in his Abendmusik (Evening Music) concerts. On approving his abilities, Buxtehude suggests that Bach replace him as organist at St Mary's Church since he wishes to retire; in return for the post, however, Bach would have to marry one of his daughters. But Bach had come to listen and learn, not to search for a bride. Indeed, he already has someone in mind – his second cousin Maria Barbara, whom he marries on 17 October 1707, by which time he has shifted to Mühlhausen.

PASSACAGLIA (BWV 582) (*see Afterlives*)

After being reprimanded by the Arnstadt authorities for staying away for more than four months, Bach may have composed his organ Passacaglia and sent a copy to Buxtehude before the master dies in May 1707. Satisfied that it surpasses anything by Buxtehude, Bach never writes another one. It stands alone as a mighty pinnacle in the vast panorama of his organ music, "the single most decisive breakthrough in Bach's compositional career and a fantastic achievement".[5]

TOCCATA AND FUGUE IN D MINOR (BWV 565) (*see Afterlives*)

There is some doubt that Bach composed what becomes his most famous organ piece. If he did – which is what most musicians after Bach believe – then it is possible he wrote it in Arnstadt or Mühlhausen, where he begins to explore the melodramatic idiom that displeases his employers.

CONCERTMASTER IN WEIMAR, 1708–17

Bach returns to the Dukes of Saxe-Weimar as court organist, and devises chorale settings, as well as numerous toccatas, fantasias and fugues, for the fine instrument in the royal chapel. This, too, is a period of intense compositional activity for the harpsichord, which includes the English Suites (BWV 806–11) and the beginnings of *The Well-tempered Clavier*. By making keyboard arrangements of Antonio Vivaldi's violin concertos (BWV 592–6 and 972–87) for one of the junior dukes who is his pupil, Bach updates himself on the latest developments in Italian instrumental music.

ORGEL-BÜCHLEIN (BWV 599–644) & EIGHTEEN CHORALES (BWV 651–68)

For services in the Ducal chapel, Bach selects 164 chorales as a directory of melodies for the Lutheran calendar, with the idea of providing each chorale with a short harmonic or contrapuntal setting. In what he later calls the *Little Organ Book*, he completes forty-six chorales, including "Ich ruf zu dir, Herr Jesu Christ" ("I call to thee, Lord Jesus Christ"), with its stately hymn tune floating on a gently moving, inner part. Except for their titles, he leaves the remaining 118 chorales unfinished.

Also dating from his period, though later revised, are the Eighteen Chorales, among which are "Schmücke dich, o liebe Seele" ("Deck thyself, my soul, with gladness") and "Nun komm, der Heiden Heiland" ("Saviour of the nations, come"). Bach conceives these organ works as fantasias, with the melodies carried on contrapuntal elaborations derived from the different chorale phrases.

"SHEEP MAY SAFELY GRAZE" (BWV 208), 1713
Bach writes his "Hunt Cantata" as a thirty-fifth-birthday gift for Duke Christian of Saxe-Weissenfels, a relative of his Weimar employer and an admirer of Bach's music. The work includes the tender soprano aria "Schafe können sicher weiden" ("Sheep may safely graze") accompanied by a pair of warbling recorders.

KEYBOARD CONTEST & TEMPORARY IMPRISONMENT, 1717
Works like the Chromatic Fantasia and Fugue (BWV 903) offer a glimpse of the improvisations that earn Bach the reputation as an outstanding keyboard virtuoso. In September 1717, he is invited to the Electoral Court in Dresden to participate in a contest with Louis Marchand, the most famous French harpsichordist of the day. Marchand flees the city rather than compete with Bach, who then offers a solo recital. Shortly after, Bach accepts a more advantageous post in Cöthen without gaining permission from his Weimar employer, who then imprisons him for four weeks. According to Heinrich Nikolaus Gerber, one of his pupils, it was in this "place of ennui, and the absence of any kind of musical instrument" that Bach

begins composing the preludes and fugues of *The Well-tempered Clavier*.[6] By the end of the year, Bach has shifted to Cöthen.

COURT MUSICIAN IN CÖTHEN, 1717–23

The post of Master of the Chapel Choir and Director of Chamber Music at the court of Anhalt-Cöthen in Saxony offers Bach an ideal situation. Prince Leopold, his employer, is an educated and cultured patron who appreciates his music and provides him with an ensemble of fine players, some recruited from the recently disbanded Prussian court orchestra in Berlin.

SOLO WORKS FOR VIOLIN AND CELLO (BWV 1001–12), INCLUDING THE CHACONNE (BWV 1004) (*see Afterlives*)

An idea of the calibre of musicians available to Bach in Cöthen may be had from the Sonatas and Partitas for Solo Violin and Suites for Solo Cello. Arranged in sets of six, they are obviously written for highly accomplished players. The musical independence of the Chaconne and its suitability as a performance piece suggest that Bach may have conceived it as a standalone work and only later appended it to Partita No. 2.

BRANDENBURG CONCERTOS (BWV 1046–51), 1721
(*see Afterlives*)

In March 1719, Bach travels to Berlin to purchase a new harpsichord for Prince Leopold, where he takes the opportunity of meeting the musically cultured Margrave of Brandenburg, a close relation to the Prussian rulers. Impressed with the players in his private orchestra, Bach revises six diverse instrumental piece he has at hand and two years later binds them in a special presentation copy and sends them to the Margrave. In the accompanying note he expresses a desire "to be employed on occasions more worthy of you and your service".[7] There is no record of the Margrave ever hearing the Concertos performed: never could he have imagined that one day Bach's music would immortalise his title. Bach receives no commission.

ORCHESTRAL SUITES (BWV 1066–9) (*see Afterlives*)

Around the time he is preparing his six Concertos for the Margrave, Bach may also have written his four "Overtures", now known as the Orchestral Suites. These medleys of French-style baroque dances include the vivacious Badinerie for solo flute in Suite No. 2 and the elegiac Air for Strings in No. 3.

INVENTIONS & SINFONIAS (BWV 772–801), 1723

To develop the finger dexterity on the keyboard of his thirteen-year-old son, Wilhelm Friedemann, Bach composes his *Aufrichtige Anleitung* (*Faithful Guide*), consisting of fifteen two-part Inventions and fifteen three-part Sinfonias.

THE WELL-TEMPERED CLAVIER (BWV 846–69), 1723 (*see Afterlives*)

By adjusting (tempering) the strings of his keyboards, Bach is able to compose music in keys with more than three sharps or three flats, which otherwise tended to sound "false" when the strings were tuned according to natural harmonics.[8] To demonstrate the possibilities of his new "tempered" system, he writes pairs of preludes and fugues in the major and minor keys on all twelve notes of the octave, something that had hardly been attempted before. How precisely Bach tuned his keyboards remains a mystery, prompting one keyboard scholar to interpret the ink loops inscribed on the title page as a coded guide.[9] Whatever his system, Bach intended his preludes and fugues "for the benefit and use of the musical youth that is eager to learn as well as for the special pastimes of those already qualified in this study".[10]

TWO MARRIAGES

Bach's productive and happy time in Cöthen is marred by the death of Maria Barbara in July 1720. Eighteen months later, he marries Anna Magdalena, a professional singer, for whom he assembles a Notebook with songs and short keyboard pieces for her to practice. At the same time, his princely employer also marries. Leopold's new, much younger wife is unmusical, and Bach's activities are no longer appreciated, leading him to consider shifting to Leipzig, the principal commercial centre of Saxony, with its famous annual fairs, publishing houses and fine university.

CANTOR IN LEIPZIG, 1723–50

By no means their first choice, in May 1723 the Leipzig authorities reluctantly appoint Bach to the distinguished post of Cantor and Music Director at St Thomas's – a Latin school and conservatory that attracts students from all over Germany. Responsible for music in St Thomas's and other Protestant churches in the city, Bach undertakes a frenzied compositional schedule. Between June 1723 and March 1724, he offers more than forty cantatas for Sunday services and feast-days, as well as large-scale choral works like the Magnificat (BWV 243) for Christmas and the St John Passion for the following Easter. In the next liturgical year, 1724–25, Bach completes another cycle of cantatas, each based on the text and melody of a different Lutheran chorale.

While keeping up a constant stream of sacred music that includes the St Matthew Passion of 1727 and the Christmas Oratorio of 1734 (BWV 248), Bach also directs concerts for the Collegium Musicum, a private society that meets regularly in Leipzig's coffee gardens and houses to entertain Leipzig's cultured citizens. For these occasions, which span the years from 1729 to 1741, Bach presents instrumental works, such as his Orchestral Suites, as well as sonatas and concertos for himself to play with his sons and other talented instrumentalists. To show that he is up to date with current musical trends, in 1735 Bach publishes his Italian Concerto (BWV 971) and Overture in the French Style (BWV 831). Even so, he is criticised by Johann Adolph Scheibe, a former pupil, who reprimands Bach for his "turgid and confused style".[11]

A high point is reached in 1747, when the sixty-two-year-old composer is invited to play for Frederick the Great, leading him to compose his *Musical Offering*. During his last years, Bach devotes himself to "free artistic inclinations and pursuit of personal musical interests"[12] by completing his Mass in B Minor and puzzling out the exemplars in *Art of Fugue*.

ST JOHN PASSION (BWV 245), 1724, & ST MATTHEW PASSION (BWV 244), 1727 (*see Afterlives*)

In the Passion music he provides for Holy Week during his first four years in Leipzig, Bach creates ambitious works to be performed as part of the Good Friday Vespers service. Bach directs several repeat performances, occasionally transferring choruses and chorales from one to the other. For the 1736 Holy Week, he prepares a fresh, meticulously written score of the St Matthew Passion. When its pages later become damaged, Bach painstakingly repairs them, perhaps in the realisation that this work represents his greatest achievement in terms of length, forces required, and dramatic and expressive content. In 1749, a year before his death, he presents the St John Passion for the last time.

"SLEEPERS AWAKE" (BWV 140), 1731, & "A MIGHTY FORTRESS IS OUR LORD" (BWV 80), *C.* 1731

Among the numerous cantatas built around Lutheran chorales that Bach writes for Leipzig, two become especially well known in later times. One of these, *Wachet auf, ruft uns die Stimme (Awake, calls the voice to us*), begins with a chorale fantasia that pits the static hymn of "Sleepers Awake" against a stirringly rhythmic orchestral accompaniment. In the cantata's central section, Bach assigns the tenors the hymn tune while unison strings play a lyrical melody that weaves independently around the theme. In 1748, he makes an organ arrangement (BWV 645). Bach opens his Reformation Day cantata, *Ein feste Burg ist unser Gott* (*A mighty fortress is our Lord*) with another elaborate chorale fantasia, assigning the hymn's phrases to a trumpet proclaiming the Protestant faith high above the voices. He concludes both cantatas with stirring, four-voice chorale settings for the congregation to join in.

KEYBOARD PARTITAS (BWV 825–30), 1731

With the idea of presenting a comprehensive survey of contemporary keyboard genres and techniques, Bach embarks upon his self-funded, *Clavier-Übung* publishing project. The first part of his *Keyboard Practice* consists of six suites of stylised dances ending in a Gigue, Capriccio or Scherzo. In a bid to attract buyers, he writes opening movements in contrasting idioms that include a Fantasia and a Toccata.

KYRIE AND GLORIA, 1733

Bach dedicates his monumental choral Kyrie and Gloria to Frederick Augustus II, newly crowned in Dresden as Elector of Saxony. With its repeated mournful phrases, the majestic B minor Kyrie seems to be a lament for the death in February 1733 of Frederick's father, Augustus II "The Strong", while the jubilant D major Gloria celebrates the ascent of the son. For these movements, Bach juxtaposes epic polyphonic choruses with Italianate-style vocal arias wreathed in instrumental elaborations. Though the Kyrie and Gloria constitute the Latin "Missa" permitted in Lutheran services, there is no clear evidence of them ever being performed.[13]

BACH'S FIFTIETH BIRTHDAY, 1735

For this occasion, Bach's friends may have presented him with a glass goblet inscribed with the B-A-C-H notes, which they recognise as his musical signature (see below). The accompanying lines of poetry express an admiration for Bach's art.[14]

MUSICALISCHES GESANG-BUCH, 1736

Bach assists Georg Christian Schemelli, a former student, in bringing out the *Musical Songbook,* a compilation of the melodies, first verses or texts, and bass lines of more than 900 sacred songs. One of Bach's contributions is "Komm, süsser Tod, komm selge Ruh" ("Come, sweet death, come blessed peace") (BWV 478).

COMPOSER OF THE ROYAL COURT CHAPEL, 1736

Bach gains a formal title from Dresden thanks to the intervention of his friend, the musical connoisseur, Count Hermann Carl von Keyserlingk, Russian ambassador to the Electoral Court, to whom he now owes a favour.

GOLDBERG VARIATIONS (BWV 988), 1741 (*see Afterlives*)

Bach devotes the fourth and final part of his *Clavier-Übung* series to an *Aria with Diverse Variations* (*Verschiedenen Veränderungen*). It is his longest piece of continuous music for the keyboard and by far the most technically demanding. According to an anecdote by Wilhelm Friedemann,[15] Bach writes the Variations to alleviate the insomnia of Keyselingk, who employs as his private musician the teenage keyboard virtuoso Johann Gottlieb Goldberg, a former Bach student. Supposedly the first to play the Variations, Goldberg earns a brief but permanent place in the annals of music history.

BOOK II OF *THE WELL-TEMPERED CLAVIER*
(BWV 870–93), 1742 (*see Afterlives*)

Demand for the preludes and fugues in *The Well-tempered Clavier* persuades Bach to issue another series of twenty-four as Book II. From now on, the two sets are often referred to collectively as the "Forty-eight".

MUSICAL OFFERING (BWV 1079), 1747

The meeting on 7 May 1747 of a provincial musician with Frederick the Great of Prussia, the most powerful state in Germany, was an exceptional occasion, noticed in the official court bulletin and picked up by local newspapers. According to these reports, on learning of Bach's arrival at his residence in Potsdam, outside Berlin, Frederick interrupted his usual evening concert to summon the visitor. Allowing Bach no time to change his travelling clothes, Frederick invited the composer to try out his new, experimental fortepianos by Gottfried Silbermann. Pausing at one instrument, the king gave Bach a theme and requested him to improvise a three-part fugue on it, which Bach promptly executed, much to the astonishment of the royal entourage. Frederick then challenged Bach to improvise a fugue in six parts. Bach excused himself, explaining that he would need time to prepare, but would later set the king's theme in a fugue that would be "ordentlich" ("proper") and have it engraved in copper.-

On first hearing Frederick's long and chromatically complicated theme, Bach must have realised that it could not be manipulated on its own, but could support a variety of counterthemes, which is exactly what he sets about doing. By September, Bach completes the promised six-voice fugue, together with a keyboard fugue in three parts, a trio sonata in the fashionable galant style with a flute part for Frederick to play (he was competent on the instrument), and a veritable magic box of ten puzzle canons, all based on the

"Thema Regium". At his own expense, Bach prints 200 copies of this miscellany, sending one special presentation copy to Potsdam under the title "Musical Offering to His Royal Majesty", which he writes in German, a language that Frederick forbade at his court, insisting that French only be spoken. He receives no reply.

BACH JOINS THE CORRESPONDING SOCIETY OF MUSICAL SCIENCE, 1747

As part of his acceptance by the Leipzig-based Society of Musical Science, which boasts Georg Philipp Telemann and George Frideric Handel among its members, Bach publishes his Canonic Variations on the Christmas Hymn "Vom Himmel hoch, da komm ich her" ("From heaven above, to earth I come") (BWV 769). He celebrates the occasion by presenting the Society with an oil portrait. In it, Bach holds a leaf of music as a calling card with notes on three staves marked "Canon triplex, à 6 Voc". These resolve into three simultaneous two-voice canons (BWV 1076), a musically "scientific" feat that presumably satisfies the Society's worthy members.

MASS IN B MINOR (BWV 232), 1748–9

Wishing to contribute to Christianity's central musical genre, Bach expands his 1733 Kyrie and Credo into a Latin Mass by setting the missing sections to music borrowed from other works. For the Crucifixus in the Credo, for example, Bach adapts the opening chorus from *Weinen, Klagen, Sorgen, Zagen* (BWV 12), a cantata dating to his Weimar days, setting its "Weeping, wailing, lamenting, fearing" words to heart-wrenching, "sobbing" vocal motifs carried on a repeated, chromatically descending bass line. For the Benedictus and Agnus Dei, he repurposes arias with instrumental elaborations from other earlier cantatas. With these disparate elements, Bach forges a work of titanic proportions but never hears it performed.

ART OF FUGUE & B-A-C-H (BWV 1080), 1742–50 (*see Afterlives*)

Bach devotes his final years to investigating all the possibilities of manipulating a single musical idea, an enterprise that culminates in *Art of Fugue*. Writing the different lines of the counterpoint on separate staves, Bach produces thirteen fugues on variations of the same theme, each of which he heads with the Latin term "Contrapunctus", as well as four canons also using the same theme. Rather than an academic treatise surveying different categories of counterpoint, the work has been interpreted as Bach's "last attempt to explore the profundities of music in terms of number and feeling".[16] While puzzling out the possibilities of the last fugue, Bach introduces a new theme beginning with two pairs of semitones – B-flat and A, and C and B-natural – which in German notation spell B-A-C-H, the composer's autograph. Up to now, he has never used these four notes as an independent idea,[17] but here, at the end of his life, Bach seems to be "signing off". Some fifty bars after the theme appears, the writing abruptly ceases. Interrupted by the blindness that descends on him after two failed eye operations, Bach can no longer continue.

"DEATHBED CHORALE", 1750

Before dying of a stroke at the age of sixty-five on 28 July 1750, Bach asks a friend to play "Wenn wir in höchsten Nöten sein" ("When we are in greatest need") for him on a domestic pedal harpsichord. Listening to the chorale, he suggests that it should serve as a setting for the more appropriate hymn "Vor deinen Thron tret ich hiermit" ("Before your throne I now appear") (BWV 668).

BACH IS REMEMBERED, 1751–4

Within a year of Bach's death, Telemann, a close friend of the Bach family, pens a memorial sonnet predicting that "the candle of thy fame ne'er low will burn".[18] Around the same time, Bach's second son, Carl Philipp Emanuel, publishes *Art of Fugue*, together with the "Deathbed Chorale" as "compensation" for its unfinished, final contrapuntal exemplar. Barely twenty copies are sold. In his 1753 *Essay on the True Art of Playing Keyboard Instruments*, Emanuel refers to his father's teaching method, innovative keyboard fingering, and emphasis on invention. (The *Essay* is to have considerable influence on Mozart and Beethoven.) The following year, Emanuel collaborates with Johann Friedrich Agricola, who had trained with Bach and married one of his daughters, in bringing out the *Nekrolog*. Disclosing details of Bach's life story and family origins, as well as listing his most significant works, the 1754 obituary serves as a fertile repository for all future writings about the composer.

AFTERLIVES

TOCCATA AND FUGUE IN D MINOR

While in this work, Bach pays homage to the virtuosic extemporisations and contrapuntal ingenuities of earlier generations of north European organists, the Toccata's gripping opening, "descending like a lightning flash",[19] is instantly recognised as being by Bach. Yet it is only by accident that the work survives: there is no signed manuscript, only an undated copy by Johannes Ringk, one of Bach's organ students. Together with the unruly structure of the Toccata and rudimentary counterpoint of the Fugue, this has led some scholars to question whether it is by Bach at all.[20] Despite their doubts, later performers and musicians respond to what they always believed to be a youthful work, brimming with a "strong and ardent spirit".[21]

Nowhere is Bach's improvisatory and free manner better heard than in the Toccata's opening proclamations that plunge downwards to a pedal D. From this bottom note rises a diminished seventh minor chord (G, B-flat, C-sharp and E), usually played as a spine-chilling, dissonant arpeggio. After a resolution in D major comes rapid figurations and scales that also pause on diminished minor chords, allowing Bach opportunities to offer expressive, recitative-like declarations. The Fugue is equally exciting, being built on a theme with rapid oscillations around the notes of D and A, recalling the open strings of a violin. Contrapuntal development is interrupted by melodramatic arpeggios running across the keyboards. The work concludes with a reprise of the Toccata's recitatives set between thunderous chords.

The relentless momentum of Bach's passages inspires later composers to identify the toccata format with what Sergei Prokofiev describes as a piece "with rapid running figurations that only touch [*toccare*] the keys briefly".[22] There is no shortage of examples.

1826 Oscillating chords and runs across the keyboard in Carl Czerny's Toccata in C Major recall Bach's organ figurations.

1833 Together with the musicologist Adolf Bernhard Marx, Mendelssohn publishes the Toccata and Fugue in *Little-Known Organ Compositions by Bach*.

1833 Chordal oscillations in Robert Schumann's Toccata in C Major mimic Bach's organ figurations.

1860s Piano transcription by Carl Tausig, Franz Liszt's most talented pupil.

1872 Charles-Marie Widor begins his Organ Symphony No. 4 with a toccata and fugue, and finishes his later Organ Symphony No. 5 (1879) with another toccata, now Widor's most popular work.

1901 Claude Debussy concludes his suite of baroque dances *Pour le piano* with a toccata.

1912 Sergei Prokofiev's Toccata in D Minor.

1913 Max Reger quotes Bach's opening bars at the beginning of his *Nine Pieces for the Organ*.

1927 Orchestration by Leopold Stokowski; in 1940 he is filmed conducting it in Walt Disney's animated film *Fantasia*.

1929 Henry Joseph Wood, founder of the hugely popular London Promenade Concerts, conducts his orchestration under the pseudonym Paul Klenovsky.

1930 The ninth section of Kaikhosru Shapurji Sorabji's mammoth *Opus Clavicembalisticum* is a toccata. He follows this with a Toccata Seconda (1934) and a Toccata Quarta (1967).

1931 Toccata movement in Igor Stravinsky's Violin Concerto in D Major.

1931 & 1962 Bach's Toccata is heard during the credits to the movie *Dr. Jekyll and Mr. Hyde*, then in the soundtrack of *The Phantom of the Opera* and in Andrew Lloyd Webber's musical remake (1986).

1973 The Toccata Concertata movement in Alberto Ginastera's 1961 Piano Concerto No. 1 is taken up by Keith Emerson of the English progressive band Emerson, Lake & Palmer.

1980 The pop group Sky improvises on Bach's Toccata.

1982 In *Bach Onto This*, Jon Lord, co-founder of the rock band Deep Purple, quotes Bach's opening flourishes.

1998 Donald Hunsberger's arrangement for the Eastman Wind Ensemble of Rochester University.

2013 The American rapper Eminem reproduces snatches of Bach's Toccata in his horror song "Brainless".

2013 The German family rock group Falk & Sons perform their version of the Toccata.

2014 Arrangement by the Spanish electric guitar orchestra Sinfonity.

2017 *Baroqueswing* album issued by the Charl du Plessis Trio includes an improvisation on the Toccata.

2018 Rainer Hersch fuses Bach with Bernstein in *Toccata Mambo in D Minor*.

2023 Orchestration by Andrew Davis for the BBC Philharmonic.

2.

BACH DISCOVERED

FROM GLUCK & TWO BACH SONS TO MOZART & FORKEL'S BIOGRAPHY

As the eighteenth century progressed, Bach's complex, polyphonic compositions infused with rich chromatic harmonies began to sound "difficult", even old-fashioned. Audiences now preferred elegantly decorated melodies in simple harmonic settings written in the newly popular "galant" style. Though Bach's music was at first neglected in the years after his death, philosophers, artists and writers began thinking about their place in history, a development which led to an interest in older music. In this way, Bach's music came to be "discovered" and once again appreciated.

CHRISTOPH WILLIBALD GLUCK (1714–87)

Abandoning the long-standing conventions of baroque opera seria, Gluck forged a new type of music drama based on Greek tragedy – an unlikely context perhaps to come across one of the earliest recorded Back to Bach journeys. And it is in an aria of exceptional emotional intensity that Gluck first references Bach. This was not an aria from one of the cantatas or Passions, which were hardly ever performed by now, but a vigorous Gigue from the keyboard Partita No. 1 in B-flat Major (BWV 825) that Bach had published in 1731 in the first part of his *Clavier-Übung* series.

ARIAS IN *ANTIGONO*, 1756, & *IPHIGÉNIE EN TAURIDE*, 1779

Gluck's first commission for Rome, *Antigono* is based on a play authored by Jean Racine in 1670. The opera's high point is an impassioned recitative sung by the heroine, the Egyptian princess Berenice, when she is separated from her lover Demetrius as he is about to die. In "Berenice, che fai?", Gluck conjures up a ten-minute portrayal of the heroine's deranged state as she veers from reflection and longing to fury and agony, and ultimately delirium. For the aria's climax, Gluck provides an agitated orchestral accompaniment with a relentless pulse based on Bach's Gigue. Responding to the momentum of Bach's hopping keyboard figurations, Gluck creates a vivid orchestral backdrop to the heroine's emotional turmoil, converting Bach's relentless triplets into nervous string tremolandos with rapid upbeat ornaments, accentuated by brass on Bach's downbeat pairs of semitones.

More than twenty years later, in 1779, Gluck returns to the same Gigue in *Iphigénie en Tauride*, based on another Racine play, which is to become one of his greatest triumphs in Paris. The climax occurs when the heroine sings "Je t'implore et je tremble" as she is about to plunge a dagger into the neck of a sacrificial victim, not knowing that he is her brother, Orestes. Calling on Diana, goddess of the hunt, to assist her in this gruesome task, Iphigénie sings a tormented aria against the same instrumental setting of Berenice's despair. For Gluck, Bach's Gigue never lost its dramatic power.

JOHANN CHRISTIAN BACH (1735–82)

In 1755, at the age of twenty, Bach's youngest son, Johann Christian, settles in Italy, converting to Catholicism to accept employment as organist at the Milan Cathedral. By 1762 he has relocated to London, where he establishes himself as "The English Bach", providing Italian operas for the King's Theatre, as well writing galant style symphonies, concertos and sonatas for public concerts. Among his students is the nine-year-old Mozart. During the year he spends in London in 1764–5, Mozart learns nothing about the music of Johann Christian's father, whom his teacher refers to dismissively as "the old perruque [wig]".[23] Yet before he shifts to London, Johann Christian has composed organ fugues, including one based on B-A-C-H. But was he paying respect to his father or proclaiming himself?

ORGAN FUGUE ON B-A-C-H, C. 1760

Johann Christian had little interest in contrapuntal manoeuvrings and seemingly no feeling for the emotive potential of multi-voice polyphony. Even so, this work for the organ betrays a thorough training in counterpoint in the household of his youth. Johann Christian begins with the B-A-C-H semitones on four equal notes, followed by predictable answers until all four voices are busily exchanging the theme in repetitive patterns. Though he never aims at musically engaging counterthemes, Johann Christian's harmonies occasionally result in startling chromatic transitions. Around the midpoint, he altogether abandons the counterpoint for oscillating arpeggios like those he employs in his instrumental sonatas and concertos. Similar arpeggios carried on B-A-C-H in the deep pedals bring the fugue to a noble conclusion.

WILHELM FRIEDEMANN BACH (1710–84)

While Johann Christian's fugue may not be compared with his father's masterpieces, the same cannot be said of the contrapuntal compositions of his older half-brother, Wilhem Friedemann, Bach's first son. After an unstable career in Halle and Braunschweig, Friedemann ends up in Berlin in 1774, where he takes on keyboard pupils. They include the talented Sara Levi, who, together with other members of the city's cultured elite, is developing an interest in "old" music, especially that of Bach. Friedemann is also introduced to Princess Anna Amalia, a sister of Frederick the Great, who is a fine keyboard player and modest composer. Hoping for a commission, Friedemann presents the princess with a set of fugues, the first four written in C major, C minor, D major and D minor, an arrangement of keys that suggests he is planning a chromatic series modelled on those in *The Well-tempered Clavier*. Lacking resolution, he never completes more than eight of the projected twenty-four. In the opinion of his younger brother, Carl Philipp Emanuel, this was not for want of talent; as Emanuel lamented, "he could have replaced our father".[24]

KEYBOARD FUGUE IN F MINOR, 1778

Friedemann's fugues are rigorously contrapuntal, with clearly defined ideas. That he is experimental when it comes to harmony is nowhere better expressed than in the one in F minor, with its downward-trending chromatic theme carried on a stately countertheme that migrates into remote keys. Listening to it performed on the organ without pedals (Friedemann only scores it on two staves) is to be ushered into a meditation on life's bitter disappointments, sustained on a continually evolving pulse. Here, Friedemann seems to be recalling the expressive intensity of the three-voice Sinfonia No. 9 in the same F minor key (BWV 795), which Bach had written as a practice piece for the son he always regarded as the most promising.

GOTTFRIED VAN SWIETEN INTRODUCES BACH TO VIENNA

In 1770, this cultured Austrian aristocrat with a sincere interest in "old music", is appointed Hapsburg ambassador to the Prussian court. In Berlin, the Baron takes lessons from Johann Philipp Kirnberger, a former pupil of Bach, and is welcomed into Princess Anna Amalia's cultivated circle, where the music of Bach and

Handel is studied and played. Acquiring as many scores as possible during his seven years in Berlin, the Baron returns to Vienna in 1777, and in the musical matinees that he then hosts in his palace, introduces Bach and Handel to music lovers in the capital and welcomes talented new arrivals like Mozart.

WOLFGANG AMADEUS MOZART (1756–91)

Something of Mozart's excitement at his discovery of the preludes and fugues of "Sebastian Bach" is communicated in an enthusiastic report he sends his father, Leopold, in April 1782: "I go every Sunday at twelve o'clock to Baron van Swieten, where nothing is played but Handel and Bach".[25] Mozart's interest in Bach is further encouraged by his pupil Karl Alois, Prince Lichnowsky, who had attended Göttingen University, where the Director of Music, Johann Nikolaus Forkel, is working on a biography of Bach. Lichnowsky brings copies of Bach's keyboard works back to Vienna, which he shares with Mozart.

If the preludes in van Swieten's copy of The Well-tempered Clavier seemed old-fashioned to Mozart, the fugues promised exciting possibilities. Indeed, he is no novice when it comes to fugal writing. Leopold had ensured that the young Mozart was thoroughly trained in counterpoint, basing his instruction on Gradus ad Parnassum, an academic treatise by Johann Joseph Fux. (It is from Fux that Mozart derives the themes beginning with four full-bar-long notes for the fugato episodes that he inserts into some of his later compositions.) Determined to absorb what he has discovered in Bach, Mozart arranges fugues from The Well-tempered Clavier and Art of Fugue, as well as the one in F minor by Wilhelm Friedemann (just mentioned) for him to play in string trios and quartets at van Swieten's musical afternoons (K. 404a and 405). When it comes to the Fugue in E-flat Minor from Book I, an awkward key for strings, Mozart transposes it down a semitone into the more manageable D minor, substituting Bach's prelude with a newly composed Adagio of his own.

Arranging Bach's fugues stimulates Mozart to write his own, encouraged by his new wife, Constanze, who expresses a craving for "this most artistic and beautiful" music.[26] She may not have expected a complete fugue, and for a time she did not get one, since Mozart leaves most of his first efforts unfinished. They include the one in his Fantasia in C Major (K. 394), based on the theme of the fugue in the same key in Book I of *The Well-tempered Clavier*. Only when he comes to write a fugue for two pianos does Mozart successfully integrate Bachian contrapuntal rigour into his own musical idiom.

FUGUE FOR TWO PIANOS (K. 426), 1783

By the time he comes to write this piece, Mozart has already composed a concerto and a sonata for these twin instruments to present in concert with his sister or a talented female student. This work, however, is a private exercise, in which Mozart feels free to invent music with four independent parts, to be executed with four hands on two keyboards. For his theme, Mozart sources the majestic Thema Regium in the *Musical Offering*, a work he would have found in the Baron's library. While accepting Bach's C minor key and basic outline, rising from C to A-flat then dropping to B-natural, followed by a series of downward chromatic steps, Mozart subjects the theme to radical revision. He begins by introducing a pair of insistent notes on the dominant (G) and then accelerating the descent by inserting adjacent notes and tiny breaks. The result is shorter, more rhythmically alive, more Mozartian; significantly, it is also more contrapuntally flexible. He can now manipulate the transformed theme with inversions and overlaps and even give it the right way up and upside down at the same time! Animating his contrapuntal antics with a vigorous trill that serves as a countertheme, Mozart extracts chromatic passages from the Thema Regium to glue his ideas together. The result is one of Mozart's most tautly written, harmonically daring compositions. It is also one of his most urgent: with almost manic energy, he drives the counterpoint relentlessly onward until it reaches a melodramatic climax.

Mozart must have considered his two-piano fugue a triumph, as five years later, in 1788, he recasts it for strings, without specifying whether for a quartet or a larger ensemble, but adding an Adagio in the manner of a French baroque overture (K. 546). With its oscillations around a single note and jagged leaps passing between the upper and lower strings, this functions as a Bachian-style prelude to Mozart's longest, most ambitious contrapuntal creation.

POLYPHONIC FINALE IN THE SYMPHONY NO. 41 ("JUPITER") (K. 551), 1788

Inspired by his discovery of Bach, Mozart finds places for counterpoint in his high-spirited instrumental finales. Wishing to consult Bach's preludes and fugues whenever needed, Mozart obtains his own copy of The Well-tempered Clavier, which, according to his English student Thomas Attwood, who took composition lessons from Mozart in 1786, he keeps beside his piano.[27] Mozart's effort to integrate Bachian counterpoint into his own compositions reaches fruition in the trio of mighty symphonies that he completes during six weeks in the summer of 1788. The Molto Allegro last movement of No. 41 in C Major, a work that rapidly attracts the name "Jupiter" from its opening "thunderbolt" announcements, begins with a quotation from Gradus ad Parnassum (No. 88). After mimicking its first four full-bar notes, Mozart converts the remainder of Fux's exercise into cheerful figurations to create an eight-bar idea enlivened with his own rhythmic energy. Mozart then introduces four short, entirely new themes, developing each separately in imitative patterns, before combining them in different combinations together with the original theme to achieve an exhilarating contrapuntal climax to his entire symphonic output.

CHORALE PRELUDE IN *DIE ZAUBERFLÖTE* (K. 620), 1791

By joining one of the Masonic lodges of Vienna, whose humanistic ideals he is in sympathy with, Mozart hoped to benefit from opportunities for social advancement and professional networking, on which he relied as a freelance musician once he had moved to the Austrian capital. Shortly after being inducted as a Master Mason into the Lodge of Beneficence in 1784, Mozart celebrated the event by composing the *Masonic Funeral Music* in memory of two fellow brethren who had recently died (K. 477). In this short, dirge-like instrumental piece, Mozart incorporates Masonic musical symbols, like the "triple-knock" chords with which the rites begin. He also includes two phrases of a simple, hymn-like melody to be played by oboes and clarinets based on a chant sung by lodge members

In the months before his death in December 1791, Mozart returns to Masonic themes in *Die Zauberflöte*. The opera opens with two sets of triple chords that imbue the overture with gravity, even though Mozart soon morphs them into cheerful, fugato-like episodes more suitable for what is intended as a musical entertainment. In the opera's second act, the triple pronouncements are heard once again, this time in sombre woodwinds and trombones, to introduce the trials of fire and water that Tamino and Pamina must undergo before being united. As the opera's hero and heroine prepare for their ordeal, two men in armour sing of the eternal wandering and suffering that leads to salvation. Mozart sets their words "Der, welcher wandert diese Strasse voll Beschwerden" ("He who walks this path weighed down with cares") to the Lutheran chorale "Ach Gott, vom Himmel sieh darein".

Brought up as a Catholic, where can Mozart have learned about this Protestant hymn? The answer seems to have been in a treatise on composition by Johann Philipp Kirnberger illustrated with different harmonic settings of "Ach Gott".[28] Mozart would have come across Kirnberger's treatise among the scores that the van Swieten had brought back from Berlin. The text that replaces the chorale's original Lutheran message (unknown to Mozart) was probably authored by Karl Ludwig Giesecke, an actor with literary pretensions who, together with the opera's impresario, Emanuel Schikaneder, cobbled together the libretto for *Die Zauberflöte*. Giesecke borrowed the chorale's text from *Life of Sethos*, a volume published in German in 1778 that purported to convey the mysteries of ancient Egypt, something which Mozart's lodge brethren were always fascinated with.[29]

That Mozart introduces a Bachian chorale into this most serious moment in *Die Zauberflöte* is partly explained by his visit to Leipzig in the spring of 1789, on the way to Berlin in search of a commission from Friedrich Wilhelm II of Prussia, an energetic patron of the arts and a competent cellist. After Mozart had paid respect to Bach by playing on the master's own organ in St Thomas's, the then Cantor of the church, Johann Friedrich Doles, who had trained under Bach some forty years before, had the choir perform for the visitors the motet *Singet dem Herrn ein neues Lied* (*Sing unto the Lord a new song*) (BWV 225). Johann Friedrich Rochlitz, who was one of the choristers, later recalls Mozart asking to examine the vocal parts, exclaiming excitedly, "Now, there is something one can learn from!"[30] If this anecdote is to be believed, it testifies to Mozart's instant recognition of Bach's mastery.

Mozart asks for copies of the Bach motet to be sent to him in Vienna. It is tempting to imagine that he also received the music of another motet, *Jesu, meine Freude* (*Jesus, my joy*) (BWV 227). Its central "Gute Nacht" ("Good night") section is scored for two sopranos and a tenor exchanging imitative, stepped passages that frame a chorale melody sung by the alto: it is a pattern that resembles the one in Mozart's opera duet. For this, Mozart writes overlapping, occasionally dissonant steps in the strings, as if to depict the "path weighed down with cares" to be followed by the hero and heroine in their trials. As they proceed, the two men in armour sing the chorale melody in parallel octaves, reinforced with doleful woodwinds and trombones. The debt to Bach was not lost on Richard Wagner, who, some eighty years later, judged the duet as "Bachian in feeling".[31]

FANTASIA IN F MINOR FOR A MECHANICAL CLOCK (K. 608), 1791

Mozart never loses his fascination with Bachian counterpoint. In his last year, desperate as always for money, he accepts a commission to provide music for an organ mechanism inserted into a clock. This mechanical curiosity is to be installed in a newly opened "Mausoleum", in which visitors will pay to view wax-plaster effigies of deceased national heroes, while being imbued with suitable veneration by artful lighting and special "funeral music" that sounds on the hour. Despite misgivings about writing for such an instrument, Mozart produces for it one of his most accomplished contrapuntal compositions.

Mozart begins with abrupt, rhythmic motifs landing on minor and diminished seventh chords alternating in different registers, a melodramatic device intended to attract visitors' attention. Significantly, Bach's Partita No. 2 in C Minor (BWV 826) opens with similarly arresting ideas. The chromatic theme of the four-voice fugue that follows, however, is Mozart's own, even though the countertheme, which oscillates around a single note, recalls Bach's figurations for the organ – another mechanical instrument. After a contrasting, calm Andante section in A-flat major, Mozart returns to F minor for a repetition of the fugue, propelling its obsessive figurations to a forceful conclusion. Though the Mausoleum and its clock lasted barely a year, Mozart's Fantasia lived on as a piano duet.

GIOVANNI PAISIELLO (1740–1816)

Mozart is not the only composer to reference the Thema Regium in the *Musical Offering*; others, like Paisiello, however, are generally content to quote its first five notes only, ending with the abrupt drop of a diminished seventh (from A-flat to B-natural in Bach and Mozart). For Paisiello, it is the theme's royal association rather than its melodic contour that is relevant. A long-time rival of Mozart in securing commissions for operas, Paisiello attracted the attention of Catherine the Great, who in 1776 persuaded him to shift to St Petersburg. There, over the next eight years, he produces music for state occasions, church services and stage entertainments, including the enormously successful *Il Barbiere di Siviglia* of 1782 (a precursor to the now much better-known opera by Gioachino Rossini). Though enjoying the benefits of regular employment and courtly comfort, Paisiello yearned for the adulation of audiences in Paris, Vienna and Naples. On gaining permission to leave the imperial service, he remembers his favourite keyboard student, Catherine's daughter-in-law, the Grand-Duchess Maria Feodorovna, by presenting her with a farewell piece based on a royal theme borrowed from Bach – an eminently appropriate choice. While expressing Paisiello's affection for his aristocratic pupil, this musical gift exhibits no sign of Bach's challenging counterpoint.

CAPRICCIO: "LES ADIEUX DE LA GRANDE-DUCHESSE", 1784

Written as a violin-piano duet in the galant style favoured at Catherine's court, Paisiello's *Capriccio* begins with the first phrase of the Thema Regium, transposed from Bach's C minor into D minor. Paisiello converts its first five strident notes into a gracefully inflected melody, which he then modifies and modulates to mark the work's different sections. Their elegant arpeggios and rapid passages were probably intended for the royal pupil to exhibit her keyboard skills, with her teacher accompanying her on the violin.

It is likely that Paisiello would have come across a copy of the *Musical Offering* in the Imperial Public Library in St Petersburg. Both Catherine and Maria Feodorovna grew up in Germany and were musically educated, so this would be unsurprising. Furthermore, they surely would have known that Bach's work was based on a theme by Frederick the Great, a monarch with whom Catherine corresponds but never meets. It is unlikely, however, that Catherine and her daughter-in-law would have made the connection between Paisiello's *Capriccio* and Bach's similarly titled *Capriccio on the Departure of his Most Beloved Brother* (BWV 992). But could Paisiello have come across this "farewell" keyboard piece that Bach wrote in about 1705, supposedly for his brother Johann Jacob? There is no record.

Paisiello's interest in Bach does not survive his departure from St Petersburg. The *Solemn Mass* he composes for the magnificent coronation of Bonaparte Emperor Napoleon I in Notre Dame in Paris in December 1804 exhibits no influence.

DISPERSAL OF BACH'S HERITAGE, 1780s

To supplement his meagre earnings, Wilhelm Friedemann sells off the scores he has inherited from his father one by one. By the time he dies in 1784, they have all been dispersed. Carl Philipp Emanuel, who spent his last years in Hamburg directing music in the city's most important churches, is a more responsible caretaker than his elder brother. After Emanuel's death in 1788, his manuscript collection finds its way into the hands of musical connoisseurs in Berlin, making this city the first to host a Bach revival. Some of Emanuel's scores are purchased by Carl Friedrich

Zelter, who later uses them to rehearse Bach's sacred works with the Berlin Singakademie, a choral society founded in 1791.

PUBLICATION OF *THE WELL-TEMPERED CLAVIER* & SOLO VIOLIN WORKS, 1801–02

Bach printed only a fraction of his output. Even so, some of his organ and keyboard music becomes well known, especially the two books of *The Well-tempered Clavier*, which circulate widely in hand-written copies, much in demand by teachers and students. In 1801, more than fifty years after Bach's death, the preludes and fugues are issued in printed form by Simrock (Bonn and Paris), Nägeli (Zurich) and Hoffmeister & Kühnel (Leipzig and Berlin), as though these three publishers were in competition with each other. Soon after, Simrock brings out the Sonatas and Partitas for Solo Violin, thereby launching the Chaconne from Partita No. 2 on its independent career.

THE FIRST BACH BIOGRAPHY, 1802

Knowledge about Bach receives considerable stimulus from Johann Nikolaus Forkel's *On Johann Sebastian Bach's Life, Genius and Works*.[32] Based on the *Nekrolog* and the author's meetings with Bach's two oldest sons in Berlin and Hamburg, as well as his own interpretation and evaluation of the music, it is the first such study of any composer, living or dead. Forkel conceives his account within an unfolding succession of musical styles, one more advanced than the previous one, reaching an apex of perfection in Bach. The work appears in the middle of the Napoleonic Wars, when feelings of nationalism were high – hence the subtitle: "For Patriotic Admirers of Genuine Musical Art". By bringing together the national and historical aspects of Bach's art, the biography underscores the growing appreciation of Bach in Germany. By 1820, it has appeared in English.

AFTERLIVES

SOLO VIOLIN CHACONNE

It is tempting to imagine Bach writing his Chaconne for a virtuoso like Johann Paul von Westhoff, whom he befriended in his first post in the court orchestra at Weimar. Westhoff had already published his six solo violin Partitas, offering Bach a model for his own set, which he divides between three Sonatas and three Partitas. For his Partitas, Bach assembles sets of stylised baroque dance movements ending with a lively Bourrée or Gigue. After the Gigue in No. 2 in D Minor, Bach appends a grandly scaled "Ciaccona", better known today by its French name "Chaconne". It takes about fifteen minutes to play, making it one of Bach's longest continuous pieces of music.

Bach's theme is in a minor key (D), with four bars in triple time, with pauses on the second beat. On its harmonic support, as represented by the bass notes that step down from the tonic to the dominant (D to A), Bach writes no less than sixty-four variations. Held together by four-bar repetitions, the variations increase in musical complexity and rhythmic variety to exploit the full range of violin textures: lyrical melodic lines; rapid scales; dashing chords; multiple voices; arpeggios across the strings; and so on. A reprise of the opening theme marks the midpoint of the Chaconne, after which Bach sets off in the major key. He returns to D minor for the last set of variations, concluding with the opening bars of the Sarabande theme, thereby ending where he had begun.

Obviously intended for a consummate artist to excite an audience, the work's musical independence and desirability as a performance piece have always been recognised. Little wonder that of all Bach's solo string works, the Chaconne enjoys the most robust afterlife.

1802 Publication of the Sonatas and Partitas for Solo Violin, by which time they are sufficiently well known for Bach's biographer, Forkel, to recommend them as "the best means of giving eager pupils complete mastery of their instruments".[33]

1840 When wishing to perform the Chaconne in public, Ferdinand David asks Felix Mendelssohn to supply a piano accompaniment.

1853 Robert Schumann's piano accompaniment for Joseph Joachim.

1856 Together with Joachim, Johannes Brahms plays Schumann's duet version at the memorial concert held four months after the composer's death.

1873 Symphonic transcription by the German composer Joachim Raff.

1879 Brahms dedicates his left-hand piano version to Clara Schumann.

1894 Ferruccio Busoni's piano transcription.

1909 Max Reger models his Chaconne for Solo Violin on Bach's.

1919 In his Sonata for Solo Viola No. 1, Paul Hindemith appends a movement titled "In Form and Time as a Passacaglia".

1930 & 1935 Orchestrations by Leopold Stokowski and Alfredo Casella.

1942 José Limòn's choreographic realisation of the Chaconne fuses contemporary dance with baroque gestures. Since then, there have been many balletic versions.

1944 In his Sonata for Solo Violin, Béla Bartók follows Bach by heading the opening movement as "Tempo di ciaccona".

1946 Max Steiner's orchestration of the opening bars of the Chaconne is heard during the credits for the horror movie *The Beast with Five Fingers*.

1959 Ernö (Ernst von) Dohnányi takes the Chaconne as a model for his Passacaglia for Solo Flute.

1968 In his opera *The Passenger,* the Russian composer Mieczyslaw Weinberg includes a scene in which a Jewish prisoner plays the Chaconne, with tragic consequences.

2010 Erich Kunzel, conductor of the Cincinnati Pop Orchestra, transforms the Chaconne into a high-spirited concerto featuring the jazz trumpeter Doc Severinsen.

2010 In *Morimur*, Christoph Poppen performs the Chaconne with the Hilliard Ensemble, who intone chorale phrases supposedly "concealed" in Bach's music.

2017 Illia Bondarenko's jazz-tango Chaconne.

3.

BACH ROMANTICISED

FROM BEETHOVEN & MENDELSSOHN TO CHOPIN & SCHUMANN

Removed from courtly salons and church naves, Bach's music was now heard in public concert halls, where it aroused feelings of veneration and awe. After listening to a recital of Bach's organ works, the poet Johann Wolfgang von Goethe imagined it was "as if the eternal harmony were communing with itself, as might have happened ... shortly before the creation of the world".[34] The new veneration of Bach accorded with the romantic notion that "music, like all art, should elevate the soul – that artists were spiritual leaders of humanity".[35] At the same time, Bach came to be regarded as the quintessential German artist, to be treated with national pride; he was even labelled the "the Albrecht Dürer of German music".[36]

LUDWIG VAN BEETHOVEN (1770–1827)

At almost the same time that Mozart is discovering *The Well-tempered Clavier* in Vienna in 1782, the twelve-year-old Beethoven is in Bonn, practising the preludes and fugues under the watchful eye of his teacher, Christian Gottlob Neefe. So thorough is Neefe's supervision that once Beethoven arrives in Vienna ten years later, his mastery of Bach is immediately noticed by van Swieten, who had earlier welcomed Mozart to the Austrian capital. At the end of his Sunday matinees, the Baron compels Beethoven to stay on into the evenings to play one prelude and fugue after another for him. This early facility with *The Well-tempered Clavier* instils in Beethoven a lifelong reverence for the master. As he was to quip in later years: "Not *Bach* (brook) but *Meer* (sea) should be his name".[37]

As he comes to perfect the classical idiom in his sonatas, quartets, concertos and symphonies, Beethoven never abandons his commitment to Bach, urging publishers to bring out an edition of the keyboard works, to which he offers to subscribe. He learns about the chromatically descending bass line in the Crucifixus chorus in the Mass in B Minor,[38] and makes several attempts to procure his own copy of Bach's score. Becoming increasingly deaf and socially isolated in later years, Beethoven consults Bach as he sets off on a compositional path that distances him from the norms of classical music. He makes string arrangements of two fugues from *The Well-tempered Clavier* as preparatory exercises for devising fugal finales for his Cello Sonata No. 5 (Op. 102, No. 2) of 1815, and the Piano Sonatas Nos 29 and 31 that follow. He also investigates the possibilities of the B-A-C-H motif, inserting it into the first version of the Agnus Dei chorus of his *Missa Solemnis*, intended for the investiture of his aristocratic patron, friend and pupil Archduke Rudolph as Archbishop of Olomouc in 1819. In the end, Beethoven discards the idea, but not before composing a Benedictus with a transcendental violin solo, with floating triplets modelled on a similar violin solo in the same G major key in the Benedictus of the Mass in B Minor.[39] For a time, he contemplates writing a symphonic overture on B-A-C-H, and even scribbles the B-A-C-H semitones onto the preliminary drafts for his last string quartets. Realising that quoting this motif is a compositional dead-end, he manipulates its two pairs of semitones to create altogether new ideas, as in the *Grosse Fuge* and the opening fugal movement of the String Quartet No. 14. With the chorale prelude in the deeply felt Adagio of his String Quartet No. 15, Beethoven's solitary Back to Bach journey reaches its ultimate destination.

FUGAL FINALE IN PIANO SONATA NO. 29 IN B-FLAT MAJOR ("HAMMERKLAVIER") (Op. 106), 1817

For the Allegro Risoluto finale of what at the time is his longest and most revolutionary keyboard work (which he titles "Hammerklavier", as a German alternative to "pianoforte"), Beethoven writes an elaborate fugue. Following an expressive Largo interlude, he announces his theme as a series of aggressive trills that lead to rapid passages broken up into descending intervals. Reducing the trills and passages to fragments, he develops them into prolonged contrapuntal episodes. After a tranquil D major section, he reprises the main theme in an individual, forceful manner by presenting it both back to front and upside down. The trill arriving on the semitone above, with which Beethoven announces his fugal theme, resembles the abrupt opening of the Fugue in F-sharp Major in Book II of *The Well-tempered Clavier*, which is where he may have sourced this surprising idea.

FUGAL FINALE IN PIANO SONATA NO. 31 IN A-FLAT MAJOR (Op. 110), 1821

While in the "Hammerklavier" fugue Beethoven presented players and listeners with perplexing transitions (not always resolved), the fugal Allegro finale in the Piano Sonata No. 31 is sonorously coherent. That Beethoven is concerned here with intense feeling is revealed in the heartfelt Arioso "recitatives" that divide the counterpoint into two almost equal parts. His A-flat major theme in triple time is based on a stately sequence of three pairs of notes, each rising an interval of a fourth, a pattern that mimics the rising fourths in the Fugue in A Major in Book I of *The Well-tempered Clavier*. Unlike Bach, Beethoven sets his fugal theme against continuous triplets and then gives the theme and the triplets upside down in the unrelated key of G major. This two-part scheme, with the second part in inversion, is familiar from Bach, who regularly employs it in the triple-time gigues of his keyboard Partitas and Suites. As the sonata's finale progresses, Beethoven returns to the home key of A-flat. After reverting to the theme's original configuration, he elevates it on brilliant arpeggios to bring the movement to a majestic close.

VARIATIONS FINALE IN PIANO SONATA NO. 30 IN E MAJOR (Op. 109), 1820

Beethoven's study of the Goldberg Variations stimulates him to conclude his two last piano sonatas with variation movements charged with deep emotion. He marks the theme of the finale of Op. 109 as "Molto cantabile ed espressivo", adding (in German) that it should be played "with the greatest inwardness of feeling". The sonata's noble, unhurried theme is in a major key and triple time, with stresses on the second beat, recalling Bach's Sarabande-like Aria. While Bach initiates his theme on a downward scale progression, Beethoven chooses an upward scale. Even so, he follows Bach by dividing his theme into two eight-bar sections, to be repeated, resulting in the same thirty-two-bar length.

At first, Beethoven seems to be echoing Bach, but as the variations develop, he sets off on his own. On the way, he offers some deliberate references. In Variation I, Beethoven shares groups of notes or chords between the hands to give the impression of unbroken melodies or harmonies, as Bach does in No. 29. With its staccato notes progressing in contrary motion against more rapid notes, Variation III recalls the patterns in Bach's Nos 1 and 8. Variation IV has imitative patterns carried on double sets of six notes, as in Bach's No. 3, which is a canon on the unison. (Identical six-note clusters are also found in the Prelude in G-sharp Minor in Book I of *The Well-tempered Clavier*.) Beethoven's Variation V begins with a fugato, with notes at successively downward intervals held across the bar, one building upon the other, much like Bach's No. 18, which is a canon on the interval of a sixth. In his final variation, Beethoven dissolves the theme in dramatic trills, arpeggios and rapid passages that encompass the entire register of the piano. He then remembers Bach by restating his theme, to be played "cantabile" without repeats, as in the Aria da Capo of the Goldbergs. Never had Beethoven reprised a theme in this manner at the end of a work.

VARIATIONS FINALE IN PIANO SONATA NO. 32 IN C MINOR (Op. 111), 1822

A peaceful mood suffuses the Adagio variations in Beethoven's otherwise tempestuous Piano Sonata No. 32. In a nod to Bach's Aria in the Goldbergs, Beethoven styles his last sonata as an "Arietta". The movement ends with the theme wreathed in ascending tremolandos and trills marked "sempre pianissimo". Where could Beethoven have sourced the idea of dissolving his theme into such transparent textures? Once again, the Goldbergs offer a precedent, as in No. 28, where Bach submerges his theme in written-out, intricate trills. Bach presents his variation as merely one among a spectrum of keyboard effects; for Beethoven, however, this variation is an ultimate destination, not only of the movement but of the entire sonata. Beethoven's filigree textures in the piano's highest register leave listeners suspended in an otherworldly domain. For Lewis Lockwood, the composer is aiming at the "starry heavens above" – words from the philosopher Immanuel Kant that Beethoven had copied two years earlier into one of his Conversation Books.[40]

DIABELLI VARIATIONS (Op. 120), 1819–23

Beethoven was always receptive to patriotic sentiment, and so readily agrees to a proposal by Anton Diabelli, an entrepreneurial, Vienna-based musician, to help raise funds for orphans and widows of the Napoleonic Wars by contributing to a compendium of variations by prominent Austrian composers on a waltz of Diabelli's own invention. Admittedly, Diabelli's waltz is musically trivial, yet Beethoven is sufficiently attracted by the project to expand his variations on it into a mighty edifice that comes to rival the Goldberg Variations. When, in 1823, he finally delivers not the expected single variation but thirty-three, Diabelli recognises a marketing opportunity and issues them in a separate volume accompanied by an introduction that proclaims "all these … will entitle the work to a place beside Sebastian Bach's famous masterpiece in the same form".[41] Diabelli assumed that potential buyers In Vienna would understand his reference to the Goldbergs, since by this time the Goldbergs had entered popular fiction. In his widely read *Kreisleriana* (1814–15), the German romantic author E.T.A. Hoffmann has his character Kapellmeister Johannes Kreisler play Bach's Variations while remarking, "I would now be happy to stop, but … the theme urges me irresistibly onward".[42]

The *33 Variations on a Waltz by Anton Diabelli* and the Goldbergs are often regarded as the two greatest keyboard variations. Parallels are not hard to find.[43] To begin with, Beethoven follows Bach by calling his variations "Veränderungen", rather than the more usual "Variationen". Like the Goldbergs for Bach, the Diabelli Variations are Beethoven's longest single keyboard work, taking performers and listeners on a survey of all the compositional possibilities and performance techniques of the day. (It is perhaps also worth remembering that when they were writing their variations, Bach and Beethoven were both fifty or thereabouts and at the pinnacle of their art.) Diabelli's waltz resembles the Goldberg

Aria in certain essentials: it is in a major key (C) and triple time; furthermore, its thirty-two bars are divided into two equal sections to be repeated, a pattern that Beethoven retains throughout. Like Bach, Beethoven often inverts his ideas in the second half of his variations, thereby creating audible symmetries. And whereas Bach builds his variations on the Aria's unvarying harmonic support, Beethoven never loses sight of Diabelli's melody.

Occasionally, Beethoven directly references Bach: as in the rapid scales and oscillating chords in No. 23; the textbook fughetta of No. 24; the gentle pulses on a moving bass of No. 25; and, in No. 26, the flights of triplets passing continuously between the hands in the same direction and then in contrary motion. But it is the eloquent Largo (No. 31) in the minor key that suggests the closest affinity with the Goldbergs by serving as a calm interlude towards the end of a vast musical span. Beethoven's penultimate variation is an extended double fugue in E-flat major. While this has no parallel in the Goldbergs, the aggressive repeated notes of its countertheme recall those in the double fugue in Bach's organ Passacaglia. Beethoven's last variation is a graceful Minuet (No. 33), a counterpart to Bach's cheerful, concluding Quodlibet. Abandoning the rhythmic urgency of the waltz that has propelled all his variations, Beethoven cloaks the original theme in transparent arpeggios to be played "sempre pianissimo" before a rapid upward scale brings the work to a resolute conclusion.

"HOLY THANKSGIVING SONG" IN STRING QUARTET NO. 15 IN A MINOR (Op. 132), 1825

It is after recovering from a bout of intestinal illness during the winter of 1824–5 that Beethoven came to write a chorale of gratefulness that references Bach. This is the Adagio Molto movement that Beethoven calls a "Heiliger Dankgesang eines Genesenen an die Gottheit" ("Holy thanksgiving song of a convalescent to the Deity"). Beethoven must have regarded the string quartet as an appropriate medium for this deeply personal testament since its four instruments resemble the four-voice chorales that he would have been familiar with from his Protestant upbringing in Bonn. To endow his prayer with a suitably antiquated atmosphere, Beethoven writes it in the Lydian mode, in the belief that in ancient times this idiom was considered a remedy for "the fatigue of the soul and the body". He learns about the Lydian mode from the sixteenth-century theorist Gioseffo Zarlino, whose writings he consults in Archduke Rudolph's library.[44]

Like the slow movement in his Symphony No. 9 in D Minor ("Choral") (Op. 125) completed the year before, Beethoven's "Heiliger Dankgesang" is also marked as "Adagio Molto" and consists of alternating episodes in contrasting tempos and moods. Beethoven begins with a noble chorale of five phrases, each with eight long notes, which he harmonises in chords based on the Lydian scale in F (the F major scale with B-natural instead of B-flat). In between the phrases, Beethoven inserts interludes based on a countertheme, fragments of which he overlaps polyphonically between the different instruments. After giving all five phrases of the chorale, Beethoven introduces an Andante episode in an animated triple time written in the "optimistic" key of D major, which he marks as "Neue Kraft fühlend" ("Feeling new strength"). He then returns to the Adagio chorale, which he varies by floating its phrases high above the other players, who now exchange shortened versions of the countertheme in increasingly intricate counterpoint. After this second chorale variation, Beethoven repeats his "feeling new strength" interlude. In the third and final chorale variation, Beethoven reduces its melody to its opening phrase, which he passes between the four instruments, while compressing the countertheme so that its upward, yearning contour takes on a life of its own. As each instrument enters,

Beethoven adds "mit innigster Empfindung" ("with the greatest inwardness of feeling"), an instruction that confirms the poignancy of his prayer. (He had marked the same sentiment over the theme of his piano variations Op. 109, written five years earlier.)

Beethoven's "Heiliger Dankgesang" owes much to Bach. By altering the countertheme of the chorale to add momentum its static melody, Beethoven follows Bach in his chorale preludes. While his chorale bears an overall similarity to those with scale-like stepped melodies that Bach arranged for the organ, such as "Ach Gott und Herr" ("Ah, God and Lord") (BWV 714), Beethoven is more interested in Bach's habit of moving the hymn tune around the different voices, often in canonic imitation; at times, he even displaces it to the bottom of the quartet. Beethoven derives his countertheme from fragments of the chorale itself, which he assembles in increasingly complicated patterns. Found nowhere else in his music, such procedures are typical of Bach's chorale fantasias. By alternating Bachian references with his more dynamic, "feeling new strength" episodes, Beethoven suggests the progress of healing in fulfilment of his prayer.

GROSSE FUGE (Op. 133), 1825

That Beethoven continued to rethink the possibilities of Bachian formats is evident from the fugal finale of the String Quartet No. 13 in B-flat Major (Op. 130). When the work was first rehearsed, the finale's huge proportions and musical independence overwhelm the quartet's other movements, bewildering both players and audience. This led the publisher, Matthias Artaria, to persuade Beethoven to issue the fugal movement separately as the *Grosse Fuge* and to provide a replacement finale for the quartet. Beethoven readily agrees, no doubt induced by the additional fee. The work then appears two years later, by which time Beethoven was dead. (It is perhaps worth recalling that Bach's Chaconne for solo violin also overwhelms a set of previous movements. However, in contrast to Beethoven's fugal movement, it probably began life as an independent composition and was only later appended to Partita No. 2.)

The *Grosse Fuge* is often compared to *Art of Fugue*.[45] For Lewis Lockwood, it sums up Beethoven's "sense of purpose as both inheritor and innovator".[46] Unlike Bach's separate propositions, however, Beethoven divides his *Grosse Fuge* into a series of connected episodes, beginning with an "Overtura" and concluding with pair of Codas. This multi-sectional scheme recalls the episodic chorale finale of the Symphony No. 9 ("Choral") that he completed the previous year. If the overall structure of the *Grosse Fuge* departs from *Art of Fugue*, the master's presence is detected in the principal theme, which is based on pairs of adjacent semitones derived from B-A-C-H. Since Beethoven requires a longer and more forceful idea to underscore this ambitious movement, he extends Bach's two pairs of semitones into four pairs, arranging them into an overall ascending series separated by wide intervals. This pattern recalls the chromatically climbing theme of the Fugue in B Minor in Book I of *The Well-tempered Clavier*. (Some years earlier, Beethoven had transcribed this same fugue onto four separate staves, as if for a string quartet.) Departing from Bach, Beethoven accelerates the last pair of semitones to achieve a tense, emotional charge.

Beethoven announces his fugal theme in the unrelated key of G major, before modulating it into the home key of B-flat major, where he juxtaposes it against an exuberant countertheme. This takes the form of a relentless, dotted rhythm with jagged upward leaps of an interval of a twelfth that soon morph into rippling triplets. Sharing these ideas between the four instruments, Beethoven subjects his theme and countertheme to continuous fragmentations and transformations. Following their forceful first appearance, they contribute to an episode with a mild, rapid note pulse, followed by a march in a boisterous triple rhythm. In a slower central section, Beethoven pits sustained notes against rapid passages to develop a strident rhythmic pattern. In the final Allegro, Beethoven embellishes his theme and countertheme with rapid trills that eventually take on a life of their own. The light-hearted spirit of the "con brio" Coda is a reminder that Beethoven originally conceived his *Grosse Fuge* as a finale to five previous movements, which is how some groups now choose to perform it.

FUGAL ADAGIO IN STRING QUARTET NO. 14 IN C-SHARP MINOR (Op. 131), 1826

In his last compositional year, Beethoven accords the fugal form an even greater prominence by beginning a multi-section work with an extended contrapuntal exercise. The fugal theme of the Adagio in the String Quartet No. 14 begins with four adjacent semitones, a major third apart. While these resemble the B-A-C-H motif, the semitones are closer to those in the five-voice Fugue in C-sharp Minor in Book I of *The Well-tempered Clavier*, also built from two pairs of adjacent semitones. Beethoven's reference to this Bach fugue can be no accident, since C-sharp minor is a key found almost nowhere else in his music – the Piano Sonata No. 14 ("Moonlight") (Op. 27, No. 2) of 1801 being a notable exception. Beethoven would also have consulted the Mass in B Minor: the adjacent semitones and rhythmic pattern of his Adagio theme recall the fugal theme in Bach's second Kyrie in the related key of F-sharp minor. The second part of Beethoven's fugal theme consists of four descending and three ascending notes in E major, which Beethoven shares between the instruments in close imitation. Almost identical episodes are found in the Fugue in B Minor in Book I of *The Well-tempered Clavier*, the same work he had already referenced in the *Grosse Fuge*. With these Bachian allusions, Beethoven interweaves his themes, both whole or fragmented, into continually evolving episodes, modulating them into different keys, even as distant as E-flat minor, in what he himself describes as "a new kind of voice-leading".[47] The result is a musical journey that transports players and listeners into a sublime realm far removed from worldly concerns.

The Adagio is followed by six movements to be played without a pause. They present a panorama of musical formats: rustic dance; short recitative; Andante variations; brilliant Scherzo; furious Allegro. By building the Allegro finale on a rhythmic idea with semitones that recall those in the Adagio's fugal theme, Beethoven invests the quartet with an overall cyclical form, a musical structure that only now does he begin to explore.

FRANZ SCHUBERT (1797–1828)

As he lay dying in his brother's Vienna apartment in November 1828, Schubert asked to the hear Beethoven's String Quartet in C-sharp Minor,[48] just published one year before. Succumbing to the transcendental spirit of its fugal Adagio, he is supposed to have remarked, "After this, what is there left for us write?"[49] If Schubert recognised that this quartet represented the culmination of Beethoven's Back to Bach journey, he must also have realised that his own journey had barely begun. He was two months short of his thirty-second birthday.

Drawn naturally to melodies and harmonic textures of the greatest originality, Schubert had little need for Bach. If Bachian polyphony is remote from his art, Schubert is perfectly capable of combining exquisite themes in a romantically inflected counterpoint, as in the lyrical exchanges of ideas between piano, violin and cello in the Andante of the Piano Trio No. 1 in B-flat Major completed in January 1828. There are even occasions when Schubert composes conventional fugues, like the one in

E minor for himself to play on the organ of the Abbey Church at Heiligenkreuz outside Vienna, to which he made a pilgrimage during his last summer. Its theme repeats the first notes of the fugue in the same key in Book II of *The Well-tempered Clavier*, so there is a Bach connection here. But the double fugue with two themes in his Fantasia in F Minor dating from the same year, which propels the four-hand piano duet towards its thrilling climax, is pure Schubert.

In the Mass in E-flat Major that he was revising up to his death, Schubert inserts choral fugues that suggest an awareness of Bach. Dissatisfied with his command of counterpoint, Schubert approaches the reputed Viennese theorist Simon Sechter but is too ill to manage more than a single lesson. That Schubert is concerned at the peak of his creativity to improve his contrapuntal skills is revealed by the surviving sketches for his last, unfinished symphony. They offer a tantalising glimpse of a tragically interrupted Back to Bach journey.

CUM SANCTO SPIRITU & AGNUS DEI IN MASS NO. 6 IN E-FLAT MAJOR, 1828

Two choral fugues in Schubert's last sacred work bear comparison with Bach. The theme of his Cum Sancto Spiritu replicates the first notes of the E Major Fugue in Book II of *The Well-tempered Clavier*, though extended to accommodate the full Latin text. Schubert follows Bach by overlapping the theme at ever-closer intervals. For the opening of the Agnus Dei, Schubert spreads the words across two pairs of adjacent semitones separated by an interval of a major third (C, B, E-flat, D). It is a pattern that imitates the chromatic theme of the Fugue in C-sharp Minor from Bach's Book I, transposed down a semitone, itself almost the same as B-A-C-H. Schubert has the choir singing this theme accompanied by a vigorous countertheme that emphasises the third beat of the bar, while the brass punctuates the second beat. These rhythmically stirring episodes alternate with calmer, more homophonic choruses to achieve an impassioned plea to the Lamb of God.

"DER DOPPELGÄNGER", 1828

Schubert seems unable to escape referencing the B-A-C-H semitones: the chromatic motif he employed in his Agni Dei chorus recurs in a song written only weeks before his death, which was to appear posthumously in the *Schwanengesang* cycle. In "Der Doppelgänger" ("The Double"), set to a poem by Heinrich Heine, the poet is horrified to observe himself standing in front of the house where his beloved once lived. The singer intones Heine's text against four chords in B minor built on two pairs of adjacent semitones (B and A-sharp, and D and C-sharp). Repeating these chords throughout the song in the lower register of the piano, Schubert creates a chilling backdrop that complements the claustrophobia of Heine's words.

SKETCHES FOR SYMPHONY NO. 10, 1828

If Schubert's Symphony No. 8 in B Minor is known as "Unfinished", then his last symphony might be characterised as "Hardly Begun". Even so, the surviving sketches show Schubert starting to explore polyphonic possibilities inspired by Bach. This is most evident in the Scherzo, which employs a lively accented theme accompanied by triplets. Abandoning this idea after only a few bars, Schubert fills the following pages with exercises testing the compatibility of his theme by inversion, augmentation and fugato. He even attempts to superimpose his Scherzo theme with the one he is developing for a central Trio section. Such ingenuities are hints of a Back to Bach journey that Schubert was unable to follow.

FELIX MENDELSSOHN (1809–47)

As might be expected in the most remarkable musical prodigy of the age, Mendelssohn's Back to Bach journey began in his earliest years. In fact, it dates to before he was born. Mendelssohn's great-aunt on his mother's side, the musically talented Sara Levy, who had studied with Wilhelm Friedemann in Berlin, instils in the juvenile composer a lifelong commitment. By the time Mendelssohn reaches his teenage years, he and his older sister Fanny have been trained in Bachian counterpoint by Karl Friedrich Zelter, director of the Berlin Singakademie. Averse to Bach's rich chromatic harmonies and complicated polyphony, Mendelssohn translates Bach into an "easier" language that he believes will evoke suitably uplifting sentiments in the players and listeners of his day. Wishing to give evidence of his sincere Protestant faith without denying his Jewish heritage, he devotes much time to producing grandly scaled, Judeo-Christian oratorios modelled on Bach's Passions. Divorced from any liturgical context, they constitute what has been described as "imaginary church music".[50]

As one of the leading organists of his generation and principal champion of the St Matthew Passion, Mendelssohn takes opportunities of introducing Bach's organ works to audiences throughout Germany and England. To this end, he collaborates with the musicologist Adolf Bernhard Marx in preparing for publication the chorale preludes in the *Orgel-Büchlein*, as well as a compilation titled *Little-Known Organ Compositions by Bach*. In addition to such editorial tasks, Mendelssohn imports Bachian chorales into his oratorios and instrumental music. Based on German texts and melodies, the chorales declare Mendelssohn's Protestant convictions as well as his nationalist feelings, especially when his works are given at the new, popular music festivals that are springing up across Germany.

ORGAN PASSACAGLIA, 1823

Already in his earliest compositions, like this passacaglia for
the organ dating to his fourteenth year, Mendelssohn looks to
Bach. His ostinato theme is unapologetically indebted to Bach's
exemplar: it is in the same key of C minor and is eight bars long,
but in quadruple time, stepping up to the dominant (G). Following
Bach, Mendelssohn presents the theme alone on the pedals before
adorning it with rapid scales and arpeggios. The melodramatic
chordal statement of the theme towards the end, however, is very
much his own. There is no fugue.

REVIVAL OF THE ST MATTHEW PASSION, 1829

At the age of fifteen, Mendelssohn inherits the score of the St Matthew
Passion from Sara Levy. (It is probably a copy of the original owned
by Wilhelm Friedemann.) Fired by enthusiasm for the work, he
persuades Zelter to allow him to prepare it for performance, and
on 11 March 1829, a week before Good Friday, the twenty-year-old
Mendelssohn directs the epoch-making revival in the Singakademie.
Attended by Prussian royals, civic nobles, and eminent authors and
writers, the event is a sensation and has to be repeated twice.

According to Fanny: "the crowded hall looked like a church.
Everyone was filled with the most solemn devotion".[51] Part of the
revival's success with an audience who had never sat through
two hours of Bach's music was partly due to Mendelssohn's
"improvements" – these included employing a massive chorus of
150 singers; introducing clarinets and a piano; and omitting arias
that distracted from the overall narrative. Two years later, in 1831, the
Berlin publisher Adolf Martin Schlesinger brings out the St Matthew
Passion, not in Mendelssohn's curtailed version, but according
to Bach's manuscript. In 1841, Mendelssohn re-introduces the
St Matthew Passion to the congregation of St Thomas's, for whom
Bach had last directed it in 1742, just over 100 years before.

CHORALE CANTATAS *JESU, MEINE FREUDE*, 1828, & *VOM HIMMEL HOCH*, 1831

As he is rehearsing the St Mathew Passion, Mendelssohn begins writing chorale cantatas in which he adapts Bach's formats to his own romantic sensibility. In *Jesu, meine Freude* (*Jesus, my joy*), for example, Mendelssohn suspends a soprano chorale melody upon a web of imitative counterpoints in the lower voices and strings. Significantly, he sets the chorale in E minor, the same key as in Bach's motet on the same chorale (BWV 227). But when it comes to the words "Lamb of God, my bridegroom", he modulates the voices into E major to achieve a reflective interlude. Three years later, Mendelssohn produces his chorale cantata *Vom Himmel hoch* (*From heaven above*), a more ambitious work scored for a full orchestra, divided into six movements, each devoted to a different stanza of Luther's Christmas song. It begins with a glorious proclamation of the hymn tune accentuated by brilliant trumpet tones floating over contrapuntal choral passages. Thereafter, the cantata proceeds with lyrical arias for bass and soprano soloists alternating with straightforward chorale renditions.

REFORMATION SYMPHONY, 1830

At the age of twenty-one, Mendelssohn accepts a commission to write a symphony for the tercentenary of the Augsburg Confession. Failing to meet the deadline, he eventually completes the symphony but judges it unworthy of publication. Not until 1868, more than twenty years after his death, does it appear as Symphony No. 5.

Since Mendelssohn intended the symphony to memorialise a momentous event in the Protestant Reformation, it is hardly surprising that he should source Luther's rousing "Ein feste Burg ist unser Gott" ("A mighty fortress is our Lord"), from Bach's Reformation Day cantata (BWV 80). (Published in 1821, it is the first of his cantatas to appear in print.) At the beginning of the symphony's fourth and final movement, Mendelssohn announces the chorale in woodwinds alone to create the effect of organ pipes. He then shifts it to the brass against excited, pulsating strings, before converting its proclamations into one of his typical, high-spirited finales. A reprise of the chorale for the full orchestra brings the work to a triumphant close.

"Ein feste Burg" is not the only chorale to be heard in the *Reformation Symphony*. In the slow opening introduction, Mendelssohn quotes the Dresden Amen, an anthem invented by Johann Gottlieb Naumann for the Catholic court in Dresden towards the end of the eighteenth century, and therefore unknown to Bach. With its rising four notes landing on the fifth note of the scale, the Amen communicates a sense of closure, which is what Mendelssohn requires when he gives it in celestial pianissimo strings after "battle cries" on the brass. As an expression of hope, it anticipates the ultimate triumph conveyed by "Ein feste Burg" at the end of the symphony. The effect of spiritual ascent in these quotations was not lost on Wagner, who many years later follows Mendelssohn by incorporating the Dresden Amen into his final music drama *Parsifal*.

PAULUS (ST PAUL), 1836

By pioneering revivals of the St Matthew Passion in 1829, and then in 1833 of George Frideric Handel's *Israel in Egypt*, Mendelssohn was well equipped to author his own musical realisations of biblical narratives. The death of his father Abraham in 1835 prompts Mendelssohn to write *St Paul*. The seven-year-old Felix had been baptised along with his siblings at the orders of his father, so a story of religious synthesis and conversion seemed a suitable tribute. With *St Paul*, the twenty-seven-year-old composer achieves his first international success, with performances all over Germany, as well as in Liverpool and Birmingham in an English translation.

In *St Paul*, Mendelssohn strives to reconcile the free religious spirit of a Handel oratorio with the more circumscribed liturgical form of a Bach Passion. His Overture begins with a solemn orchestral version of the opening phrases of "Wachet auf, ruft uns die Stimme" ("Awake, calls the voice to us"), drawn from the concluding chorale in Bach's cantata of the same name (BWV 140). Mendelssohn then creates a sense of expectation by writing a fugue with a plaintive theme that rises through the first five notes of a minor triad (A to E in the first enunciation) before dropping an interval of a seventh (to F). It is a pattern that recalls the first phrase of the Thema Regium in the *Musical Offering*. The oratorio's fugue begins listlessly in the strings but steadily gathers momentum and drama until it is arrested by woodwind and then brass announcements of "Wachet auf" to usher in the oratorio's first scene. Mendelssohn must have regarded "Wachet auf" as crucial to the narrative since he has the chorus sing the full chorale punctuated with brass fanfares as a prelude to the miraculous transformation of Saul of Tarsus into the Apostle of early Christianity (No. 16).

A more extended, elaborate chorus in the second part of *St Paul* proclaims another conversion – that of the Gentiles (No. 35). Beginning in the lower register, the voices accumulate in contrapuntal urgency, as in the epic opening chorus of the St Matthew Passion. The allusion is strengthened when Mendelssohn introduces a soprano part in sustained notes singing a chorale, as Bach had done in his Passion chorus. To proclaim the newfound faith of the Gentiles, he chooses the Lutheran hymn "Wir glauben all an einen Gott" ("We all believe in one God"), which Bach had used in the organ chorale preludes in the third part of his *Clavier-Übung* (BWV 680 and 681). To portray Paul's spiritual awakening, Mendelssohn supports the majestic polyphony of the vocal parts with woodwinds, and then in forceful brass and kettledrum pronouncements.

SIX PRELUDES AND FUGUES FOR PIANO, 1837

While engaged with *St Paul*, Mendelssohn explores other ways of reconciling his romantic sensibility with Bach's contrapuntal rigour, as represented by *The Well-tempered Clavier*. The result are these six pieces with lyrical preludes in the manner of *Songs Without Words*, three books of which Mendelssohn had already completed by this time, accompanied by fugues that rapidly dissolve into pianistic showpieces. This eclectic approach is already in evidence in the first of the series, No. 1 in E Minor. The prelude features a passionate melody engulfed in arpeggio cascades, while the accompanying, sorrowful fugue accelerates into crashing octaves that eventually morph into the chorale "Was mein Gott will, das g'scheh allzeit" ("What my God wills should happen always"). Mendelssohn's inclusion of this chorale is explained by the fact that he had already composed the fugue ten years earlier as a memorial to his teenage friend August Hanstein, who died in 1827. The theme of the fugue that follows the Prelude No. 2 in D Major recalls the one in the same key in Book I of *The Well-tempered Clavier*, though denuded of Bach's ornaments and dotted rhythms, while that of No. 5 in F major mimics the tripping rhythms of Bach's keyboard gigues.

PIANO ACCOMPANIMENTS TO BACH'S SOLO VIOLIN WORKS, 1840

For more than twenty years up to 1834, when he retired from the concert platform, Niccolò Paganini had proved that audiences were willing to listen to a solo violin if it was played with sufficient skill and theatrical flair. Even so, he never included Bach in his recitals. This was left to another virtuoso, Ferdinand David, who hesitated to present the solo Sonatas and Partitas in public. In 1840, he reaches out to Mendelssohn, who obliges with a piano accompaniment for the Chaconne that offers deep chords to anchor the violin line without interfering with Bach's rapid runs and cross-string arpeggios.

ALL-BACH ORGAN RECITAL IN ST THOMAS'S, 1840

On 6 August 1840, Mendelssohn gives a recital on the master's own instrument to raise money for a Bach monument in Leipzig; it is to be the first to any composer, living or dead. Robert Schumann is in the audience. After hearing Mendelssohn play the Passacaglia on this occasion, he pens a passionate response to its twenty variations "entwined so ingeniously that one can never cease to be amazed".[52]

VARIATIONS SÉRIEUSES, 1841

Intended as a contribution to an *Album Beethoven* to raise money for a monument for the composer in Bonn, his birthplace, this project parallels the one for Bach that Mendelssohn had initiated the previous year in Leipzig. Instead of modelling his variations on Beethoven's piano sets, however, Mendelssohn turns to Bach by writing what is sometimes considered his most significant work for the piano. That he himself thought so is indicated by the title, with which Mendelssohn seeks to distance his variations from the more trivial sets that were so popular at the time.

Mendelssohn's theme is eight bars long, broken into two parts, each further divided into two-bar phrases. The musicologist Glenn Stanley suggests that this pattern recalls a Bach organ chorale, notably "Christ lag in Todesbanden" ("Christ lay in the bonds of death") in the *Orgel-Büchlein* (BWV 625).[53] Not only does this chorale have an identical, eight-bar length divided into two-bar phrases, it is in the same D minor key as the *Variations sérieuses*. Stanley identifies elements of Bach's harmonisation in the four-part writing, with its active inner voices, wandering from one semitone to another to achieve expressive chromatic effects – something found hardly anywhere else in Mendelssohn's music. After announcing his theme, Mendelssohn embarks upon a broad spectrum of pianistic devices, some technically demanding and obviously intended for a composer who is also an outstanding performer. In this regard, the *Variations sérieuses* may be compared to the Goldberg Variations, another bravura performance piece written by a virtuoso keyboard artist.

SIX ORGAN SONATAS, 1845

Named after Bach's Sonatas for the organ (BWV 525-530), Mendelssohn's Sonatas are also arranged in a series of six. They survive as among the most accomplished works for the instrument of the nineteenth century and a required repertory of organists to this day (though apparently not for the composer, who never performed them in public). Rather than conforming to Bach's unvarying, fast-slow-fast formats, Mendelssohn alternates fugues, toccatas and chorale settings, like those he finds throughout Bach's keyboard works, with his own, more lyrical idioms, in yet another illustration of his eclectic approach to Bach.

Sonata No. 1 is notable for its powerful F minor opening, its strident figurations interrupted by "Was mein Gott will", the chorale that Mendelssohn had already used in the first of his Six Preludes and Fugues. The Sonata concludes with dazzling, toccata-like passages spanning the entire range of the organ. In No. 2, Mendelssohn writes a duet between soprano and middle "voices" in his most tender manner against a dark meandering background, before progressing to a chorale-like proclamation and a static fugue. Sonata No. 3 opens with a sequence of fast-moving passages and counterthemes that frame the chorale "Wenn wir in höchsten Nöten sein" ("When we are in deepest need"), which Mendelssohn would have discovered in the *Orgel-Büchlein* (BWV 641). Dashing passages lend the opening of Sonata No. 4

a toccata-like character, enhanced by dotted rhythmic motifs. This is followed by a chorale-type interlude, an Allegretto with a lovely song announced in the soprano and tenor registers, and finally a duet with a flowing accompaniment. The concluding Allegro Maestoso incorporates a fugue with a descending theme, reinforced with oscillating fast notes.

Each of the last two Organ Sonatas begins with a grandly harmonised chorale; in No. 5, this is Mendelssohn's own invention. For Sonata No. 6, Mendelssohn provides an extended set of variations on "Vater unser im Himmelreich" ("Our Father in heaven's realm") also from the *Orgel-Büchlein* (BWV 636). Mendelssohn embellishes the theme with faster-moving notes before offering a fortissimo reprise of the theme in the pedals and then in the soprano register that brings his set of Organ Sonatas to a resolute conclusion.

PIANO TRIO NO. 2, 1845

On at least on one occasion, Mendelssohn imports a Bach chorale into a chamber work. In the Allegro Appassionato of his second piano trio, he quotes "Gelobet seist du, Jesu Christ" ("Praise be to you, Jesus Christ") from the *Orgel-Büchlein* (BWV 604), although in his own harmonisation. At a moment when the finale's restless motion dies down, Mendelssohn has the piano play the hymn-like phrases of the chorale as tranquil interludes between fragments of the movement's agitated theme in the violin and cello. This sequence is then reversed when the strings proclaim the hymn in forceful chords that contrast with quieter passages in the piano. Such proclamations invest the trio with an air of sacred celebration that is unique in Mendelssohn's chamber music.

ELIJAH, 1845

The second of Mendelssohn's Judeo-Christian oratorios has its premiere in an English translation at the annual Birmingham Festival, after which it becomes one of his most frequently performed works. Though Handel's oratorios offered Mendelssohn the most obvious models, Bach is already present in the Overture's extended fugue with a sorrowful theme in D minor, its terse contrapuntal lines in the strings supported on trombones. Not unlike the opening of the St John Passion (in the related key of G minor), Mendelssohn injects the music with growing excitement, plunging without a break into the forceful declarations of the opening chorus.

Two of Mendelssohn's solo arias reveal further Bach references. The B minor soprano lament "Hear ye, Israel!" (No. 21), which opens the second part of *Elijah*, recalls the alto aria in the same key with which Bach begins the second part of the St Matthew Passion (No. 30). The other example is the F-sharp-minor bass aria "It is enough" (No. 26). Its downward trending vocal line embellished with mournful cello passages framing an agitated central section has its counterpart in the St John Passion, in the alto aria with similar words, "Es ist vollbracht" ("It is fulfilled"), accompanied by a viola da gamba (No. 30). Inspired by Bach, these two heart-wrenching arias represent emotional highpoints in the overall panorama of Mendelssohn's most ambitious religious work.

CHRISTUS, 1847

Mendelssohn's last, unfinished oratorio comprises a handful of musically realised episodes cobbled together after his death on 4 November 1847. Though Mendelssohn omitted chorales in *Elijah*, one section of *Christus* includes an unaccompanied four-voice setting of "Wie schön leuchtet der Morgenstern" ("How lovely shines the morning star"). Mendelssohn's setting is in F major, the same key that Bach had used in the concluding chorale of his cantata of the same name (BWV 1). Among other Bach allusions in *Christus* is the melodramatic chorus calling for Jesus to be crucified instead of Barabbas. Here, Mendelssohn employs disturbing, tremolando strings to support the chromatic vocal lines of "Let him die", as in the corresponding scenes in Bach's two Passions. For the closing chorus ("He reflects on…"), he writes a specially invented chorale intended to mirror those in the St Matthew Passion. Such references sum up Mendelssohn's repurposing of Bach's choruses and chorales for a work based on a variety of biblical sources.

IGNAZ MOSCHELES (1794–1870)
& JOHANN NEPOMUK HUMMEL (1778–1837)

As Mendelssohn is devising preludes and fugues for the piano and organ, other composers who also had careers as pianists and teachers disengaged Bach's preludes from his fugues to produce sets of twenty-four preludes in the spirit of *The Well-tempered Clavier.* By now, most pianos are tuned to a standard, equal-tempered system, so the only purpose in writing pieces in all the major and minor keys is to style them as technical demonstrations and call them "Studies". So firmly did this paradigm of twenty-four pieces in all the keys imprint itself on the piano repertoire that many such sets now begin to appear, such as the *Preludes and Exercises* of Muzio Clementi in 1811, and the *24 Studies* of Friedrich Kalkbrenner in 1816. However, it is those of Moscheles and Hummel that prove the most influential.

ÉTUDES DE PERFECTIONNEMENT, 1824

One of the outstanding virtuosos of his day, the Prague-born Moscheles was a friend of Beethoven and teacher of the teenage Mendelssohn, who later invites him to become a professor of piano studies in his newly established Conservatorium of Music in Leipzig. Before he settles in Leipzig in 1846, Moscheles produces much piano music with pedagogic intent. They include the twenty-four *Studies of Perfectioning*, which he subtitles "For the attainment of perfect equality and great brilliance of touch" – not unlike Bach's "for the improvement of musical youth" inscription in *The Well-tempered Clavier*. Aiming at developing the player's technique, Moscheles highlights specific pianistic problems. In the first four studies, for example, he calls on expertise with speedy right-hand passages, dense chord clusters, rapid chromatic scales, and arpeggios over several octaves.

Though Moscheles preferred composing according to the fashion of the day, he never forgets *The Well-tempered Clavier*. In 1861, towards the end of a long career, he transcribes twenty of Bach's preludes for one or two pianos with a supporting cello line. By labelling these arrangements as *Studies in Melodious Counterpoint*, Moscheles discloses his romantic approach to Bachian polyphony.

24 GRANDES ÉTUDES, c. 1834

Like Moscheles, the Austrian composer and pianist Hummel was also intent on producing a set of twenty-four pedagogical exercises. In 1818, he authors *A Complete Theoretical and Practical Course of Instruction on the Art of Playing the Pianoforte*, a treatise that is to influence future generations of teachers and students. About sixteen years later, he brings out his *24 Great Studies*, each focusing on a particular technical problem to be mastered when played at the greatest speed: scales in contrary motion (No. 1); continuous thirds (No. 3); flowing arpeggios (No. 5); oscillating sixths (No. 14); sustained trills (No. 22); and so on. Though he calls his pieces "studies" rather than "preludes", Hummel occasionally has *The Well-tempered Clavier* in mind: the jagged rhythms in his G minor Etude (No. 4), for instance, recall those in Bach's prelude in the same key in Book II, while the four-voice "Fughetto" in the D minor Etude (No. 6) is based on a theme vaguely resembling that of the Fugue in C Major in Book I. Rather than following Bach's chromatic sequence, however, Hummel organises his studies in pairs of major and minor keys on the same note in ascending cycles of fifths (C major and C minor; G major and G minor; etc.).

FRÉDERIC CHOPIN (1810–49)

The Back to Bach journeys of Moscheles and Hummel are dominated by sets of twenty-four pieces in all the keys that would present players with a variety of technical challenges: they make no attempt to match the range of musical ideas in *The Well-tempered Clavier*. This was left to Chopin, who integrated what he had learned from Bach into his own unique poetic sensibility. Chopin constantly practiced Bach's preludes and fugues, ordering his students in Paris to do likewise, ensuring them "that this will be your best means to make progress".[54]

Between 1829 and 1835, Chopin composed two sets of *12 Études* that explore the twenty-four-piece format. Though these did not systematically cover all the major and minor keys, references to Bach are unmistakable. The first set begins with Étude No.1 in C Major, in which Chopin converts Bach's two-hand, single-position arpeggios in the first prelude in Book I of *The Well-tempered Clavier* into a dazzling, right-hand sweep up and down the keyboard. The second sets ends with a B-A-C-H tribute in Étude No. 12 in C Minor, which features arpeggios in both hands to be executed "al fuoco". As this fury of fast-track passages takes off, the notes E-flat, D, F and E-flat are clearly heard. When repeated, Chopin raises the last note to E-natural, thereby replicating the B-A-C-H semitones transposed down a perfect fifth. As the study proceeds, these semitones are extended into a variety of themes, thereby maintaining Bach's presence.

Full coverage of all the keys is only achieved in the later *24 Préludes*, in which Chopin systematically pairs major and related minor keys in cycles of fifths (C major and A minor; G major and E minor; etc.), in the belief that this arrangement would be better facilitate performing the preludes as a group – something Bach had never imagined. During a miserable two months on the island of Majorca in the winter of 1838–9, Chopin applies the finishing touches to his *24 Préludes*, "encouraged" by a copy of *The Well-tempered Clavier* that forms part of his luggage.

24 PRÉLUDES, 1839

Chopin's miniature masterpieces occupy an unrivalled place in the piano repertoire, admired to this day for their musical originality and exquisite pianistic textures. While each prelude explores a single idea, Chopin intends them to be performed in a sequence. For this reason, he often aims at striking contrasts between adjacent preludes: for example, between the reflective, simplicity of the A Major Mazurka-like Andantino and the rapid passages of the F-sharp Minor Molto Agitato that follows; between the noble grandeur of the E Major Largo and the intricate filigree of the Molto Allegro in C-sharp Minor; and between the wild fury of the E-flat Minor Allegro to be executed at top speed and the lyrical phrases of the D-flat Major "Raindrop" Sostenuto. For the final D Minor prelude, Chopin writes an Allegro Appassionato in a heroic Beethovian manner supplied with brilliant trills and runs. Like Bach, Chopin encompasses the greatest range of musical formats, while at the same time surveying techniques that expand the acoustic and technical possibilities of the piano, just about the only instrument for which he ever composed.

Among Chopin's affinities with Bach are discrete references to *The Well-tempered Clavier*: the broken chords concealing inner voices in Chopin's C Major Agitato parallel those of the prelude in the same key in Book I; the left-hand passages in Chopin's G major Vivace resemble those in the E Minor Prelude (also in Book I); and the harmonic ambiguities of Chopin's A Minor Lento recall Bach's chromaticism in the A Minor Prelude in Book II. Some preludes recall other works of Bach: the pulsating chords in Chopin's E Minor Prelude are based on a chromatically descending bass line that recalls that in the E minor Crucifixus chorus in the Mass in B Minor; the repeated A-flat/G-sharp notes in the D-flat Major Prelude resemble a pedal point in one of Bach's organ toccatas; the rapid, abrupt outbursts in the C Minor Prelude recall Bach's improvisatory flourishes in the Chromatic Fantasia. Other preludes reveal a hint of Bachian counterpoint, as in the lyrical melody concealed in the incessant triplets in the E-flat Major Prelude, or the multiple voices in the dreamy Piu Lento section of the F-Sharp Major Prelude. Like Bach, Chopin creates musical lines that serve both as a harmonic support and an expressive melody, as in the eloquent B Minor Assai Lento.

With his *24 Préludes*, Chopin does not entirely exhaust his Back to Bach journey. In 1841, he writes his Fugue in A Minor for two voices alone, one for each hand. Its drooping chromatic theme recalls that in the similarly two-voiced Fugue in E Minor in Book I of *The Well-tempered Clavier*. Published only after his death in 1849, this solitary fugue reveals Chopin's enduring preoccupation with Bach.

Chopin's *24 Préludes* contribute to the long-lasting afterlife of this Bachian keyboard archetype. Among the many successors are the *25 Preludes in All the Major and Minor Keys*, written in 1844 by the French composer and virtuoso pianist Charles-Valentin Alkan. (The increase in number is explained by the addition of a second C major prelude.) Styling his technically demanding preludes as character pieces, Alkan gives them whimsical titles such as "In the Gothic Style" and "I was asleep, but my heart was awake". He also introduces Jewish themes that reflect his religious background, as in his "Old Synagogue Melody" prelude.

LOUIS SPOHR (1784–1859)

As this German musician was developing his career as a virtuoso violinist and prolific composer, especially of concertos for him to perform (he wrote eighteen), Spohr promoted Bach, directing the first complete performance of the St Matthew Passion in Kassel on Good Friday in 1833, and again in 1845 and 1851. When it came to writing his own Passion oratorio, *The Saviour's Last Hours* (1835), Spohr follows Bach's format with the words of Christ assigned to a bass singer, with other soloists taking the roles of the characters and the choir providing support. But there is, however, little musical influence other than the eloquent fugal introduction. Soon after, however, he conceives the novel idea of a symphony that would convey a panorama of music history, beginning with Bach, who is accorded first place as the "ancestor" of everything to come.

HISTORICAL SYMPHONY, 1839

Spohr's Symphony No. 6, subtitled "In the Style and Taste of Four Different Periods", presents a chronology of movements from "Bach-Handel Period, 1720" to "Very Latest, 1840". Rather than directly quoting from composers, Spohr transforms their musical ideas into new symphonic materials. The first movement opens with a Largo introduction before proceeding to an Allegro moderato fugue. Both are based on a theme that reproduces the stepped outline and rhythmic pattern of the Fugue in C Major from Book I of *The Well-tempered Clavier*, though expanded into four bars and transposed into G major. Spohr's contrapuntal competence is much in evidence in the thematic overlaps with which he creates an orchestral richness far removed from Bach. In the movement's central Pastorale section, Spohr sources "He shall feed his flock like a shepherd" from Handel's *Messiah*, after which he returns to Bach. Departing from the conventional first movement of a classical symphony, this tripartite scheme serves Spohr's purpose of incorporating past ideas into his own idiom.

ROBERT SCHUMANN (1810–56) & CLARA SCHUMANN (1819–96)

Bach plays a central role in Robert Schumann's courtship of Clara Wieck, who he would eventually marry in 1840. Writing to her in 1839, Robert imagines a future happiness, in which she would "love Bach in me".[55] After their marriage in Leipzig (vehemently opposed by Clara's father, Friedrich Wieck, who had trained his daughter to become one of the finest pianists of the day), the couple devote themselves to studying the preludes and fugues, often spending evenings playing four-hand piano arrangements of Bach's organ works. "Let The Well-Tempered Clavier be your daily bread", Robert counsels Clara,[56] who complies by including Bach in her concert recitals. Meanwhile, Robert scrutinises the preludes and fugues, and even begins authoring a treatise on fugal composition. In 1842, he displays his contrapuntal competence in the Piano Quintet in E-flat Major by contriving a fugal climax that ingeniously combines themes drawn from the work's first and last movements.

Robert and Clara each compose fugues as part of what Clara described as a mutual "Fugenpassion".[57] Suffering from increasing bouts of physical weakness and mental instability, Robert discovers that counterpoint brings welcome relief in what becomes, in effect, a therapeutic Back to Bach journey. Recovering from a distressing episode towards the end of 1844, he writes fugues and canons for the keyboard, many intended for a pedal piano, a domestic instrument with foot pedals. Schumann finds places for canons in his instrumental music, as in his Piano Trio No. 2 of 1847, and even conceals a canon in the so-called "Ghost Variations" that he completes just days before being admitted to an asylum on 4 March 1854. When, during the previous year, his friend, the violinist Joseph Joachim, wished to give Bach's Chaconne in concert, Schumann produces a piano accompaniment, which he eventually does for almost all of Bach's solo string works.

Clara outlives Robert by forty years and is much in demand on concert platforms throughout Europe. Though regularly presenting compositions by her husband, she avoids the Bach-inspired contrapuntal pieces, perhaps in the belief that they were conceived as private exercises.

TOCCATA IN C MAJOR, 1833

This piano work stands as one of the earliest markers along Schumann's Back to Bach journey. The Toccata begins with strident proclamations before progressing to relentless, oscillating chords to be played at the highest speed. Though imitating similar passages in Bach's majestic organ works, the syncopations and chromatic dissonances are Schumann's own, as are the captivating refrains that replace Bach's recitative-like phrases. By the time he completes his Toccata, Schumann can no longer play it, having permanently damaged two fingers on his right hand. From now on, he devotes himself exclusively to composition, much encouraged by Clara, with whom he is falling in love.

FOUR FUGUES, 1845

In these contrapuntal exercises for the piano, Schumann sources ideas from *The Well-tempered Clavier*. He builds the theme of No. 1 in D Minor, for example, on stately triple notes that progress upwards and downwards in intervals of fourths and sixths, much like those in the Fugue in A Major in Bach's Book I. Schumann's No. 2, also in D minor, begins with a downward interval of a fourth followed by a leap upwards of a minor ninth (D to A to a high B-flat): this is a pattern that replicates the theme of the five-voice

Fugue in B-flat Minor in Book I. While the other two fugues make no such references, Schumann's contrapuntal inventiveness and harmonic richness are much in evidence, best seen in the counterthemes that take on a life of their own. In the Fugue No. 4 in F major, Schumann alters and expands his theme until it evolves into a new idea that he then develops independently.

THREE PRELUDES AND FUGUES, 1845

As Robert is writing his *Four Fugues*, Clara is occupied with her set of three, each of which exhibits musical independence from those of her husband. Clara's first prelude features a serene, though restless, syncopated motif in four parts, progressing from A-flat major to C major, concluding in the home key of C minor. The three-voice fugue that follows is structured from a new theme with rapid notes, which are then inverted and doubled in sixths in a manner recalling Bach. In contrast, the tender melody floating on lightly scored arpeggios in the second prelude is very much Clara's own. The third prelude and fugue each employ the same pair of double-beat notes followed by four repeated, single-beat notes. While this motif appears calmly in the prelude, it is chromatically extended in the fugue before appearing in one-bar stretto overlaps.

SIX STUDIES IN CANONIC FORM, 1845

These strictly contrapuntal works for the pedal piano represent a highpoint in Robert's Back to Bach journey. Intrigued by the canons in the Goldberg Variations, Schumann devises six of his own, investing each with a melodic facility that conceals the two-part, imitative structure. Pleased with the results, he sends a copy of his Six Studies to Heinrich Dorn, his first counterpoint teacher.

Schumann makes no attempt to match Bach's catalogue of canons on all the notes of the scale. Satisfied with writing those on the unison and the intervals of the fifth and octave only, he creates a medley of forms that represent, in miniature, the scope of his musical art. Two of the Six Studies are instrumental, with persistent toccata-like oscillating passages, or vigorous, repeated staccato punctuations; another two are conceived as vocal duets for overlapping voices that display Schumann's irrepressible lyricism; the last recalls a stately chorale.

The infectious charm of the Six Studies guarantees them an enduring afterlife: Georges Bizet arranges them for piano duet in 1873, while Claude Debussy proposes two pianos in 1900. Since then, there have been several instrumental versions.

SIX FUGUES ON B-A-C-H, 1845

Schumann works diligently on these fugues for an organ or pedal piano, in the belief that they might complete Bach's unfinished *Art of Fugue*. As in Bach's last project, Schumann pursues the possibilities of using a single theme (in this case, the B-A-C-H motif) by altering its melodic and rhythmic contour by augmentation, diminution and stretto. In his fourth fugue, he even quotes it back to front, marking it "tema retrograde".

Each of Schumann's *Six Fugues* is based on a version of B-A-C-H that generates an independent "character piece". Schumann here gives reign to his poetic sensibility, as expressed in flowing harmonies and sensitive melodies. Both are apparent in the first fugue, where Schumann directs the four stately, half-bar B-A-C-H semitones upwards at progressively higher intervals. In the second fugue, he transforms B-A-C-H into a jagged, restless motif, setting it within oscillating, repeated passages that recall one of Bach's organ toccatas, but rearranges the semitones in downward steps in the fourth fugue, before extending the theme with two additional pairs of semitones. In the fifth fugue, Schumann submerges B-A-C-H in flowing triplets that recall

Bach's high-spirited keyboard gigues. To conclude his set with suitable seriousness, he offers a chorale-like version of B-A-C-H in the final fugue.

SYMPHONY NO. 3 ("RHENISH"), 1850

That Schumann's Back to Bach journey could lead beyond preludes, fugues and canons to freer contexts is demonstrated in this symphony, which was premiered in Düsseldorf on the Rhine. Though its first audiences understood the work as a salutation to the majestic flowing river (hence its lingering title), Schumann did not offer an explanatory programme. Even so, its majestic fourth movement, marked "Feierlich" ("Solemnly"), reminded listeners of the grandeur and atmosphere of Cologne Cathedral. This impression is suggested by the counterpoint based on a sombre theme, announced at first on lower brass and woodwinds, before being taken up in overlapping layers by the other instruments to achieve a monumental, towering effect. Schumann's theme consists of a sequence of three rising intervals of a fourth, a pattern that reproduces the one that Bach employs in the contrapuntal episode in his Prelude in the same key (E-flat major) in Book I of *The Well-tempered Clavier*. Bach's counterpoint begins with single-beat notes followed by double-beat notes, a progression that Schumann reproduces, while translating its stately progressions into dark orchestral colours to serve as an imposing "prelude" to his cheerful, concluding fifth movement.

VIOLIN SONATA NO. 2, 1851

Having sourced a Bach fugal theme for a symphonic movement, Schumann turns in his second violin sonata to a Bach chorale for a set of variations based on "Gelobet seist du, Jesu Christ". (This was the same chorale that Mendelssohn had used six years earlier in his second piano trio, from where he must have got the idea.) Schumann transforms Bach's chorale into a wistful melody, featuring a triple pulse divided into hymn-like phrases, with the violin in pizzicato or double stops carried on delicate piano chords, running notes or flowing arpeggios. The result is an intermezzo that functions as a calm interlude between two more vigorous movements.

SEVEN PIECES IN FUGHETTA FORM, 1853

A year before he is confined to an asylum, Robert returns to counterpoint in this set of modest fugal compositions for the piano. Among the Bachian devices that he explores here are the chromatic theme in the second fughetta and the stretto overlap of the theme in the third fughetta. Even so, Schumann cannot supress his lyrical expressiveness, as in the meandering melodies with falling, diminished seventh intervals on rapid flowing notes in the fourth fughetta, or the intimate melodiousness in the fifth fughetta.

With the gentle mood of the Seven Pieces, Schumann seems to be steadying his spirit as his illness progresses. While the fughettas survive as the last manifestations of his Back to Bach journey, Schumann may have found consolation in the asylum by scribbling contrapuntal exercises before dying there on 29 July 1856.

CARL CZERNY (1791–1857)

As one of Beethoven's most brilliant pupils, the twenty-one-year-old Czerny gives the premier of his teacher's Piano Concerto No. 5 ("Emperor") in Vienna in 1812. In later years, he becomes a prolific composer, theorist and pedagogue, authoring multiple volumes of piano exercises, such as *The School of Velocity* (1833 and 1838). Czerny also edits Bach: his version of *The Well-tempered Clavier*, issued in 1837 by C.F. Peters in Leipzig, is marked with fingerings, tempos, dynamics and phrasings gleaned from Beethoven's renditions, which he had noted as a student.

48 PRELUDES AND FUGUES, 1857

Motivated by his understanding of Bach as the supreme master of counterpoint, Czerny brings out his own *48 Preludes and Fugues in All the Major and Minor Keys*, dedicating them to his former pupil Franz Liszt. Significantly, these are the first complete set of preludes coupled with fugues to be written after Bach. Arranged like Chopin's cycle in ascending intervals of fifths, the publication is subtitled "The Pianist in the Classical Style", to explain that Czerny conceives his preludes and fugues in accordance with contemporary musical taste. While emulating Bach's overall scheme and underlying didactic purpose, Czerny makes no attempt to approach Bach's contrapuntal ingenuity or harmonic inventiveness. Rather, he recasts the idea of *The Well-tempered Clavier* in the pianistic idiom of the day, with attractive melodies for the preludes and clearly articulated lines for the fugues, frequently interspersed with virtuosic rapid octaves and scales. Czerny's B minor prelude, for instance, presents a passionate melody supported on running triplets in the manner of Mendelssohn, while the associated fugue has overlapping figurations with rising triplets, somewhat like theme of the Fugue in A Major from Bach's Book I. Here, as elsewhere, Czerny is concerned to please the listener while encouraging the dexterity of the player.

AFTERLIVES

ORGAN PASSACAGLIA

Bach's titanic work follows the tradition of passacaglias and chaconnes based on repeated "ostinato" ("obstinate") bass lines, like those of Dieterich Buxtehude that Bach had studied in his junior years. Expanding Buxtehude's four-bar ostinatos to eight bars, Bach has his theme step up and down a C minor triad, in alternating short and long notes in triple time, ending in a perfect cadence (G to C). Bach begins by announcing his rugged ostinato alone on the pedals, something Buxtehude had never thought to do. He then introduces "sorrowful" downward-trending motifs in the keyboards, "stumbling" across the bars. Could Bach have been thinking of his arduous journey to Lübeck to visit Buxtehude? If so, after two ostinato repetitions, the music lifts off, as though Bach has safely arrived. The rising passages lead to a sequence of variations, one leading without interruption into the next, illustrating the full range of organ effects, from cascading arpeggios and crashing chords to rapid scales running up and down the keyboards. After reaching the midpoint, Bach relocates his ostinato to the upper keyboard, where he clads it in further embellishments. After twenty repetitions of these eight-bar episodes, Bach plunges without a break into the fugue that forms a massive pendant to the Passacaglia, and which lasts almost as long. For its principal theme, Bach repurposes the first eight notes of the ostinato, pitting it against two counterthemes: one with stepped notes proceeding in contrary motion, the other with rapid oscillations. With these contrasting musical materials, Bach constructs an epic fugue, driving its complex counterpoint relentlessly onwards until it reaches a climax on a melodramatic "Neapolitan sixth" chord (F, A-flat and D-flat), followed by a final C minor utterance.

As an antiquated musical form, Bach decides against including his Passacaglia among the organ works he assembles in the third part of his *Clavier-Übung* survey. Even so, it becomes one of Bach's most celebrated compositions for the instrument, stimulating later composers to respond to its obsessive structure by writing their own Bach-influenced passacaglias.

1823 The teenage Felix Mendelssohn's models his organ Passacaglia on Bach.

1840 Mendelssohn includes the Passacaglia in his all-Bach concert in Leipzig.

1849 The "Ad Nos ad Salutarem" hymn in Giacomo Meyerbeer's *Le Prophète* resembles Bach's ostinato, as does Liszt's 1850 *Fantasy and Fugue on "Ad Nos"*.

1867 Publication of the Passacaglia in the Bach Gesellschaft volume.

1885 Johannes Brahms styles the Allegro finale of his Symphony No. 4 as a colossal orchestral passacaglia.

1902 Max Reger models his Passacaglia in F Minor on Bach's.

1908 Anton Webern's *Passacaglia for Orchestra*.

1912 In his path-breaking *Pierrot Lunaire*, Arnold Schoenberg includes a passacaglia, as if to link past traditions with those yet to come.

1922 Leopold Stokowski's orchestration.

1923 Arthur Honegger's orchestral *Pacific 231* is structured as a passacaglia.

1925 Berthold Goldschmidt's *Passacaglia for Large Orchestra* wins the prestigious Mendelssohn Prize.

1930 Ottorino Respighi's orchestration.

1934 Dramatic passacaglia interlude in Dmitri Shostakovich's *Lady Macbeth of Mtsensk*.

1936 In *An Anti-Hitler Symphony*, Hanns Eisler sets a text referring to the imprisonment of political dissidents to an instrumental passacaglia.

1938 Paul Hindemith provides a monumental passacaglia for the last scene in *Nobilissima Visione*.

1941 The Adagio movement in Honegger's Symphony No. 2 is a lamenting passacaglia.

1942 R.H. Blyth proposes Bach's Passacaglia as an example of Zen paradox.

1945 Benjamin Britten includes an ominous passacaglia interlude in *Peter Grimes*.

1948 & 1956 Passacaglia movements in Shostakovich's Violin Concerto No. 1 and String Quartet No. 6.

1959 *Passaglia to the Memory of Arthur Honegger* by Maurice Jarre.

1960 Arrangement for double orchestra by the Polish–French composer and music theorist René Leibowitz.

1962 Ronald Stevenson's *Passacaglia on DSCH* pays tribute to Shostakovich.

1968 Passacaglia finale in Shostakovich's Sonata for Violin and Piano.

1986 Donald Hunsberger's wind band transcription.

1993 Ron Nelson's *Passacaglia (Homage on B-A-C-H)* for wind band.

4.

BACH ROMANTICISED, CONTINUED

FROM MEYERBEER & LISZT TO WAGNER & BRAHMS

As the nineteenth century progressed, Bach's music was exported to civic auditoriums and, under Meyerbeer and Wagner, even opera houses, where his complex polyphony was translated into grandly scaled, orchestral formats to add drama to stage plots. Nor was Bach's organ music neglected since it inspired impressive symphonic and keyboard variations. In 1850, the centenary of Bach's death, the Bach Gesellschaft was founded in Leipzig to bring out everything that Bach had written. It was the most ambitious publication project ever conceived for a composer. By the time the forty-ninth volume appeared in 1899, Philipp Spitta had completed his monumental biographical study, laying the foundation for all later Bach research.

GIACOMO MEYERBEER (1791–1864)

As Mendelssohn was finding places for Bach chorales in his instrumental and choral music to achieve a suitable mood of seriousness, the German-born Meyerbeer (originally Jakob Meyer Beer) embarked upon a similar course in his stage works. He was well qualified to do so: during his early years in Berlin, he had studied with Carl Friedrich Zelter, the same teacher who had instructed the juvenile Mendelssohn. Dividing his time between Berlin and Paris, Meyerbeer establishes himself as the premier exponent of the grand operas that dominate Europe's theatrical houses and in two of his greatest successes he references Bach.

LES HUGUENOTS, 1836

Spectacular choruses, processions and scenography in *Les Huguenots* guaranteed the popularity of a love story invented by Meyerbeer's librettist Eugène Scribe set against an actual historical event – the persecution of Protestants by French Catholics in 1572. To represent the Huguenots, Meyerbeer quotes Luther's defiant "Ein feste Burg ist unser Gott" ("A mighty fortress is our Lord"), which, like Mendelssohn, he discovers in Bach's cantata BWV 80. (It is surely a curious coincidence that two composers of similar Jewish background should each have sourced this chorale.) Meyerbeer uses "Ein feste Burg" both as a sung hymn and as an instrumental background to events taking place on stage. After announcing the chorale in the opera's overture in mournful woodwinds and brass (not unlike Mendelssohn at the beginning of his *Reformation Symphony*), Meyerbeer employs it to declare the sincere faith of the Protestant hero Marcel in Act I. Towards the end of the opera, Meyerbeer reprises the same chorale to express the defiance of the Protestants who are about to be massacred, thereby investing "Ein feste Burg" with potential tragedy.

LE PROPHÈTE, 1849

Thirteen years later, in *Le Prophète*, Meyerbeer returns to the idea of a chorale on stage. This time, however, instead of borrowing one from Bach, he invents one of his own that sounds like Bach. This was for the three Anabaptist priests to sing "Ad nos, ad salutarem undam" ("Bring us to the wave of salvation") to incite the common people to revolt against the tyrannical prophet mentioned in the opera's title. Meyerbeer divides his chorale-like hymn into two mournful phrases, each consisting of four bars in triple time, with upward and downward steps in alternating longer and shorter notes. It is a pattern found in many of Bach's chorales, as well as in the Passacaglia, by now one of his best-known organ pieces. Significantly, Meyerbeer writes his chorale in C minor, the same key as Bach's ostinato, which most likely serves as the model.

CHARLES GOUNOD (1818–93)

Meyerbeer is not the only composer of grand opera to be drawn to Bach. After winning the prestigious Prix de Rome at the age of twenty-one in 1839, Gounod travels around Europe, pausing in Leipzig to visit Mendelssohn, who encourages his interest in Bach. Returning to Paris in 1843, Gounod embarks upon a precarious, but eventually fruitful career as an opera composer, while at the same time producing much church and concert music. This includes a piece for violin or cello with a Bach prelude as a piano accompaniment that was to achieve immortality when Gounod converts it into a sung prayer.

MÉDITATION SUR LE 1ER PRÉLUDE DE PIANO DE S. BACH, 1853, & *AVE MARIA*, 1859

It is on the Prelude in C Major from Book I of *The Well-tempered Clavier* that Gounod superimposes his own expressive melody. Originally conceived for a string instrument, Gounod adapts it for a soprano singing the words of the Latin prayer Ave Maria in an expressive lyric that emerges naturally from the prelude, as if latent in Bach's arpeggios.

GIOACHINO ROSSINI (1792–1868)

As the most renowned opera composer of his generation, Rossini has little need for Bach – that is, until many years after he retires in 1829. Settling in Paris in 1855, he amuses himself by turning out charming, miniature salon pieces, which he calls *Sins of Old Age*, and devoting himself to the delights of gourmandising. At the age of seventy-one, he accepts a commission for a sacred work to be performed in a private home by writing his *Petite messe solonnelle* for a small vocal ensemble, two pianos and a harmonium. While the work betrays Rossini's long-standing experience with Italian arias and operatic choruses, the keyboard piece he inserts for the Offertory reveals an unexpectedly, expressive Back to Bach journey.

PRÉLUDE RELIGIEUX, 1863

Though he calls the keyboard interlude in his *Little Solemn Mass* a "Religious Prelude", Rossini writes it as a prelude and fugue, even if he reduces the prelude to a series of sonorous chords. From this introduction, he progresses to a three-voice fugue in F-sharp minor and triple time, deriving his theme from the stepped accompaniment in the bass aria in the same key and tempo in Bach's *Ach Gott, wie manches Herzeleid* (*Oh God, how much heartache*) (BWV 3). Rossini learns about this cantata from Camille Saint-Saëns, who had made a piano arrangement of its opening chorus two years earlier.

With their downward intervals of a sixth pausing on the semitones beneath, Rossini's phrases resemble those of Bach's, though they are somewhat shorter; even so, they remain faithful to Bach's sorrowful mood. While his counterpoint is admittedly rudimentary, Rossini introduces rich chromatic harmonies that are not to be found elsewhere in his operatic oeuvre.

FRANZ LISZT (1811–86)

As an international celebrity pianist, Liszt tours concert halls and private salons, launching a veritable, Europe-wide "Lisztomania". In his pyrotechnical performances, Liszt finds places for Bach, including piano arrangements of many of the harpsichord and organ works. Such transcriptions form part of a broad corpus of music by other composers, both past and present, that Liszt draws on as part of a lifelong pursuit of new musical realms. Occupying a central role in this quest is a Back to Bach journey that challenges traditional canons of harmony through a series of piano and organ variations.

FANTASY AND FUGUE ON "AD NOS, AD SALUTAREM", 1850

Soon after its premiere in Paris in April 1849, Meyerbeer's *Le Prophète* toured German opera houses, attracting Liszt's attention, particularly the "Ad Nos, ad salutarem" hymn sung by the Anabaptist priests. Knowing that Meyerbeer had quoted a Bach chorale in *Les Huguenots*, Liszt probably believed that the "Ad Nos" hymn was also by Bach. If he had doubts, these did not inhibit him from writing a Fantasia and Fugue on the hymn, his longest and most grandly conceived organ composition. (It seems that Liszt was not adept on the organ and was reluctant to perform the work in public.)

In Meyerbeer's opera, the Anabaptists sing the hymn unaccompanied. This leaves Liszt free to immerse the theme in rich chromatic chords and to envelop it in a vast panorama of musical ideas. In the brilliant outer movements of the *Fantasy and Fugue*, Liszt directs the C minor chorale through unpredictable keys, embellishing it with violent cascades, arpeggios and rapid triplets, and interspersing it with horn-like fanfares and reflective recitatives. The central Adagio, in the remote key of F-sharp major, leads to a lyrical Andante, from where Liszt progresses to an Allegro fugue in C minor based on an animated, fragmented version of the hymn set against a jagged countertheme. The counterpoint is eventually overwhelmed by gigantic chordal leaps and speedy accompaniments until Liszt reprises the choral for the last time in the blazing key of C major.

TRANSCENDENTAL STUDIES, 1852

As a precocious fourteen-year-old, in 1825, Liszt published his *Study in Twelve Exercises* as the first part of a series intended to cover all twelve keys, in the manner of *The Well-tempered Clavier*. Revising them several times over more than twenty-five years, Liszt eventually issues them as his *Transcendental Studies*. That they encompass ideas far removed from Bach is clear from their programmatic titles, such as "Mazeppa" (No. 4), in which Liszt portrays the fury of the galloping horse on which the Ukrainian hero is strapped in punishment. In "Will-o-the Wisps", "Evening Harmonies" and "Sleigh Ride", Liszt reveals a poetic sensibility attuned to the works of Lord Byron and Victor Hugo. Varying from vast and mysterious to heroic and passionate, the *Studies* are audacious technical and acoustic experiments, ranging from top-speed leaps, scales and arpeggios up and down the keyboard, to chordal clusters, tremolandos and trills. Like Bach's demands on the players of his time, they expand the technique of contemporary keyboard practice.

Liszt wrote his *Transcendental Studies* in the major and related minor keys on twelve notes only. More than fifty years later, in 1905, his plan for a complete set of twenty-four was realised when the Russian pianist Sergei Lyapunov contributed his own *Transcendental Studies* in all of Liszt's missing twelve keys. Like his predecessor, Lyapunov adds imaginative headings like "Dance of the Ghosts" and "Bell Peals", ending with an "Elegy in Memory of Franz Liszt".

FANTASY AND FUGUE ON THE THEME B-A-C-H, 1855

Schumann's organ fugues on B-A-C-H inspire Liszt to contribute one of his own, while at the same time providing a piano version. Liszt was long acquainted with *Art of Fugue* and its B-A-C-H motif. Soon after settling in Paris with his mistress Marie d'Agoult in 1836, he invites his mother to visit, entreating her to bring with her the score of *Art of Fugue* from his personal library in Vienna.[58] As in his *Fantasy and Fugue on "Ad Nos"*, Liszt selects a theme on which to create an exploratory, multi-section work with continuously evolving harmonies. Liszt announces B-A-C-H as in Bach's original, beginning on B-flat, and then repeats it on all the other notes of the octave. Between these successively higher appearances, he inserts arpeggio cascades, rapid passages and crashing chords before reaching a triple-forte climax. For his fugal theme, which he marks "misterioso", Liszt extends the two pairs of semitones of B-A-C-H to four pairs, followed by another four pairs of quicker, descending semitones. Liszt treats this expanded theme freely by adding bravura effects to achieve huge masses of sound that often overwhelm the counterpoint. After directing his theme with harmonic abandon, he progresses to a forceful conclusion in B-flat major, which is where he began.

BACH TRANSCRIPTIONS, 1859–63

After being appointed in 1846 as "Capellmeister Extraordinaire" to the ducal court orchestra in Weimar, Liszt develops an interest in the organ-playing tradition preserved in the nearby churches of Thuringia harking back to Bach's time. Among the organ works he transcribes for the piano during these years are the Prelude and Fugue in A Minor, with its thrilling oscillations (BWV 543), and the Prelude and Fugue in E Minor, nicknamed "The Wedge", from the outward motion of its fugal theme incorporating increasingly greater intervals (BWV 548). In these and other such arrangements,

Liszt makes few alterations, aside from adding bass octaves to better render the low register of the organ or its pedals, and occasionally doubling passages to strengthen the inner voices. Striving for ever-more impressive pianistic effects, he introduces octaves, sixths and thirds into his version of the Fantasia and Fugue in G Minor (BWV 542). By adding dynamics, accents and phrasings, Liszt draws attention to what he imagines to be the drama inherent in Bach's improvisational manner.

Liszt leaves the celebrated Toccata and Fugue in D Minor (BWV 565) to his most talented pupil, the Polish-born Carl Tausig, who completes a virtuosic version shortly before his death at the age of twenty-nine in 1871.

VARIATIONS ON WEINEN, KLAGEN, SORGEN, ZAGEN, 1859 & 1862

Nine years after completing his Fantasy and Fugue on "Ad Nos" on what he believed to be a Bach chorale, Liszt composes another large-scale keyboard work, this one based on the "Weinen, Klagen, Sorgen, Zagen" chorus from the cantata of the same name (BWV 12) published in the 1852 Bach Gesellschaft volume. As originally written for the piano, Liszt takes inspiration from the chromatically descending, repeated stepped bass line supporting the "weeping, lamenting" voices. After the tragic death of his eldest daughter, Blandine, in September 1862, the words seemed especially appropriate for expressing his personal grief, leading Liszt to expand the variations and recast them for the organ, transforming Bach's theme into ever-evolving "suffering" motifs.

Liszt begins his organ version of the *Variations on Weinen, Klagen...* with an arresting statement of Bach's chromatic bass figure in D-flat major before modulating it into F minor, the original key in the cantata chorus (not Bach's E minor adaptation of it for the Crucifixus in his Mass in B Minor). As in the Goldberg

Variations, with which he is familiar, Liszt writes exactly thirty variations on Bach's chromatic bass line, subjecting it to continuous rhythmic and thematic distortions to create striking contrasts of dynamics, registers and harmonies. The result is a work that ranges from calm, recitative-like episodes and delicate rippling textures to melodramatic utterances engaging the full forces of the organ, as Bach had so often done in his own organ music. Following Bach at the end of his cantata, Liszt concludes his variations with a noble harmonisation of the Lutheran chorale, "Was Gott tut, das ist wohlgetan" ("What God does, that is well done"). Liszt must have found its message comforting.

RICHARD WAGNER (1813–83)

Bach purists may be surprised to learn that Bach played a crucial role in Wagner's quest for a revolutionary musical language. Never one to acknowledge a debt, in later years Wagner did come to admit what he owed Bach. In 1878, after listening to the Fugue in F-sharp Minor from Book II of *The Well-tempered Clavier* played for him at one of the frequent Bach evenings that he hosts in Wahnfried, his newly built villa in Bayreuth, the sixty-five-year-old composer confesses that here, "as if in a dream, the unending melody [of mine] seems to have been predestined".[59] By what he calls his "unendliche Melodie", Wagner is referring to the music of infinite expansion that he was perfecting in his operatic dramas. By claiming Bach as a precursor, he exposes the significance of his Back to Bach journey.

It is a journey that dates to his junior years when Wagner takes keyboard and composition lessons from Christian Theodor Weinlig, Cantor of St Thomas's, the same post that Bach had occupied some 100 years before. Though complaining of having to invent fugues and canons for Weinlig, Wagner receives a thorough grounding in Bachian counterpoint. At first, though, he is attracted

to the improvisatory keyboard works. The Fantasia in F-sharp Minor
for piano, written in 1831 when Wagner is eighteen years old, begins
with melodramatic flourishes and recitative-like pauses that mimic
those in the Chromatic Fantasia and Fugue (BWV 903). Wagner's
Fantasia also bears comparison with Bach's Toccata in the same
key of F-sharp minor (BWV 910): both are juvenile compositions with
somewhat incoherent sequences of contrasting sections.

As Wagner pursues an exploratory musical path, his
compositional method becomes more powerfully persuasive, more
structurally linear. This is expressed in his manipulation of musical
ideas, usually labelled leitmotifs: to identify particular personalities
and objects in his stage works; to emphasise specific dramatic
and psychological moments; and to reflect on the narrative taking
place. From *Das Rheingold* onwards, Wagner presents his leitmotifs
in the broadest range of instrumental sonorities, distorting them
rhythmically, and modulating them into remote keys. At the same
time, he piles leitmotifs one on top of another to create a richly
complex, symphonic counterpoint. Wagner displays his Bach-
informed polyphony most obviously in the Prelude that introduces
the medieval world of *Die Meistersinger von Nürnberg*, the music
of which he later referred to as "angewendeten" ("applied") Bach.[60]
Even more contrapuntally complex is the orchestral texture in the
scene of Brünnhilde's immolation that brings the four operas of *Der
Ring des Nibelungen* cycle to a transcendental conclusion, and in
the Transformation Music in *Parsifal* that introduces the moment
in which the Holy Grail in Montsalvat Castle is first revealed to the
hero. That the opening scene of Act III of *Parsifal*, in which the hero
is anointed, takes place on Good Friday suggests a comparison
with the St Matthew Passion. Bach's portrayal of Christ's last
hours, written for the 1727 Good Friday service in St Thomas's, is
imbued with a sincere profession of faith, while in his "Festival Play
for the Consecration of the Stage", premiered more than 150 years

later in the newly completed opera house of Bayreuth, barely 200 kilometres to the south of Leipzig, Wagner mingles theatrical drama with deepest mystery to present a symbolic profession of faith.[61]

PRELUDES, CHORALES AND INTERLUDE IN
DIE MEISTERSINGER VON NÜRNBERG, 1862 & 1868

Premiered in a concert performance six years before he completes his music drama, Wagner's Vorspiel (Prelude) to *The Mastersingers of Nuremberg* presents in musical terms the two contrasting worlds of the opera's narrative: the "old" style, representing the conventions of the guild of Mastersingers; and the freer "new" style, epitomised by the lyrical Prize Song with which the courtly hero Walther wins the hand of Eva. For the world of the Mastersingers, Wagner conjures up a quasi-medieval atmosphere by exploiting the contrapuntal language, not of the sixteenth century, during which the opera's story takes place, but of the eighteenth century – the era of Bach. Certainly, there is much of Bach in his high-spirited overture, especially in the superimposition of three of the opera's principal themes: that representing the corporation of the Mastersingers, with which the Prelude begins; an excerpt from the Prize Song; and a quotation of the Mastersingers' ceremonial march, based on an actual sixteenth-century song.

The Prelude runs without interruption into the church service with which Act I of *Die Meistersinger* begins. While Walther and Eva exchange amorous glances, an off-stage chorus sings what sounds like a noble Lutheran hymn in one of Bach's settings. In fact, both the words and harmonies are Wagner's. Ernest Newman, who authored one of the classic books on Wagner's operas, judges it as "the only really first-rate thing in that genre …. since the great days of German Protestant chorale-writing".[62] Wagner's chorale begins with a drop of a fourth (from C to G), followed by a scale ascending a sixth (to E). This simple progression corresponds with the first phrase of the chorale that concludes Bach's cantata *Allein zu dir, Herr Jesu Christ* (*Oh you alone, Lord Jesus Christ*) (BWV 33). The reference to John the Baptist in Wagner's text locates the opera's story at the Feast of St John on Midsummer's Day, which is when the song contest that will decide the fate of the lovers is to take place. Wagner's opening words, "Da zu dir der Heiland kam" ("That the Saviour came to you"), recall those of Luther that Bach used in his St John's Day cantata, *Christ unser Herr zum Jordan kam* (*Christ our Lord came to the Jordan*) (BWV 7).

Bach is also a distant presence in the night-time street riot between the different apprentices and outraged citizens of Nuremberg that brings Act II of *Die Meistersinger* to a close. For this disorderly scene, Wagner resorts to a large-scale fugato built on two themes: one derived from the ungainly song which Beckmesser, Walther's rival, tries unsuccessfully to woo Eva; the other from the hammering motifs administered by Hans Sachs, the opera's central character, that interrupt Beckmesser's song. Wagner repeats these two musical ideas in progressively manic overlays shared between the orchestra and the twelve-part chorus. The result is an astonishing repurposing of Bachian counterpoint in the service of stage action.

To introduce Act III of *Die Meistersinger*, Wagner provides a Prelude that begins with another fugato, this one built on the "Wahn" ("Folly/Delusion") motif identified with Hans Sachs, which anticipates the brooding monologue that he sings soon after the curtain rises. As the "Wahn" motif rises through the strings, it assumes a mournful drop of a minor sixth (from G to B-flat in one version), then a descent of a semitone before rising a diminished fifth (A to E-flat). Wagner describes this haunting melody in his usual overblown manner as "the perturbation of a profoundly-stirred soul, finally allayed and calmed."[63] What he does not reveal is that he derives the "Wahn" motif from the Fugue in G Minor from Book I of *The Well-tempered Clavier*, which begins in a similarly sorrowful manner. After building up the motif in the strings, Wagner introduces horns and bassoons to suggest the mighty chorale in the opera's final scene, sung by Nuremberg's citizens to celebrate the Mastersingers and the happy outcome of the song contest. The chorale begins with the words of Luther's well-known hymn "Wachet Auf" ("Awake"), here compressed into the two syllables of "Wach Auf". For its melody, Wagner sources a song by the historical Hans Sachs greeting Luther and the Reformation in a harmonisation that recalls Bach's mightiest proclamations.

IMMOLATION SCENE IN *GÖTTERDÄMMERUNG*, 1874

For the concluding scene of *Twilight of the Gods*, Wagner harnesses an astounding array of leitmotifs, merging one into another before combining them contrapuntally to achieve an unparalleled, dense orchestral texture. This serves as a perfect vehicle for expressing the transformative act of Brünnhilde's sacrifice by fire to liberate her father, Wotan, and her lover, Siegfried, from the deadly curse of the dwarf Alberich. Here, Wagner assembles three contrasting ideas: the flickering Fire motif; the rippling wave-like arpeggios of the Rhine motif; and the lilting Song of the Rhine Maidens. Into this symphonic apotheosis Wagner inserts yet further ideas: the jagged leaps of Brünnhilde as a Valkyrie warrior riding through the skies; the majestic chords of Walhalla, Wotan's aerial castle; and the rising notes of Siegfried's stirring fanfare. Wagner even briefly quotes the ominous Curse motif of Alberich as he attempts to seize the ring before drowning in the Rhine. The scene concludes with Brünnhilde returning the ring to the Rhine Maidens fashioned from the gold that Alberich had stolen from them at the beginning of *Das Rheingold*.

Soaring above this accumulation of leitmotifs is the melodic arc of Brünnhilde's Redemption by Love motif, pausing on the first two notes of the scale before dropping an interval of a seventh. As the scene unfolds, Wagner elevates this motif to the flutes and violins where, in expanded double time, it floats high above the rippling triplets of the Song of the Rhine Maidens in the woodwinds, while the lower strings and no less than six harps (!) are busily engaged in portraying the "waves" of the Rhine. In drawing out the contour of Brünnhilde's motif, writing what, in effect, is a Bachian chorale prelude, Wagner offers a sacred hymn that spreads "consoling wings over not merely the present scene but the whole stupendous drama".[64]

TRANSFORMATION MUSIC IN *PARSIFAL*, 1882

In *Parsifal*, completed a year before his death, Wagner creates a pervasive soundscape that represents the culmination of his Back to Bach journey. Much of the opera's instrumental score is constructed from a spectrum of leitmotifs freighted with symbolical meaning and psychological force derived from the majestic "Grundthema" ("basic theme") with which the Prelude to *Parsifal* begins. For the musicologist Carl Dahlhaus, the Grundthema recalls Bach's Fugue in F-sharp Minor,[65] to which Wagner had drawn attention five years before. Like Bach's fugal idea, Wagner's Grundthema begins mysteriously, with the notes of a triad floating free from the main beats of the bars.

While much of *Parsifal*'s music proceeds independently of the voices, it illuminates the inner emotive world of the principal characters both on-stage and off it. This is especially true of the orchestral interlude in Act I, known as the Transformation Music, which portrays Parsifal's sense of awe as he first approaches the Hall of the Grail. Before he enters, the chief knight, Gurnemanz, who assumes the role of an Evangelist-like narrator, explains that "here time is one with space".[66] Wagner highlights this mystical convergence with unprecedented contrapuntal splendour. In three mighty enunciations, between which are heard bell-like peals from Monstalvat castle, Wagner introduces three of the opera's principal musical ideas. To begin with, there are the transcendental cadences of the Grail motif, which he sources from the Dresden Amen. (These were already used by Mendelssohn in his *Reformation Symphony*, from where Wagner most likely got the idea.) Then comes the Faith motif, which proceeds in imitative steps, building up in ever-higher pitches propelled by additional triplet figurations. To these, Wagner adds the descending chromatic passages of the Suffering motif that express the agony of Amfortas, the wounded Grail king, with whom Parsifal is about to empathise. At crucial moments, Wagner includes yet another agitated idea, with rapid scales and jagged upward leaps on the violins. He supports all these interlocking ideas on a bass line that moves around a cycle of intervals of a fifth, a harmonic progression that reminds one commentator of "Bach at his most majestic".[67] In harnessing Bachian expressive counterpoint for this most tremendous moment, Wagner achieves what has been described as *Parsifal*'s "central sonorous image".[68] It is a convincingly epic conclusion to his Back to Bach journey.

JOHANNES BRAHMS (1833–97)

Wagnerian opera is alien to Brahms, who prefers the instrumental and vocal works of past masters, especially those of Bach, which occupy a hallowed place in his extensive library. Brahms studies, performs and directs a great deal of Bach's music. He makes piano arrangements of the organ and harpsichord works to include in his recitals – the Chromatic Fantasia and Fugue (BWV 903) being one of his favourites – and between 1872 and 1875 prepares the Christmas

Oratorio and St Matthew Passion for the concerts he organises for the Society of Friends of Music in Vienna.[69] Brahms advises the editorial board of the Bach Gesellschaft, scrutinising the volumes as they appear year after year. He considers the completion of this project, together with the unification of Germany in 1871, the two greatest events of his lifetime.[70]

As he confesses, "in old Bach, there is always something astonishing … and always something to be learned".[71] In demonstration, Brahms morphs Bach's fugal themes from *Art of Fugue* into melodies for a cello sonata and then makes a piano transcription for left-hand alone of the Chaconne for Solo Violin. When he turns to choral compositions like the *Begräbnisgesang* and *A German Requiem*, he consults Bach. However, it is in the monumental, passacaglia-like finale of his Symphony No. 4 that Brahms reveals his true seriousness. At the end of his life, he pays final tribute by writing a set of choral preludes for the organ in the manner of Bach.

BEGRÄBNISGESANG, 1858

Two years after Robert Schumann dies, Brahms composes the sombre *Burial Song* as a testament to the musician who had nurtured his early career. Unusually scored for choir with winds, brass and percussion, but without strings (so that it could be performed outdoors at a graveside interment), the work is based on verses by the sixteenth-century Lutheran theologian Michael Weisse. Bach is present in the work's central section, in which Brahms shares the text between the sopranos and altos and then the tenors and bass, before linking them up into a pattern of alternating short phrases modelled on the doleful, soprano-alto duet in *Christ lag in Todesbanden* (*Christ lay in the bonds of death*) (BWV 4). At the time, Brahms is rehearsing this very cantata with the choir and orchestra of the court at Detmold in northwest Germany. The cantata is included in the first volume of the Bach Gesellschaft edition, a copy of which Brahms receives as a Christmas gift in 1855 from Clara Schumann. If Brahms had consulted Forkel's biography, he would have learned that *Christ lag in Todesbanden* was written when Bach was twenty-two years old, only a little younger than Brahms when he accepted the post in Detmold the previous year.

CELLO SONATA NO. 1, 1865

Brahms's markings on his copy of *Art of Fugue* testify to his detailed scrutiny of Bach's fugal propositions. Looking beyond the B-A-C-H motif in the last unfinished fugue, he imports Bach's other ideas into this sonata as "an act of homage".[72] For the opening theme of the first movement, announced in the bottom register of the cello, Brahms turns to Contrapunctus 4, modulating its theme into E minor, omitting Bach's first note, altering the rhythm, adding an ornament, and converting Bach's descending line into one that rises. The result is an altogether new and eloquent melody shared between the cello and piano, on which Brahms builds a conventional, sonata scheme movement.

More dependent on *Art of Fugue* is the Allegro Fugato finale. Borrowing the idea of ending a cello sonata with a fugal movement from Beethoven's Cello Sonata No. 5, Brahms conceives his finale as series of vigorous contrapuntal episodes alternating with more freely composed, lyrical sections. For his principal theme, he borrows that from Contrapunctus 13, one of the two mirror fugues, reproducing Bach's forceful octave leap downward followed by rapidly rising triplets. As he does in the sonata's first movement, Brahms omits the leading note of Bach's theme before transposing it into E minor. He then juxtaposes it with a countertheme with stepped notes to create bold, two-against-three patterns – one of his favourite rhythmic devices. As the movement proceeds,

Brahms follows Bach by inverting his theme, with upward octave leaps and downward trending triplets, but ends by driving his two-against-three figurations to a frenzied conclusion.

A GERMAN REQUIEM, 1865–8

As he begins writing what is to become his most significant choral composition, Brahms turns to Bach. As remembered by the conductor Siegfried Ochs, Brahms mentioned to him that the "whole work was, essentially, founded on the chorale "Wer nur den lieben Gott lässt walten"' ('Who only allows beloved God to rule')".[73] Brahms would have found its melody in the cantata *Ich hatte viel Bekümmernis* (*I had much grief*) (BWV 21), which had appeared in the 1855 Bach Gesellschaft volume. The opening phrase of Bach's chorale, which is in F minor, wanders up and down an interval of a minor third (from F to A-flat), a pattern that provides Brahms with the eloquent D minor melody with which he begins the *Requiem*'s sombre introduction. By repeating this at successively higher intervals, Brahms creates a quasi-polyphonic texture, first in the lower strings, then in the chorus that follows. In the march-like dirge sung by unison voices in the *Requiem*'s second movement, he recalls the same chorale phrase with greater clarity. Here, Brahms lowers the second note of the B-flat minor scale (from C to C-flat) to emphasise the melancholy spirit of "Denn alles Fleisch, es ist wie Gras" ("For all flesh, is as grass"). For the sixth movement, Brahms sets the words "Dann es wird die Posaune schallen" ("Then will the trumpet sound") to an almost identical passage, though in C minor, adding a triplet figure on the second syllable of "Posaune". Bach had employed the same C minor setting of the melody in triple time in the opening chorale of *Wer weiss, wir nahe mir mein ende?* (*Who knows, how near to me my end?*) (BWV 27), a cantata that Brahms would also have discovered in the 1855 Bach Gesellschaft volume.

Another point of contact with Bach is found in the fugue with which Brahms concludes the sixth part of the *Requiem*, which one commentator has compared with the six-voice fugal Credo in the Mass in B Minor.[74] Following Bach, Brahms employs a rugged theme consisting of alternating long and short notes, which he overlaps in increasingly complicated counterpoint, supported on a continuously moving bass line. Such Bach derivations by no means rob *A German Requiem* of a musical individuality that is compatible with texts that avoid any mention of Christian dogma, which Brahms extracted from Luther's Bible.

WARUM IST DAS LICHT GEGEBEN DEM MÜHSELIGEN?, 1878

Brahms conceives the motet *Why is the Light Given to the Weary?* as an obituary for Hermann Goetz, a composer friend who had recently died of tuberculosis. In recognition of its Bach references, he dedicates what is his longest unaccompanied vocal composition to this friend Philipp Spitta, who five years before had published the first volume of his biographical study of the composer. Since the motet focuses on Job's heartfelt questioning of his sufferings as described in the Bible, Brahms begins with a meandering fugue with the voices singing "Warum?" ("Why?"). He concludes with "Mit Fried und Freud ich fahr dahin", a chorale that Brahms sources from the cantata *Gottes Zeit ist die allerbeste Zeit* (*God's time is always the best time*), also known as "Actus Tragicus" (BWV 106), issued two years before in the 1876 Bach Gesellschaft volume. Attracted to the cantata's funerary atmosphere as expressed in the dolorous tones of its recorders and viola da gambas, Brahms transposes "Mit Fried und Freud" into his own D minor harmonisation. The chorale's opening line, "In peace and joy I now depart", must have seemed an appropriate closure to what in essence was a musical memorial.

PIANO ARRANGEMENT OF THE CHACONNE, 1879

Brahms is familiar with the Chaconne from playing Schumann's piano accompaniment to Bach's score together with Joachim at the memorial concert for Schumann held in Hamburg in November 1856, four months after the composer's death. When, twenty-three years later, Clara Schumann suffered from a bout of tendonitis in her right hand, Brahms arranges the Chaconne for the left hand alone for her to give in concert. In the letter to her that accompanies the score, he proclaims the "world of deepest thoughts and the most powerful feelings" that he discerns in Bach's violin writing.[75] Could this be a covert declaration of what Brahms has always felt for Clara?

Brahms transfers Bach's violin writing to the piano without sacrificing the Chaconne's musical character. Virtually devoid of intervention, he locates Bach's figurations and chords in the piano's middle register, substituting a darker and richer sound for the violin's higher, brighter tone. For Bach's exhilarating chords and cross-string passages, Brahms proposes equally thrilling passages for the left hand, replicating on the piano the struggle of the violinist to overcome Bach's formidable difficulties. As rendered on the piano, Bach's harmonic progressions often sound more chromatically audacious than those employed by Brahms and his contemporaries in their own compositions for the instrument.

PASSACAGLIA FINALE OF SYMPHONY NO. 4 IN E MINOR, 1885

As far back as 1869, Brahms recognised that the ostinato of Bach's organ Passacaglia might permit him to "invent something actually new",[76] and so begins imagining it in the sonority of a full orchestra. But only when he comes across the chaconne-like, final chorus in Bach's cantata *Nach dir, Herr, verlanget mich* (*For thee, Oh Lord, I long*) (BWV 150), which had just appeared in the 1884 Bach Gesellschaft volume, does he act. In the presence of his friend, the conductor Hans von Bülow, Brahms plays the chorus on the piano, enthusing: "What would you say to a symphonic movement written on this theme one day? But it is too lumpish, too straightforward. It would have to be chromatically altered in some way".[77]

Indeed, this is exactly what Brahms sets out to do in the "Allegro energico e passionato" finale of his Symphony No. 4. But so substantial are his modifications that, while privately acknowledging Bach, he does not consider his chaconne "borrowed": in the end, Bach's ostinato is hardly recognisable. While maintaining the triple measure and minor key of the original (transposed from B into E), Brahms expands Bach's stepped four-bar theme ascending an interval of a fifth by inserting a sharpened fourth (A-sharp) and a repeated dominant (B), allotting each note a full bar. The result is an eight-bar theme that serves as the foundation for thirty variations, precisely the same number as those in the Goldberg Variations. However, Brahms is not interested in Bach's separate propositions; instead, as in Bach's Passacaglia and Chaconne for Solo Violin, he embeds his variations in a single musical span.

Though restricting himself to a repetitive eight-bar format, Brahms creates an epic movement that ranges in mood from forceful energy to reflective lyricism. He first announces the theme as a rising, scale-like melody in the woodwinds carried on brass chords, which is then repeated in pizzicato strings. Brahms achieves momentum with "unstable" harmonisation: the theme's first note (E) is not supported, as might be expected, on the chord of E minor, the key which governs the whole movement; instead, it forms part of an inversion of A minor (C, E and A). Only in the last bar of the theme is the E minor chord given in its fundamental form (E, G and B). As the variations progress, Brahms moves the theme around the orchestra, altering its instrumental colour and rhythmic pattern to achieve an overall tripartite scheme. In the first section, the violins play eloquent passages, oscillating in Bachian fashion around a single note (an open E string), before being shared with the woodwinds. An eloquent flute solo ushers in a middle section in E major, which recalls a similar major key section in Bach's Chaconne. Brahms reprises his original theme in the third section of his finale but interrupts it with forceful string interventions. Then come aggressive triplets in the high strings followed by gentle, waltz-like phrases in the woodwinds. In the coda, Brahms accelerates the tempo, compressing the theme into four bars and modulating it through a variety of keys while directing it ever upwards. A frenzied arpeggio cascade propels the finale to its dramatic conclusion.

CHORALE PRELUDES FOR ORGAN, 1896

Brahms's Back to Bach journey reaches its destination in the chorale preludes for the organ that he composes soon after learning of Clara's death on 20 May 1896. In addition to mourning the loss of a friendship that has endured more than forty years, the pieces suggest an atmosphere of grief and a reconciliation with death. While Brahms had written preludes and fugues for the organ in his early years, now, at the age of sixty-three, he returns to Bach, selecting nine chorales from the *Orgel-Büchlein* for his eleven settings, permeating them with his own rich harmonic language. Following Bach, he shares the static themes between the upper keyboards and bottom pedals, fleshing out the harmonies with flowing melodies or with contrapuntal ideas derived from the theme itself, while marking the chorale words on the pages.

In Chorale Prelude No. 1, "Mein Jesu, der du mich" ("My Jesus, who has called me"), the most extended of the set, Brahms presents the melody in the pedals, with each verse preceded by a fugal exposition, while in No. 8, "Es ist ein Ros entsprungen" ("A rose breaks into blossom"), he altogether dispenses with the pedals, dissolving the chorale into a flowing melody. Brahms treats the melody of No. 11, "O Welt, ich muss dich lassen" ("Oh world, I must leave you"), with which he concludes the set, in successive lines of great harmonic richness, each phrase followed by a double echo, the last "touchingly elongated".[78] With this expression of submission, Brahms takes leave of his life's work. He was to die the following year.

NIKOLAI RIMSKY-KORSAKOV (1844–1908)

A celebrated figure in Russian musical life, much sought after for his expertise in orchestration, Rimsky-Korsakov is usually associated with Orientalist extravaganzas like *Scheherazade* and the *Russian Easter Festival Overture*. Yet in 1871, at the age of only twenty-seven, he is appointed Professor of Composition at the Conservatory of St Petersburg where he embarks upon a systematic study of Bach's counterpoint in the belief that "all modern music owed everything to Bach".[79] As if in illustration, Rimsky-Korsakov writes his *Six Fugues* (1875) for the piano, each built on a theme that mimics one from *The Well-tempered Clavier*. Two years later, he progresses to his *Fugue on the Theme B-A-C-H in G Minor*, a somewhat severe exercise in which the four long-held notes of the motif are juxtaposed against a variety of counterthemes. Rimsky-Korsakov's most creative engagement with B-A-C-H, however, is a set of delightful piano variations.

SIX VARIATIONS ON THE THEME B-A-C-H, 1878

Wishing to show how Bach's musical signature might be incorporated into the music of his day, Rimsky-Korsakov marks the B-A-C-H letters over the four semitones whenever they first occur in each of his variations. The set begins with a "Valse", which has a limpid melody in triple time carried on full-bar B-A-C-H notes. A central section features running notes in the inner voice with four-bar-long B-A-C-H notes above. In the following Intermezzo, rapid figurations cascade downwards from B-A-C-H notes before these are displaced to the left hand. The third variation, which is a light-hearted Scherzo, has playful, jagged motifs floating above B-A-C-H in the middle register. The fourth variation is in the style of a Chopin nocturne, with B-A-C-H discretely embedded in an elegiac melody embellished with trills supported on a flowing accompaniment.

For his last two B-A-C-H variations, Rimsky-Korsakov reprises Bach's prelude and fugue format. The fifth variation consists of multiple voices expressed in continuous rapid notes, the middle group touching all four semitones. Cadenza-like flourishes lead directly to the sixth variation, which is a three-voice fugue built on B-A-C-H in half-bar notes, extended with descending pairs of semitones. Rimsky-Korsakov rounds off his fugue, and indeed the whole variation set, with an augmented form of B-A-C-H in the bass.

CÉSAR FRANCK (1822–90)

In 1889, the Belgian-born Franck declared: "Before I die, I am going to write some organ chorales, just as Bach did, but on a quite different plan".[80] The *Three Chorales* that he completes just a few months before his death the following year are not, as Franck predicted, like those of Bach, founded on well-known Protestant hymns; instead, they are variations on melodies of his own invention set in rich chromatic harmonies with shifting tonal centres. Though devoid of any specific liturgical message, they communicate the composer's sincere Catholicism and tendency towards mysticism.

Employed for much of his life as organist at Sainte-Clotilde in Paris, Franck gives frequent recitals of Bach's works on the basilica's superb instrument, recently installed by the most famous organ builder of the day, Aristide Cavaillé-Coll. Franck's familiarity with Bach influences his own compositions, which display chorale-like melodies divided into regular four-bar phrases, as well as fugues with step-like chromatic themes. The melodies pivoting around a single note, and dense chromatic harmonies with continuously shifting centres, however, are very much his own.

PRELUDE, CHORALE AND FUGUE, 1883

Despite his years in the organ loft, Franck composes numerous pieces for the piano, including this one, which the British-born pianist Stephen Hough judges "the most deeply felt and serious work for the instrument to come out of France in the nineteenth century".[81] He might also have added that it is a masterly demonstration of how Bachian formats may be translated into an epic, romantic piano work.

At the heart of Franck's composition is a chorale of his own invention, framed between a freely composed prelude and a more strictly structured fugue to create an extended work on a modified Bachian scheme. The prelude opens with shimmering, cascading arpeggios adorning an expressive theme in B minor, consisting of four closely spaced notes (F-sharp, E, G and F-sharp to begin with) that closely resembles the B-A-C-H semitones (transposed). At the theme's conclusion, Franck introduces an upward-trending idea that grows in emotive power until it is subdued by the phrases of a majestic chorale carried on rippling chords in the unrelated minor keys of C and E-flat. A cadenza-like interlude leads to the fugue in B minor. Its theme is based on three sets of semitones descending more than a full octave, a pattern that recalls the passacaglia-like ostinato of the Crucifixus chorus in Bach's Mass in B Minor. Franck develops the fugue in multiple voices but occasionally interrupts the counterpoint with pianistic displays.

Towards the end, Franck combines the arpeggios of the prelude with the theme of the chorale, and then with the fugal theme itself. The resulting contrapuntal overlay serve as a bravura climax, while at the same time investing the work with a cyclical structure, something with which Franck was always concerned.

CHARLES-MARIE WIDOR (1844–1937)

During the years that Franck is responsible for organ music at Sainte-Clotilde, Widor is similarly engaged in the nearby church of Saint-Sulpice. As the most influential French organist of the era, Widor enjoys a long career as performer and teacher. Trained in Brussels with the Bach specialist Jacques-Nicolas Lemmens, he becomes one of the leaders of the Bach revival in France, directing the first complete performance of the St Matthew Passion in Paris for the Concordia Choral Society in 1885. He also contributes a preface to the 1905 edition of Schweitzer's monumental study of Bach, and between 1912 and 1924, together with Schweitzer, brings out five volumes of what is intended as a definitive collection of Bach's organ works, adding his own commentaries.

ORGAN SYMPHONIES, 1872 & 1879

The superb organ at Saint-Sulpice, also by Cavaillé-Coll, offered a range of dynamics and tones that rivalled those of a full orchestra, suitable for richly chromatic harmonies and modulations. No wonder, then, that Widor calls his most ambitious organ compositions "Symphonies", even if he bases many of their movements on Bach's polyphony and keyboard figurations. Symphony No. 1 in C Minor, for example, opens with a contrapuntal prelude and ends with a fugue that vaguely recalls Bach's organ Fantasia and Fugue in C Minor (BWV 537). Symphony No. 2 in D Major features a joyful "Gigue Fugato" in a triple measure that vaguely references Bach's keyboard suites.

Symphony No. 3 in E Minor begins with a prelude with interweaving lines that ascend and descend in chromatic steps in the manner of a Bach prelude, while in No. 4 in E Minor, Widor offers a Toccata and Fugue that revisits Bach's jagged rhythms, crashing chords and recitative-like episodes. Its finale has a central section that begins somewhat like the Prelude in E Major in Book I of *The Well-tempered Clavier*.

When, seven years later, Widor comes to write another set of Symphonies, Bach's presence has lessened, although there are occasional allusions. No. 5 in F Minor concludes with a Toccata conceived in the spirit of Bach's monumental organ exemplars. The movement makes a tremendous impact through repeated, staccato pairs of chords against relentless sextuplets that modulate through just about all the keys. By locating it at the end of his Symphony, the Toccata serves not as an introduction, as is usual in Bach, but as a jubilant finale. Today, it is Widor's best-known organ composition, frequently played at church weddings.

BACH'S MEMENTO, 1925

At the advanced age of eighty-one, Widor returns to Bach by transcribing for the organ six pieces sourced from the master under the title *Bach's Memento*. The last of these, "Mattheus-Final", is a stirring arrangement of the closing chorus from the St Matthew Passion. Here, as in the other *Memento* transcriptions, Widor sticks closely to Bach, even when he transposes the originals into keys that he considers more suitable for the organ. For example, the F-sharp minor "Miserere mei", which Widor marks "Lento", is adapted from the Prelude in D Minor from Book I of *The Well-tempered Clavier*, while the E-flat minor "Sicilienne" is based on the G minor movement from the Sonata for Flute in E-flat Major (BWV 1031). With these modest revisions of his most beloved Bach pieces, Widor pays a final homage.

AFTERLIVES

THE WELL-TEMPERED CLAVIER

Bach's most influential work looks both forwards and backwards in time. By writing two "Books" of preludes and fugues in the major and minor keys on all twelve notes of the octave, Bach paves the way for all future harmonic developments. In both Books, Bach organises his pairs of preludes and fugues in ascending chromatic order (C major and minor, C-sharp major and minor, D major and minor, etc.) to demonstrate the workings of his system of tuning ("tempering"). He never imagines that one day they might be performed as entire groups.

In his freely styled preludes, Bach draws on melodic and rhythmic ideas drawn from German and Italian toccatas, French overtures, popular courtly dances, even arias in contemporary operas. He realises this musical panorama in a range of keyboard techniques: continuous arpeggios, running passages, hopping figurations, sustained chords, and so on. In his strictly composed fugues, Bach brings the long-standing tradition of polyphony to unsurpassed perfection in the contrapuntal manipulations of (mostly) three or four voices. Imbuing his themes and counterthemes with musical individuality, Bach achieves a variety of moods: the jovial spirit of the Fugues in G major and A minor; the stern proclamations of the one in D major; the soulful melodies of those in G minor and G-sharp minor – and these are only from Book I. Touching on all twelve semitones of the octave, the gravely serious theme of the Fugue in B Minor in Book I ends a musical journey that had begun with the mellifluous arpeggios in the Prelude in C Major.

Manuscript copies of the preludes and fugues circulate widely in response to demands from teachers and their pupils, offering what has been described as a comprehensive "correspondence course in melody, harmony, and counterpoint".[82] No composer or musician after Bach could ignore these lessons; indeed, they treat the preludes and fugues as "springboards" for countless adaptations and improvisations.

1782 After discovering *The Well-tempered Clavier* in the library of Baron Gottfried van Swieten in Vienna, Mozart arranges three preludes and five fugues for string trio or quartet.

1782 Mozart adapts the theme of the Fugue in C Major in Book I in his Fantasia in C Major.

1783 The Cum Sancto Spiritu chorus in Mozart's Mass in C Minor recalls the theme of the Fugue in E Major in Book II.

1801 The Preludes and Fugues are brought out separately by three different publishers.

1817 The fugal theme in the finale of Beethoven's Piano Sonata No. 29 ("Hammerklavier") begins with the same abrupt trill as in the Fugue in F-sharp Major in Book II.

c. **1815** Beethoven transcribes fugues from Book I into four separate parts as a private exercise.

1824 Twenty-four *Studies of Perfectioning* by Ignaz Moscheles.

1826 The theme and episodes in the fugal Adagio of Beethoven's String Quartet No. 14 recall those in C-sharp minor and B minor in Book I.

1837 Felix Mendelssohn's Six Preludes and Fugues for the piano.

1837 Carl Czerny brings out an edition annotated with Beethoven's tempos, dynamics and phrasings.

1839 Frédéric Chopin's *24 Préludes*.

1845 Robert Schumann's *Four Fugues* and Clara Schumann's *Three Preludes and Fugues*.

1850 The fourth movement of Schumann's Symphony No. 3 ("Rhenish") opens with a contrapuntal exposition based on the Prelude in E-flat Major from Book I.

1852 Franz Liszt writes his *Transcendental Studies* in twelve major and related minor keys. Studies in the remaining twelve keys are supplied in 1905 by Sergei Lyapunov.

1853 & 1859 Charles Gounod's *Méditation sur le Premier Prélude de Piano de J.S. Bach* for violin or cello supported on Bach's arpeggios becomes Ave Maria.

1857 *48 Preludes and Fugues in all the Major and Minor Keys* by Carl Czerny.

1878 Wagner proposes that the Fugue in F-sharp Minor from Book II anticipates his "unending melody". The principal theme of the Prelude to *Parsifal* is compared with the same fugue.[83]

c. **1912** Alexander Siloti's Prelude in B Minor.

1921 In his orchestral *Ragtime (Well-Tempered)*, Paul Hindemith quotes snippets from the Fugue in C Minor from Book I.

1920s The German–American artist Lyonel Feininger takes up writing fugues based on those of Bach.

1938 Keyboard spoof "Bach Goes to Town", subtitled "Prelude and Fugue in Swing", by the blind, Welsh-born, American jazz pianist Alec Templeton.

1942 Hindemith models his *Ludus Tonalis* on *The Well-tempered Clavier*.

1951 Dmitri Shostakovich pays homage in his 24 Preludes and Fugues.

1952 For the prelude to *Das Vorbild*, Hanns Eisler adapts the Fugue in G minor from Book I.

1958–67 In his *Play Bach* albums, Jacques Loussier records jazz improvisations on many of the preludes and fugues.

1962 With its preludes and fugues in all the keys, *The Well-Tempered Guitars*, written by the Italian composer Mario Castelnuovo-Tedesco for the guitar duo Alexandre Lagoya and Ida Presti, is modelled on Bach.

1963 & 1968 In their *Jazz Sébastien Bach* albums, the Swingle Singers vocalise many of the preludes and fugues.

1964 La Monte Young's *The Well-Tuned Piano*.

1964–99 *The Tempered Piano* by the Danish composer Niels Viggo Bentzon is a colossal project consisting of fourteen "books" of twenty-four preludes and fugues.

1965 Friedrich Gulda's *Prelude and Fugue in E-flat Minor*.

1967 Procol Harum quotes the Prelude in C Major in their song "Repent Walpurgis".

1968 Arvo Pärt imports the Prelude in C Major into his allegorical cantata *Credo*.

1968 Igor Stravinsky's instrumental transcriptions of four preludes and fugues.

1974 For their song "Rest in Peace", Mott the Hoople sources the Prelude in C Major from Book I.

1982 The American Christian singer and songwriter Rich Mullins introduces his "Sing your Praise to the Lord" with the Fugue in C Minor from Book I.

1982 The constant figurations in one of Tom Johnson's *Rational Melodies* recall those in the Prelude in C Major.

1984–2014 John Lewis of the Modern Jazz Quartet records all the preludes and fugues.

1985 *The Bad-Tempered Electronic Keyboard* by Anthony Burgess.

1987, 1990 The jazz pianist Keith Jarrett records the preludes and fugues: Book I on the piano, Book II on the harpsichord. Asked why he did not extemporise, he retorts: "the music doesn't need my help".[84]

1988 Nikolai Kapustin's *24 Preludes in Jazz Styles*.

1994 The opening bars of the Prelude in C-sharp Minor from Book I are heard in Tan Dun's shamanistic *Ghost Opera*.

1995 Peter Schickele's *The Short-Tempered Clavier*.

2000 In his *Bach Meets Jazz* album, Marc Matthys includes the Prelude in C Major.

2004 "They", a song by Jem (Jemma Griffiths), features the rendition of the Prelude in F minor from Book II by the Swingle Singers.

2009 Lady Gaga begins and ends her "Bad Romance" video with the Fugue in B Minor from Book I.

2011 & 2017 The French jazz classical pianist Édouard Ferlet sources ten preludes for extemporisations on his *Think Bach* albums.

2011 In Bach à la Jazz, Matt Herskowitz improvises on the Prelude in C Major.

2014 Max Richter sources the Prelude in C Major for "The Departure", the signature theme of the HBO drama series *The Leftovers*.

2015 The Prelude in C Minor from Book I is adapted by Luo Ni for the mobile game *Piano Tiles 2*.

2018 In *After Bach*, Brad Mehldau improvises on four preludes and one fugue.

2018 Jörg Achim Keller includes a selection of preludes and fugues in *Bach Goes Big Band*.

2021 Two preludes are included in *Bach Mirror*, played by the piano-marimba duo Thomas Enhco and Vassilena Serafimova.

Tag" ("Christ, who art the light of day") (BWV 766); the fughetta on "Gottes Sohn ist kommen" ("God's son is come") (BWV 703); and the chorale prelude "Lob sei dem allmächtigen Gott" ("Praise be to Almighty God") from the *Orgel-Büchlein* (BWV 602). Busoni quotes Bach's themes and accompanying passages at the beginning of each section of his Fantasia, whether in F minor or F major, as in Bach; and whenever Bach relocates the theme to the bass with figurations above, Busoni does likewise. To enrich these excerpts, Busoni adds his own arpeggios and scales, chromatic chordal supports, and modulations into unrelated keys. In addition, he creates a personal theme of mourning by using a "tolling-bell" motif with long, repeated notes extracted from a phrase of "Christ, der du bist".

FANTASIA CONTRAPPUNTISTICA, 1910–22

Over some twelve years, Busoni is preoccupied with his longest, most technically ambitious Bachian composition for the piano. (In consideration of its difficulties, Busoni issues a two-piano version and even approves an orchestral arrangement by Frederick Stock for the Chicago Symphony Orchestra.) Conceived as a tribute to *Art of Fugue*, Busoni begins his *Fantasia Contrappuntistica* with an extended chorale prelude based on a stately melody of his own invention accompanied by a range of pianistic textures. This serves as an introduction to three fugues that correspond almost note for note with each fugal episode in the unfinished exemplar at the end of *Art of Fugue*. In the process, Busoni repositions several of the voices, strengthening them with octaves, exploratory chromatic harmonies, and accelerating tempos. Busoni's third fugue, in which, following Bach, he introduces the B-A-C-H theme, continues after Bach leaves off to present a completed version. In the Intermezzo and Variations that follow, Busoni improvises on B-A-C-H and the other themes, directing them through different keys and ever-more complex figurations. A Cadenza with jagged rhythms leads to a fourth fugue, which reprises all of Bach's themes until Busoni returns to his opening chorale. Then comes a stretto built from the detached, three-note phrases extracted from Contrapunctus 11. Juxtaposing these diverse ideas in a fury of inversions and combinations, Busoni arrives at a finale supplied with dense chords in D minor, Bach's original key. With such imaginative manipulations, *Art of Fugue* constitutes a fitting destination for Busoni's lifelong Back to Bach journey.

MAX REGER (1873–1916)

By concluding that "every piece of organ music which is not at bottom related to Bach is impossible",[87] it is hardly surprising to learn that Bach features so prominently in Reger's organ compositions. By 1900, when he made this pronouncement, Reger has already set off on his Back to Bach journey by rejecting his Catholic Bavarian musical heritage in favour of the Protestant tradition. Composing fantasias, preludes, fugues and passacaglias modelled on Bach, both for the organ and the piano, Reger converts Bach's polyphony into a densely chromatic, almost atonal language, described by one musicologist as "historicist modernism".[88]

Suffering from nervous exhaustion and alcoholism between 1896 and 1900, Reger discovers that composing Bachian-inspired works has an alleviating effect. From these years onward, Reger writes sets of chorale preludes and fantasias, followed by works based on B-A-C-H. These are mostly intended for the organ, an instrument that Reger hesitates to play in public, relying instead on his friend and champion Karl Straube, organist at St Thomas's in Leipzig. Under the sway of Bach, Reger also produces a grandly scaled oratorio for choir and orchestra, and even a chaconne for solo violin.

CHORALE FANTASIAS, 1898–1900

An idea of Reger's imaginative approach to Bach's organ chorale preludes may be had from the Fantasia on "Freu dich sehr, o meine Seele" ("Rejoice greatly, oh my soul"), in which a succession of episodes is linked by repetitions of the chorale's four-bar phrases. The episodes comprise an introduction with toccata-like cascades, rapid passages and violent chords leading to a four-voice fugue based on the chorale's opening phrases. The three chorale preludes that follow repeat the melody in various rhythmic guises and increasingly complicated settings, passing from the keyboards to the pedals. While displaying his command of counterpoint, Reger seems more concerned with exploring a range of organ effects.

A multi-episodic format in a variety of chromatic settings also characterises the Fantasia on "Wie schön leuchtet uns der Morgenstern" ("How beautifully shines for us the morning star"). For its extravagant, toccata-like opening, Reger introduces the static chorale theme, first heard between meandering figurations, accelerating to ever-quicker triplets. In the following Adagio, he distorts the theme to create a lyrical melody, while in the Vivace he has groups of running notes for every single note of the chorale. Reger concludes the Fantasia with an extended fugue into which he introduces the chorale, directing its phrases around keyboards and pedals towards a glorious chorale climax. As in the Fantasia in "Feud dich sehr", Reger indicates the words of the chorale whenever they appear.

FANTASY AND FUGUE ON B-A-C-H, 1900

Throughout this work, Reger subjects the B-A-C-H motif to incessant harmonic metamorphoses and figural elaborations. At the end of the Fantasy, for example, he supports its four semitones on chords that progress audaciously from E-flat minor to E-natural major. The Fugue opens with B-A-C-H extended with pairs of chromatic semitones, into which Reger introduces a second fugal theme with running rapid notes compatible with B-A-C-H. While the counterpoint accords with Bachian procedure, with augmentations and inversions of the main theme, the abrupt contrasts of forcefulness and contemplation are Reger's own.

PASSACAGLIA IN F MINOR, 1902

Following Bach, Reger begins his Passacaglia with the ostinato announced alone on the pedals. His theme proceeds in two four-bar phrases, with alternating short and long notes running up and down a minor scale. On this base, Reger constructs a twelve-minute-long work encompassing the full range of organ textures, on one occasion relocating the ostinato to the upper keyboard. Despite this Bachian homage, Reger is not inclined to append his Passacaglia with a fugue; instead, he ends with a dazzling cluster of chromatic chords.

VARIATIONS AND FUGUE ON A THEME BY J.S. BACH, 1904

When it comes to writing this work for piano, Reger decides against using a Bach chorale, choosing instead the eloquent oboe introduction to the alto-tenor duet in the cantata *Auf Christi Himmelfahrt allein* (*On Christ's ascension into heaven alone*) (BWV 128). Reger begins with this theme, marking it "as if an oboe solo" but indicating that it is to be played at a much slower speed, thereby creating, in effect, an altogether new piece. In the variations that follow, Reger distorts the theme melodically, rhythmically and harmonically, before submerging it in a range of pianistic textures and technical extravagances. Despite the emotive eruptions alternating with calm interludes, the theme, even when fragmented, is mostly recognisable.

Reger bases his fugue on a chromatically similar but different theme in the same B minor key as the oboe melody. It begins in a Bachian manner with four clear voices before a lighter, quick-moving countertheme is introduced, with which it is then juxtaposed. Towards the end, the theme is heard in overlaps in increasingly grandiose chords. As in his organ works, Reger supplies the score with a profusion of dynamic and emotive markings, insisting that fugue's principal theme be "well marked and expressive".

THE 100TH PSALM, 1909

In this huge choral symphony for chorus, orchestra and organ set to Luther's translation, Reger fuses Bachian polyphony with his own opulent textures, chromatic modulations and dynamic melodramas. Originally commissioned for the celebration of the 350th anniversary of Jena University in 1908, Reger only completes the work in the following year, expanding it into four movements, ending with a monumental choral fugue with the voices singing "Denn freundlich is der Herr, und seine Gnade währt ewig" ("For friendly is the Lord, and his mercy lasts forever"). For its climax, Reger introduces "Ein feste Burg ist unser Gott" ("A mighty fortress is our Lord") on trumpets and trombones in forceful unison. His writing for the trumpet recalls Bach's use of the same instrument soaring above the opening chorus in his cantata based on the same chorale (BWV 80). That Reger writes his version in the same "jubilant" D major key as Bach can be no coincidence.

CHACONNE FOR SOLO VIOLIN, 1909

Reger had studied violin in his student days and acquired expertise in string writing, which he displays in later years in pieces for solo viola and solo cello. Among those that exhibit the closest affinity with Bach is the Chaconne for Solo Violin. Reger's Chaconne shares with Bach a minor key (G minor for Reger, D minor for Bach); a theme that stresses the second beat (though Reger expands Bach's four-bar theme to eight bars); and a set of continuous variations. With their frequent multiple stops, cross-string arpeggios, rapid passages and harmonics, the work challenges the limits of violin technique. Following Bach at the end of his organ Passacaglia (though not his Chaconne), Reger appends a fugue, which he models on the three-voice Fuga in the same G minor key as in Bach's Sonata No. 1 for Solo Violin (BWV 1001).

EDWARD ELGAR (1857–1934)

Elgar's experience as organist in St George's Roman Catholic Church in Worcester between 1885 and 1899 instils in him a reverence for Bach, which extends into later years, when he orchestrates one of Bach's most majestic organ pieces. By this time, he has already completed a work for strings conceived in the shadow of the Brandenburg Concertos.

INTRODUCTION AND ALLEGRO FOR STRINGS, 1905

It was after sitting through a performance of Brandenburg Concerto No. 3 at the Lower Rhine Festival in Cologne in 1904 that Elgar's close friend August Jaeger, the Anglo-German music publisher, reached out to the composer: "Why not a *brilliant* String Scherzo … such as Bach could write …. You might even write a *modern Fugue* for strings".[89] The following year, Elgar responds by completing his *Introduction and Allegro* as a showpiece for the string section of the newly formed London Symphony Orchestra.

In true concerto grosso style, Elgar disposes his musical ideas and technical difficulties equally between a solo string quartet and tutti strings. Some of their exchanges recall those in the Brandenburg Concertos, as in the staccato rapid notes passing back and forward between the players in the Allegro. Declaring his affinity with Bach, Elgar devotes the central section of the Allegro to a fugue, longer and more complicated than anything he has written before, including the contrapuntal interlude in his oratorio *The Dream of Gerontius* of five years earlier. The string fugue is based on a dance-like theme with abrupt, bouncing intervals that vaguely recall those in the Fugue in F Major in Book I of *The Well-tempered Clavier*, which Elgar juxtaposes with one of his own distinctive, sweet melodies. Skilfully manipulating these complementary ideas, Elgar reveals what he has learned from Bach.

ORCHESTRATION OF BACH'S FANTASIA AND FUGUE IN C MINOR, 1922

Following the rift between English and German composers in consequence of World War I, Elgar attempts to re-establish his friendship with Richard Strauss, who had always promoted his music, by proposing they collaborate on an orchestration of a Bach organ work, suggesting one of his favourites, the Fantasia and Fugue in C Minor (BWV 537). When they meet in 1921, it is agreed that Strauss would set the Fantasia, and Elgar the Fugue; in the end, Elgar arranges both for the Three Choirs Festival held in Gloucester the following year. His transcription calls for a huge orchestra, with full brass and percussion. While eloquent oboe passages occasionally relieve the thick instrumental textures, Elgar's tendency is for emotive climaxes accentuated by rapid woodwind, strident brass passages and even harp glissandos. Despite the tremendous excitement and lush colouration, Elgar never loses sight of Bach's contrapuntal clarity.

GUSTAV MAHLER (1860–1911)

Bach is a constant source of inspiration for Mahler. As his wife, Alma, recalled, the only music scores that Mahler kept at hand in his summer composing cabin in the Austrian Alps were the Bach Gesellschaft volumes.[90] In November 1909, when appointed music director and principal conductor of the New York Philharmonic,

Mahler paid tribute with an "Historical Cycle" of concerts, which includes the music of Bach.

BACH SUITE, 1909

By combining movements from Bach's Orchestral Suites, Mahler creates the four-part format of a classical symphony, beginning with the Overture from No. 2, and ending with the pair of Gavottes from No. 3. For the central slow movement, Mahler imports the Air from No. 3 (in Bach's original D major key), which he enhances with lush string sonorities that translate Bach's interweaving melodies into an ethereal Adagio, not unlike those in his own symphonies. Wishing to enhance the infectious flute antics in the Badinerie from No. 2, Mahler adds buoyant string pizzicatos. For the continuo, played by himself on a piano modified to sound like a harpsichord, he invents supporting chords and supplementary passages that often imitate those of the soloists. Mahler justifies his interventions by arguing that these would make Bach more appealing to the New York audience. He must have judged correctly, for he was to repeat the Suite several times before he returned to Europe in 1911.

CLAUDE DEBUSSY (1862–1918)

It is the freedom he discovers in the music that underpins Debussy's Back to Bach journey. As he once wrote: "when Bach took over the arabesque …. it was able to move forward with the free, ever fresh fantasy which still amazes us today".[91] Liberty from convention is central to Debussy's colouristic textures, exotic modes, unsymmetrical phrases and abrupt transitions. Even so, much of his piano writing conceals an intricate and subtle counterpoint, as in his *Préludes*. Like those of Bach, these eventually number twenty-four, but do not cover all the major and minor keys since Debussy prefers harmonic ambiguity and multiple key changes, often within a single work. By the time he came to write a piece for the unusual combination of two pianos, in which he quotes a Bach chorale, Debussy has accepted a commission from his Paris publisher Jacques Durand to edit Bach's Sonatas for Violin and Viola da Gamba.

POUR LE PIANO, 1901

Debussy's first mature piano composition is a suite of three pieces that he calls Prelude, Sarabande and Toccata, in an obvious nod to the baroque era. That Bach's keyboard suites may have been in Debussy's mind is suggested by the repeated, rapid note patterns of the Prelude and the triple metre of the outer sections of Sarabande, with their insistent emphasis on the second beat. Rippling passages in the Toccata recall those at the beginning of Bach's Partita No. 6 in E Minor, a movement which Bach also calls a Toccata. Marked "Vif" ("Lively"), Debussy's depiction of unrestrained motion has groups of notes running swiftly across the keyboard. Though beginning and ending his Toccata in C-sharp minor, he modulates its central section into the remote key of F major, at which point he introduces a tranquil melody on gentle arpeggios.

EN BLANC ET NOIR, 1915

The circumstances under which Debussy comes to write this work for two pianos are worth noting. Fleeing Paris during World War I, Debussy retreats for a time to the Normandy coast, where he composes *Caprice in White and Black*, later dropping the first word. With this title, Debussy was thinking of the monochrome colours in Francisco Goya's *Los Caprichos* (*The Caprices*), which includes *Los Desastres de la Guerra* (*The Disasters of War*),[92] an understandable reference at the time. Debussy dedicates the central movement to the memory of Durand's nephew who had just been killed, marking it as "Slow and sombre" and prefacing it with lines from the *Ballade contre les ennemis de la France* by the fifteenth-century poet François Villon. This literary reference to the "Enemies of France" is illustrated by pianistic renditions of bugle calls and distant rumbling guns. Into these disturbing evocations of war, Debussy inserts dirge-like phrases of "Ein feste Burg ist unser Gott", subverting Bach's jubilant chorale with dissonant chords, tremolandos and violent staccato passages. The scoring of the chorale theme in hollow octaves, mostly in the middle and lower registers of the pianos, contributes to the distressing effect.

Debussy's inclusion of a Lutheran hymn in a work premiered in Paris as the Germans are menacing the city triggers the wrath of Camille Saint-Saëns. In a letter to Gabriel Fauré, he condemns *En blanc et noir* as "unbelievable", using his objection as an excuse to bar Debussy from membership of the prestigious Institut de France.[93] But Debussy did not choose "Ein feste Burg" to celebrate German culture; rather, it was to evoke the chorale's message of resistance and comfort.

ERIC SATIE (1866–1925)

A year before Debussy deployed a Bach chorale to express his anguished response to war, another French composer altogether ignored the conflict by writing a light-hearted, satirical work recalling a Bach chorale.

CHOSES VUES À DROITE ET À GAUCHE (SANS LUNETTES), 1914

It is with a "Hypocritical chorale" that Satie begins his duet for violin and piano, cheekily titled *Things Seen to the Right and Left (Without Spectacles)*. Though here Satie invents his own spare chorale melody, its two-bar phrases recall those of Bach. Satie assigns the hymn melody to muted chords in the violin, with the piano providing a gently dissonant support. At the end, Satie added the words: "my chorales match up to those of Bach, the only difference being that they are rarer and less pretentious".[94] Satie's nod to the master is not altogether irreverent: he positions his chorale between a "Groping Fugue" and a "Muscular Fantasy", which he first thought to arrange in Bachian fashion as a fantasy, chorale and fugue. Like the two chorales he included in his earlier piano duet *En habit du cheval* (*In riding gear*) (1911), Satie translates Bach's format into his own pared-down idiom. He is to do the same in the chorale with which he begins *Parade*, the orchestral ballet score that he composes in 1917. By this time, however, he has renounced any reference to Bach.

ALEXANDER SILOTI (1863–1945)

As an inveterate transcriber, this Russian émigré pianist, conductor and teacher makes more than 200 arrangements of works of Bach. The most famous of these is an adaption of a keyboard prelude that Bach himself had also arranged.

PRELUDE IN B MINOR, *C.* 1912

This is a version of the Prelude in E Minor (BWV 855a) that Bach included among the sixty or so practice pieces that he compiled in 1720 in the *Clavier-Büchlein* for his ten-year-old son Wilhelm Friedemann. Not all these are original compositions, including perhaps even this prelude. Yet, Bach regarded it sufficiently highly to make a new version by adding a lyrical melody upon continuously running notes in the left hand and inserting it into Book I of *The Well-tempered Clavier*. For his Prelude, Siloti reverts to Bach's earlier version, transposing it into B minor and relocating the running notes to the right hand. When the prelude is repeated, as instructed, the supporting, arpeggiated chords reveal a soulful inner voice, transforming what had been a keyboard exercise into a transcendent meditation, which, as Emil Gilels demonstrated, proves irresistible to the greatest pianists.

LEOPOLD GODOWSKI (1870–1938)

The Polish–American musician Leopold Godowski is another virtuoso émigré pianist who is also an enthusiastic Bach arranger. In 1909–10, he skilfully adapts Bach's string writing in the Solo Violin Sonatas and solo Cello Suites to the acoustics of the piano, adding his own harmonic supports, extra voices and ornamental flourishes. That such interventions form part of a creative homage is borne out by the fact that Godowski finds places for B-A-C-H in his own compositions.

SONATA IN E MINOR, 1911

Into the last movement of his grandly scaled piano work, Godowski inserts a fugal section built on B-A-C-H, heading its four semitones with the relevant letters, together with the instruction that they are be played "molto espressivo". Expanding B-A-C-H into a four-bar theme, Godowski creates a triple-voice fugue that builds in volume and intensity, ending in brilliant passages in imitation and in canon, one of which has an augmented version of B-A-C-H played against itself.

PASSACAGLIA IN B MINOR, 1927

Written on the eve of the centenary of Franz Schubert's death, Godowski turns to the Symphony No. 8 in B Minor ("Unfinished") for a piano work modelled on Bach's organ exemplar. The Passacaglia consists of variations on an eight-bar ostinato borrowed from Schubert, which Godowski shifts around the different registers of the piano to explore different textures and technical challenges. His variations include an Andante espressivo "Epilogue" followed by a three-voice fugue based on Schubert's theme, which Godowski augments before abandoning the counterpoint to arrive at a stirring finale.

PRELUDE AND FUGUE ON THE THEME B-A-C-H, 1929

Godowski composes this piece for the left hand alone, presumably as a vehicle for his formidable technique. (He probably had in mind Brahms's transcription of Bach's Chaconne for Solo Violin – another left-hand piano arrangement of daunting difficulty.) In his prelude, Godowski offers an assortment of wistful melodies on fast-moving figurations, some of which recall those of Bach. The fugal theme, with the B-A-C-H notes expanded into four bars, is announced in a jaunty rhythm that mimics that of the Fugue in C Minor in Book I of *The Well-tempered Clavier*. By supplying his three-voice fugue with imitative episodes and stretto overlaps, Godowski gives evidence of his contrapuntal competence.

LEOPOLD STOKOWSKI (1882–1977)

As organist and choirmaster in churches in London and New York in his early years, Stokowski gains first-hand acquaintance with Bach. In 1912, he advances to the post of Director of the Philadelphia Orchestra, with whom, over the next thirty years, he presents countless programmes showcasing the brilliance of its players. They include more than forty Bach transcriptions, three of which should be sufficient to illustrate the famous "Stokowski sound".[95]

PASSACAGLIA, 1922

Stokowski translates Bach's organ work into symphonic drama by pitting different sections of the orchestra against each other, distinguishing the thirty variations with different instrumental textures and colours. Never is the ostinato lost, whether played on lower strings, strident brass chords, or high trumpet solo. The same instrumental articulations in the fugue highlight Bach's counterpoint, which Stokowski drives ever onward until it reaches a monumental tutti climax.

TOCCATA AND FUGUE IN D MINOR, 1927

Stokowski assigns the chords with which the Toccata begins to ominous overlays in the brass, while rustling strings navigate the intricate upper figurations of the keyboard recitatives. Before the tremendous climax that brings the Toccata to a close, Stokowski sets off on the Fugue with the violins and violas playing Bach's oscillating notes, partly on open strings, and the cellos and double basses reproducing the rumbling pedal figurations. Passing Bach's ideas between the higher strings and woodwinds, Stokowski injects the Fugue with colouristic contrasts that suggest different organ stops. He then harnesses his symphonic forces until they reach a virtual standstill, before driving the orchestra towards the conclusion, where the violins negotiate Bach's scales and arpeggios between forceful brass chords.

Stokowski's version of the Toccata and Fugue reaches worldwide audiences thanks to Walt Disney, who selects it for the opening sequence in his 1940 animated film *Fantasia*. Responding to Bach's obsessive counterpoint, Disney's artists fill the screen with abstract surging angles and swelling shapes.

CHACONNE, 1930

As in his organ orchestrations, Stokowski offers an entirely new piece of music without sacrificing a note of Bach. His version of the solo violin piece begins with gloomy lower strings and woodwinds, before progressing to eloquent oboe melodies, solemn brass pronouncements, and ecstatic staccato violin passages. At times, Stokowski's lush orchestration recalls the density of a Mahler symphony.

MYRA HESS (1890–1965)

For the concerts she organises during World War II in London's National Gallery, Hess includes many keyboard works of Bach.

JESU, JOY OF MAN'S DESIRING, 1926

By making a piano arrangement of the chorale "Wohl mir, dass ich Jesum habe" from the cantata *Herz und Mund und Tat und Leben* (*Heart and mouth and deed and life*) (BWV 147), Hess launches its stately melody framed by lilting triplets into worldwide popularity.

WOLFGANG GRAESER (1906–28)

A child prodigy who masters mathematics, philosophy, painting and musicology, the Swiss-born Graeser is the first to demonstrate that Bach's contrapuntal exemplars could be listened to as music when translated into instrumental colours.

ART OF FUGUE, 1927

Graeser presents his orchestration in St Thomas's in Leipzig, where *Art of Fugue* has never been heard before. Graeser's realisation imports Bach's fugues into the acoustic of an orchestra that includes trumpets and trombones but reserves the canons for the organ and harpsichord. Based on a meticulous study of the original manuscript, Graeser hopes his reconstruction might inspire fervent patriotism. As he writes: "the German *Volk*, in a time of serfdom, of inner and outer poverty, must remember the spirit of its great, world-historic genius".[96] One year after its premier, Graeser commits suicide: he is barely twenty-two years old.

ARTHUR HONEGGER (1892–1955)

In 1925, this French composer admits that Bach lies "at the origins of all my works",[97] a claim borne out by the central role of counterpoint underpinning Honegger's colouristic, neoclassical idiom.

MOUVEMENT SYMPHONIQUE NO. 1 (PACIFIC 231), 1923

Barely seven minutes long, Honegger's astonishingly realistic portrait of a locomotive journey begins with tremolandos in the strings and brass to produce the effect of puffing and exhaling. He then introduces more instruments in increasingly rapid figurations to suggest the gathering momentum of the train, until full symphonic forces are deployed to express the greatest speed. Screeching brass outbursts announce the brakes being applied before a final tutti indicates that the engine has come to a stop. Only after completing his *Mouvement symphonique* did Honegger think to call it *Pacific 231*, an imaginary train, under which name it comes to feature on soundtracks in Soviet and French films in 1931 and 1949.

At the time, Honegger's musical evocation of mechanical propulsion seemed an epitome of modernist optimism. Despite its audacious instrumentation and avoidance of conventional tonality, however, the work gazes backwards: in effect, it is a literal Back to Bach journey. Honegger readily acknowledged this when he described *Pacific 231* as a "big, diversified chorale, strewn with counterpoint in the manner of J.S. Bach".[98] Rather than a chorale, however, it is with a passacaglia that Honegger conveys the train's motion by repeating an eight-bar, ostinato-like theme with a rising contour to support increasingly complicated figurations. As the music accelerates and orchestral textures thicken, Honegger contracts the length of the theme, passing it between the different instruments to propel the music ever forward. At the end, he reprises it in fortissimo brass outbursts.

LES NOCES D'AMOUR ET DE PSYCHÉ, 1928

On at least one occasion Honegger's Back to Bach journey led directly to the master, as in the music he provided for the ballet *The Wedding of Cupid and Psyche* staged for Ida Rubinstein's company in Paris. For each of its movements, Honegger sources music from one of Bach's keyboard works, which he transcribes for an ensemble that includes two saxophones, harp and celesta. For the "Entrance of Psyche", for instance, he arranges the lyrical Sarabande from French Suite No. 6 (BWV 817), and for the concluding "Apotheosis", the majestic organ Prelude and Fugue in C Major (BWV 545), which he transcribes for full orchestra. Judging from the scenic designs by Alexandre Benois, Honegger's instrumental extravagances were matched by the Paris staging.[99]

PRÉLUDE, ARIOSO ET FUGHETTE SUR LE NOM DE B-A-C-H, 1932

In this modest piano work, Honegger pays tribute to Bach by writing three movements that incorporate the B-A-C-H motif in different ways. He begins with a prelude that presents arpeggio cascades progressing up and down chromatic steps, ending in four repetitions of the B-A-C-H semitones. These anticipate the motif's appearance in the Arioso as four long notes spread across two bars, which are then repeated throughout the movement in the bass. Against this, Honegger provides an eloquent, free-flowing melody shared between the upper and lower registers supported on a gentle pulse. A cadenza provides the transition to the two-voice fughetta on B-A-C-H. The motif appears in short notes bouncing over more than an octave, followed by quicker configurations. Towards the end, Honegger offers B-A-C-H in stretto in half-bar overlaps.

SYMPHONY NO. 2, 1941

Honegger never forgets the Bachian structure of his *Mouvement symphonique No. 1*, and some eighteen years later returns to the passacaglia format in the Adagio of his Symphony No. 2. Commissioned by the Swiss conductor and patron Paul Sacher, the work is only completed during the Nazi occupation of France, by which time Honegger's music is banned, except for film scores. Written for strings alone, except for a trumpet solo towards the end, Honegger's symphony is suffused with an atmosphere of deprivation and doom, as expressed in dissonant chords and jarring chromatic melodies. The "mesto" ("sad") Adagio central movement takes the form of a passacaglia based on a four-bar ostinato. This is in triple time, with a melancholy, drooping semitone motif that gradually ascends. Recalling the beginning of Bach's organ ostinato, Honegger's theme carries lamenting, chromatic melodies in the middle and upper strings. These dolorous figurations contrast with the buoyant gigue-like passages in the symphony's final Vivace. Towards the end of this movement, Honegger introduces a chorale theme of his own that sounds like one of Bach's. He gives it to the violins as well as to a trumpet, which is now heard for the first time soaring high above the strings, propelling the movement, and indeed the whole symphony, towards a "positive" D major finale. For one listener, the chorale offered "a glimmer of hope … to this desperate music".[100]

In November 1941, Honegger was invited to a week-long festival in Vienna organised by the Nazi establishment to celebrate the 150th anniversary of Mozart's death. He takes the opportunity of smuggling the manuscript of his newly completed symphony to Sacher.

PASSACAGLIA TO THE MEMORY OF ARTHUR HONEGGER, 1959

Honegger instils a lasting respect for Bach in his student Maurice Jarre, who, four years after his teacher dies in 1955, offers an orchestral tribute in the form of a passacaglia.

Though built on an unsymmetrical, seven-bar ostinato in triple metre, with pairs of short and long notes, Jarre's Passacaglia references Bach's organ exemplar, even when the ostinato is displaced by provocative, rhythmic irregularities. The work abounds in percussive outbursts, dissonances in brass chords and dense strings, as well as delicate solos for clarinet, flute and violin. Such effects anticipate those that Jarre incorporates into the film scores that he later writes for David Lean, which are to bring him fame.

FRANCIS POULENC (1899–1963)

As he accepts a commission from Vladimir Horowitz to write a miniature encore piece that the pianist could present in concert programmes, Poulenc remembers Bach.

VALSE-IMPROVISATION SUR LE NOM DE BACH, 1932

This high-spirited piece is built on a beguiling melody that Poulenc contrives from the B-A-C-H semitones. Maintaining a constant rhythmic pace, he propels his waltz to a frenzied climax with fortissimo chords hammering out the four semitones simultaneously (indicated by the letters in the score).

IGOR STRAVINSKY (1882–1971)

In 1913, Stravinsky considered Bach's music "too remote".[101] Barely five years later, he reverses his opinion and inserts a Bach chorale into *L'Historie du soldat* (*The Soldier's Tale*). Stravinsky's fascination with the music of the past is more fully expressed in 1920, when he provides witty treatments of pieces for his ballet score *Pulcinella*, which he believed to be by the eighteenth-century composer Giovanni Battista Pergolesi. From *L'Histoire* and *Pulcinella*, both written for the theatre, Stravinsky progressed to an idiom often described as "neoclassical". At the same time, he admits: "I have a predilection for Bach, who likes clear forms and chisels them perfectly, abolishing all useless and dangerous ornament".[102] Among the neoclassical works infused with Bach figurations are the Octet for Wind Instruments and the Piano Sonata. However, it is not until his Concerto in E-flat (inscribed "Dumbarton Oaks") that Stravinsky discloses his Back to Bach journey by unambiguously referencing the Brandenburg Concertos.

After the death of Arnold Schoenberg in 1951, Stravinsky begins composing "serial" music using twelve-tone rows. At the same time, he returns to Bach by making an elaborate orchestral-choral arrangement of Bach's organ variations. And as a final tribute at the great age of eighty-six, he transcribes several preludes and fugues from *The Well-tempered Clavier*.

L'HISTOIRE DU SOLDAT, 1918

In this story of a runaway soldier's encounter with the devil, as related through spoken words and sparsely scored musical interludes, some to be danced, Stravinsky follows the form of a traditional Russian folk ballad, with a narrator assuming different roles. The musical character of *The Soldier's Tale* is eclectic, with dance movements ranging from Russian folk music to waltz, tango and ragtime, all animated with Stravinsky's buoyant rhythms and dissonant harmonies. Before the "Triumphal March of the Devil", with which the work concludes, the narrator presents the story's moral, with verses set between a "Little Chorale" and a "Great Chorale", both based on "Ein feste Burg ist unser Gott". While Stravinsky retains Bach's phrases and cadences to suggest a moment of consolation, he supports these on dissonant chords to express a sense of unease, anticipating the soldier's death.

OCTET FOR WIND INSTRUMENTS, 1923

That Stravinsky models this neoclassical work on an eighteenth-century divertimento is obvious at the outset from the sonata-scheme first movement; Andante theme and variations in the central movement; and Rondo finale. The Andante's last variation is a fugue, but this displays little Bachian character. In contrast, the finale opens with a long theme, with bouncing notes jumping over large intervals separated by rippling, scale-like passages carried on a continuous step-like notes – all typical Bachian patterns. As Stravinsky later remembered: "Bach's Two-part Inventions were somewhere in the back of my mind while composing this movement, as they were during the last movement of the Piano

Sonata".[103] While the imitative passages between bassoon and clarinet in the octet's finale recall those in Bach's Inventions Nos 2 and 11 (BWV 773 and 782), they are even closer to passages in Nos 4 and 8 of the three-part Sinfonias (BWV 790 and 794). Stravinsky's fondness for recurring dissonances, however, precludes any direct quotations. Gentle, syncopated chords in an un-Bachian manner bring the octet's finale to an end.

PIANO SONATA, 1924

A Bachian spirit often infuses Stravinsky's piano writing, as in this neoclassical-style Sonata. Its first movement is built on continuous triplets, mostly spanning large intervals, played simultaneously with both hands. Stravinsky arranges them in two or three groups per bar, a pattern that recalls the incessant triplets in the gigues of Bach's keyboard suites, though lacking any harmonic or thematic connection. The same is true of the sonata's last movement, which features rapid passages, marked "not legato", as if to suggest the touch of a harpsichord. The progression upwards and downwards around an interval of a sixth in the Sonata's finale recalls Bach's keyboard writing, as in the Fugue in E Minor in Book I of *The Well-tempered Clavier*.

The Bachian elements in Piano Sonata did not escape Schoenberg, who heard it premiered at the International Society of Contemporary Music concert in Venice in 1925. In one of the *Three Satires* for choir and small instrumental ensemble that he writes shortly afterwards, Schoenberg adds the sarcastic rebuke "Little Modernsky … quite the Papa Bach".[104] Sergei Prokofiev, too, recognised the "Bach-ness" of the work.[105]

SYMPHONY OF PSALMS, 1930

Scored for choir and orchestra without violins, but with two pianos, this is perhaps Stravinsky's mostly deeply felt, religious work. It is also one of his most eclectic, as it encompasses the homophonic chants of the Russian Orthodox Church as well as the rich polyphony of the Catholic and Protestant traditions, the latter represented by Bach. Stravinsky sets the symphony's second movement, "With expectation, I have waited for the Lord", from Psalm 39, as a double fugue. The seven-bar first theme, announced on solo wind instruments, with its first two notes of the C minor triad, followed by a B-natural that drops an interval of a sixth, bears an overall resemblance to the opening phrase of the Thema Regium in the *Musical Offering*, also in C minor. Stravinsky extends his theme with rapid oscillations around the Bachian intervals of a sixth and seventh. After developing the fugue in the woodwinds, he introduces the chorus by singing a second theme. As the movement progresses, the two themes are often heard together, though the first is sometimes reduced to its opening four notes and rhythmically augmented. From these components, Stravinsky constructs a solemn, majestic movement with inventive counterpoint enhanced by the spare scoring of voices, woodwinds, trombones and lower strings.

CONCERTO IN E-FLAT ("DUMBARTON OAKS"), 1938

This concerto takes its name from the mansion in Washington DC, where it was first heard in a private performance by the owners who had commissioned the work. Stravinsky conceives "Dumbarton Oaks" as a concerto grosso for Bachian forces: single woodwinds, a pair of horns, and triple sets of violins, violas and cellos; only the clarinet would have been unfamiliar to Bach. At different moments, each player assumes the role of a soloist, as in the Brandenburg Concertos Nos 3 and 6. Stravinsky himself draws attention to the connection. As he later admits to his friend, colleague and biographer Robert Craft: "I was greatly attracted to the Brandenburg Concertos, especially the third …. The first theme of my concerto is, of course, very like Bach's ... so is my instrumentation .... I do not think, however, that Bach would have begrudged me this loan of these ideas and materials, as borrowing in this way was something he liked to do himself".[106]

"Dumbarton Oaks" opens with high-spirited, rapid configurations on the strings, some jumping onto half-beats to interlock with those on the main beats, a pattern that recalls the beginning of the Brandenburg No. 6, even though Stravinsky identifies No. 3 as the source. About halfway through the first movement, Stravinsky indulges in a fugal episode based on a playful, syncopated motif, first in the strings, then in the woodwinds and horns. The movement ends with reprise of the Brandenburg-type figurations before pensive string chords serve as a transition to a gracious Allegretto that points to the period of Haydn and Mozart. When it comes to the last movement, Bach is left far behind.

ARRANGEMENT OF "VOM HIMMEL HOCH", 1956

As he was planning the premier of his *Canticum Sacrum*, written in praise of St Mark, patron saint of Venice, Stravinsky searched for a companion piece that could be performed by the same combination of voices and woodwinds, brass, harp and lower strings. Trawling through Bach's organ works, he came across the chorale variations that Bach had presented to Mizler's learned society in Leipzig more than 200 years before. Stravinsky becomes captivated by the ingenious canons with which Bach had adorned the stately phrases of "From heaven above, to earth I come" (BWV 769). Perhaps, like Schweitzer, he understood "the maze of ascending and descending scales [as a depiction of] flying angels".[107] It was an ecstatic image perfectly suited to the gleaming interior of St Mark's.

Stravinsky begins by announcing "Vom Himmel hoch" in trumpets and trombones, in a harmonisation that recalls the chorale in Bach's Christmas Oratorio (BWV 248). For the variations, Stravinsky quests after contrasting tonalities: trombones as a background; flutes and oboes over the voices; harp and pizzicato strings below; and so on. He mostly assigns the chorale melody to the choir, which proclaims Luther's words in unison; only in the last variation does he divide the upper and lower voices to sing the chorale in Bach's two-part canon, in inversion. Such strategies clarify Bach's counterpoint as well as his rhythmic vitality, something to which Stravinsky was always drawn. He is not the only one: in 1972, another émigré Russian, George Balanchine, choreographs Stravinsky's "Vom Himmel Hoch" variations for the New York City Ballet.

RAOUL DUFY IN MEMORIUM, 1959

Stravinsky never forgot Bach's ingenious organ canons, and three years later invented one of his own for a miniature piece that he writes in memory of the French artist Raoul Dufy, whose paintings he admires. In this double canon for string quartet, Stravinsky displays a contrapuntal cunning worthy of Bach by writing two independent canons to be played simultaneously in the upper and lower pairs of strings. The twelve-tone row that he invents for the first canon begins with two pairs of adjacent semitones (F-sharp and F-natural, A and G-sharp), in an obvious nod to B-A-C-H. By inverting this theme and that of the second canon, then giving them in retrograde, Stravinsky salutes the canons in the Musical Offering.

TRANSCRIPTIONS FROM THE WELL-TEMPERED CLAVIER, 1968

As his style transitioned from neoclassicism to atonalism, Stravinsky consults Bach. In fact, Bach has always been there: according to one his biographers, Stravinsky began each day playing preludes and fugues from The Well-tempered Clavier.[108] After the composer's death in New York on 6 April 1971, Robert

Craft discovered the pages of the Prelude in E-flat Minor from Book I open on the studio piano, as if this was the last piece of Bach that Stravinsky had played.[109] Perhaps he was considering arranging it for strings and woodwinds, as he had done three years earlier with four other preludes and fugues from *The Well-tempered Clavier*. They include a string version of the Prelude and Fugue in B Minor from Book I, which takes on an expressive intensity that recalls the chromatic romanticism than Stravinsky had rebelled against in his earliest years. Bach writes the B Minor Prelude with two independent upper voices carried on a basso continuo, which Stravinsky captures on the cello. For the Preludes and Fugues in C-sharp Minor and E Minor in Book I, and in F Major in Book II, Stravinsky turns to woodwinds. The tonal clarity of the clarinets and bassoons brings Bach's counterpoint into high relief, emphasising the rhythmic patterns and interweaving lines that Stravinsky had so often employed in his own music. With these arrangements, Stravinsky's Back to Bach journey arrives at its final destination.

AFTERLIVES

BRANDENBURG CONCERTOS, BADINERIE & AIR ON THE G STRING

Bach styles the six pieces he sends the Margrave of Brandenburg in 1721 as "Concerts" (Concertos), since they conform to conventional baroque era concerto grosso formats. Each consists of a trio of quick-slow-quick movements performed by soloists pitted against a string band: three hunting horns in No.1; trumpet, recorder and oboe in No. 2; a pair of recorders with a violin in No. 4; flute, violin and harpsichord in No. 5. He restricts No. 3 to triple sets of violins, violas and cellos, while for No. 6, he harnesses deeper-toned violas, viola da gambas and cellos. Bach must have had capable players in mind, since he writes demanding parts for a solo flute in No. 2, and for solo violin in No. 4. For No. 5, he devises a bravura passage for keyboard alone, probably for himself to play, perhaps on the harpsichord he had purchased for his princely employer in Berlin in 1719. It anticipates the cadenzas in later piano concertos.

While the Brandenburg Concertos came to inspire later instrumental works, two movements from the four Orchestral Suites, which Bach calls "Overtures", being medleys of French-style dances, prove particularly popular. These are the vivacious Badinerie for solo flute from No. 2, and the elegiac Air for string ensemble from No. 3. The latter enjoys a distinguished career as the "Air on the G String", having been "invented" by the German violinist August Wilhelmj in 1871 as a solo piece to be played on the bottom string of the instrument.

1830 Felix Mendelssohn plays a version of Bach's Air for the eighty-one-year-old Goethe. The descending stepped bass line that carries its melody leads the poet to imagine "a file of well-dressed people walking in stately fashion down a great staircase".[110]

1849 The German music theorist Siegfried Wilhelm Dehn comes across the manuscript of Bach's Concertos in the Prussian Royal Library in Berlin. Bach's dedication to the Margrave leads him to publish them as the Brandenburg Concertos.

1897 Publication of the Orchestral Suites.

1905 Edward Elgar's concerto grosso-style *Introduction and Allegro for Strings*.

1909 Gustav Mahler's *Bach Suite*.

1925 Bach-inspired Concerto Grosso No. 1 by Ernest Bloch.

1927–28 Kammermusik Nos 5, 6 and 7 by Paul Hindemith.

1930–45 In his nine *Bachianas Brasileiras* written for different instrumental ensembles, Heitor Villa-Lobos fuses Bachian concerto grosso formats with the folk music of his native Brazil.

1938 Igor Stravinsky's Concerto in E-flat ("Dumbarton Oaks").

1964 The Swingle Singers vocalise the Badinerie from Suite No. 2.

1967 The Beatles quote Brandenburg-like trumpet passages in "Penny Lane".

1967 Procol Harum's "A Whiter Shade of Pale" begins with the first bars of Air on the G String.

1968 The progressive rock band The Nice issues Keith Emerson's *Brandenburger*.

1969 Air on the G String features in "Air" by the Dutch crossover band Ekseption.

1977–93 Alfred Schnittke's six Concerto Grossos.

1977 *Tabula Rasa* by Arvo Pärt.

1966–91 Air on the G String is exploited in a television advertising campaign for a brand of new cigars called Hamlet.

1989 Jazz pianist Eugen Cicero spices up the Badinerie in *Swinging Bach*.

1990 The Air is heard in "Everything's Gonna Be Alright" sung by Tina Harris.

2000 Turtle Island Quartet's *Seven Steps to Bach* is based on Bach's Air.

2019 In *Reconstructing Bach*, Marc Romboy reimagines the Badinerie with the aid of synthesiser.

2025 Joachim Horsley's African-style take on the Badinerie in "Bach Boogaloo".

6.

BACH MODERNISED, CONTINUED

FROM SCHOENBERG & WEBERN TO SHOSTAKOVICH & VILLA-LOBOS

As they were authoring their revolutionary tracts on new compositional method, Schoenberg and Hindemith referenced Bach for support, as if his music had prophesised what was to come. Together with their contemporaries, they found places for the B-A-C-H musical signature in the twelve-tone rows that regulated their serial works and, in the case of Shostakovich, even invented one of their own. Another way forward was reviving Bachian formats, like the concerto grosso and the prelude and fugue. But it was the passacaglia that proved most suitable for expressing the sense of doom that cloaked Europe as World War II approached.

ARNOLD SCHOENBERG (1874–1951)

In his radical 1911 treatise *Theory of Harmony*, Schoenberg proposes that there is nothing inherently different between consonance and dissonance, and that equal status should be accorded to pitch, rhythm and tonal colour. This leads him to abandon vertical harmony and to concentrate instead on melodic linearity through the manipulation of twelve equal tones. Regarding Bach as a precursor of his new "serial" system, Schoenberg draws attention to the twelve different pitches in the theme of the "chromatic" Fugue in B Minor in Book I of *The Well-tempered Clavier*. He went on to acknowledge the persistent "newness" of Bach, concluding that "it seems the more astonishing the more we study his music".[111]

In the following year, 1912, Schoenberg references Bach by including a passacaglia in *Pierrot Lunaire*, a miniature melodrama written in an abrasive, atonal manner. Ten years later, Schoenberg pays direct tribute by making orchestral arrangements of chorale preludes from the *Orgel-Büchlein*: notably "Komm, Gott, Schöpfer, Heiliger Geist" ("Come, God, Creator, Holy Ghost") (BWV 631) and "Schmücke dich, o liebe Seele" ("Adorn yourself, oh dear soul") (BWV 654), as well as the Prelude and Fugue in E-flat Major ("St Anne") (BWV 552). By this time, Schoenberg is writing serial music regulated by twelve-tone rows that often incorporate the B-A-C-H semitones.

SUITE FOR PIANO, 1923

In this "witty recreation of the Bachian keyboard suite in twentieth-century guise",[112] Schoenberg recalls baroque formats familiar from Bach, like the Prelude, Gavotte, Musette, Intermezzo, Minuet and Gigue, basing each on a twelve-tone row incorporating B-A-C-H. Giving these semitones in different sequences, and on one occasion in retrograde, they can barely be discerned without a close reading of the score. Even so, there are moments when B-A-C-H is clearly audible, as in the last bar of the Gavotte, the playful, staccato opening and ending of the graceful Musette, and the upward and downward leaps of the lilting Minuet.

VARIATIONS FOR ORCHESTRA, 1928

This much longer work for large forces comprises a theme with nine variations and an extended finale, also based on a twelve-tone row incorporating B-A-C-H. As in the *Suite for Piano*, Schoenberg freely rearranges its four semitones, making them difficult to hear. A further impediment to recognising B-A-C-H is that Schoenberg shares the motif between different instruments, though it can sometimes be made out in delicately scored episodes, like those for solo violin, harp, celesta and flute. In the multi-section finale, however, Schoenberg introduces audibly clearer versions in different rhythmic patterns, all beginning on B-flat, as in Bach's original. They are first heard in the violins in pianissimo tremolandos followed by aggressive chords, and then on the horns, with the semitones drawn out in retrograde to create a seven-note theme. For his final Presto section, Schoenberg offers a jaunty, jagged idea, against which the violins play B-A-C-H.

THREE SATIRES, 1926

Schoenberg is the first to observe that the theme that Frederick the Great gave to Bach on that memorable evening in Potsdam in May 1747 bore no resemblance to the galant-style melodies in the king's own concertos and sonatas, or those written for him by Johann Joachim Quantz, the flautist in his court orchestra. Schoenberg proposes that the unusual length of what Bach calls the Thema Regium, and the fact that it did not permit contrapuntal manipulation on its own, suggest that it was invented by Carl Philipp Emanuel, presumably at the king's orders, to test his father's skill so that Frederick could "win" when Bach was unable to extemporise a six-part fugue.[113] Identifying with what he understands to be Bach's embarrassing, but ultimately creative, response to the royal challenge, Schoenberg comes to write his *Three Satires* in the manner of the canons in the *Musical Offering*. The event leading to their composition is worth noting.

In 1925, the music critic Ernst Krenek publishes a negative notice about Schoenberg, accusing him of romanticism. In the following year, Schoenberg writes his *Three Satires* for four voices supported by lower strings and piano, supplied with his own texts. His rejoinder to Krenek is embodied in the third satire: "I no longer remain a romantic; I hate romantic!", a caustic remark that implies that Schoenberg has conceived his *Three Satires* in a spirit of grievance. By taking the canons of the *Musical Offering* as models, he identifies with the humiliation that he imagines Bach suffered in Frederick's palace.

Despite Schoenberg's ironic texts, and the miniature scale and small forces employed, the *Three Satires* are contrapuntally rigorous. Here, Schoenberg shows his ability to write strict canons disposed among four voices; in the second satire, he even indulges in a palindrome that can be performed front to back, or from back to front. Even if Schoenberg's tone rows lack discernible Bachian references, the obvious models are the puzzle canons in the *Musical Offering*.

ANTON WEBERN (1883–1945)

As a student of Schoenberg, Webern is directed to scrutinise the music of Bach. One outcome of this tutelage is his "re-harmonisation" of eighteen Bach chorales in 1906, in which he introduces his own counterpoint and chromatic harmonies. Webern's Back to Bach journey begins properly two years afterwards with his first published work, the *Passacaglia for Orchestra*, followed by a vivid orchestration of the six-voice Ricercar from the *Musical Offering*. As his compositional method evolves, Webern emphasises formal structures based on tone rows that often exploit internal symmetries, as when, for example, he divides his twelve notes into four groups of different pitches using inversion and retrograde. This gives Webern's compositions a musical unity, even when the melodic lines are fragmented and shared between different instruments.

PASSACAGLIA FOR ORCHESTRA, 1908

Before attending Schoenberg's composition classes, Webern is instructed by his mother. As he later confides to his fellow student Alban Berg, "all of my works from the Passacaglia on relate to the death of my mother".[114] Two years after she dies, Webern writes what turns out to be his longest and most richly scored piece of Bach-inspired continuous music. Its expressive intensity suggests a highly emotional relationship.Webern replaces the reassuring inevitability of Bach's eight-bar ostinato with unpredictability. Instead of Bach's unambiguous C minor triad, Webern presents six out of the seven notes of the D minor scale, somewhat rearranged, with the addition of a discordant A-flat, but ending firmly, like Bach, with a perfect cadence (A to D). This theme is first heard in mysterious pizzicato strings, then accompanied by haunting woodwind phrases with upward and downward leaps that recur throughout. The twenty-three variations that follow showcase Webern's early mastery of orchestral sonorities, ranging from bombastic tuttis to delicate pianissimo passages for harp, violin solo and muted trumpet, and anticipate the sparse textures of his later compositions. Whether urgent and dramatic, or lyrical and yearning, the orchestral passages are mostly reduced to interweaving fragments, which Webern marks with a superabundance of dynamics, tempos and mood indications.

ORCHESTRATION OF BACH'S SIX-VOICE RICERCAR, 1935

In this direct engagement with the *Musical Offering*, Webern re-imagines Bach's six-part fugue in twentieth-century tonalities. Webern's most daring intervention is to audibly deconstruct the Thema Regium by splitting it between different instruments: to begin with, muted trombone, horn, trumpet and harp, followed by other sections of the orchestra and even solo players. This distribution accords with the technique of "Klangfarbenmelodie" ("Sound-colour melody") that Webern is developing at the time to inject colouristic clarity into his own compositions. This fragmentation of the theme contrasts with Webern's more sustained treatment of the interweaving counterthemes, distinguishing them from the Thema Regium.

STRING QUARTET, 1938

As his music becomes increasingly compressed and abstract, Webern pursues a Back to Bach journey by finding places for B-A-C-H in his twelve-note rows, like those in his only string quartet. Lasting barely eight minutes, Webern assembles his regulating row from three groups of four semitones: the first and third groups reproduce Bach's semitones, beginning on B-flat as in *Art of Fugue*, or on G-flat; the second and fourth groups are transposed up an interval of a major fourth and then inverted. Such permutations yield the detached and leaping two- and three-note figurations that animate the entire quartet. There are even some moments when the B-A-C-H semitones are clearly audible, as when the strings alternate in pizzicato and bowing.

VARIATIONS FOR PIANO, 1936, & *VARIATIONS FOR ORCHESTRA*, 1940

Both these works are based on twelve-tone rows, in which the first and last sets of four notes have adjacent semitones separated by intervals of a major or minor third, as in B-A-C-H. The four semitones are announced in linear symmetry as palindromes, also in vertical symmetry, with chords formed from the different tones arranged around a central pitch. Such manipulations occasionally result in four-note motifs that resemble B-A-C-H, as well as the theme of the Fugue in C-sharp Minor in Book I of *The Well-Tempered Clavier*. Webern's incessant tone-row manoeuvres match the inventiveness of Bach's counterpoint; being atonal, however, they are almost impossible to hear.

Despite the mathematics, Webern imbues both his variation sets with musical individuality. Movements in the *Variations for Piano* incorporate transparent, wistful moments as well as rapid, scherzo-like episodes. In contrast, the later *Variations for Orchestra* are constructed from jagged, leaping formations that achieve abrupt, even violent changes of mood, which Webern marks with copious indications of speed and volume. That Bach's presence is somehow embedded in these musical instabilities led the American author Thomas Pynchon to claim that Webern stands "at the far end of what'd been going on since Bach".[115]

BERTHOLD GOLDSCHMIDT (1903–96)

Webern was twenty-five when he wrote his *Passacaglia for Orchestra*, setting an example for another youthful composer who had come under the sway of Schoenberg. This was the twenty-three-year-old Berthold Goldschmidt, who in 1925 submitted his *Passacaglia for Large Orchestra* for the prestigious Mendelssohn Prize. Though awarded the prize, which establishes him as one of the leading German composers at the time, it takes more than seventy years before the work is published, on which occasion Goldschmidt remembered that "it is a very north German piece which could have been born in the Marienkirche in Lübeck".[116] He was thinking of Dieterich Buxtehude, whose passacaglias written for the organ of St Mary's inspired the junior Bach.

PASSACAGLIA FOR LARGE ORCHESTRA, 1925

Goldschmidt salutes Bach's Passacaglia by devising an ostinato in triple time with alternating, long-short pairs of steps. Though these begin by dropping downward rather than upward, they span a perfect fifth (C to F) followed by a diminished seventh (D-flat to E), a progression that precisely reproduces the beginning of the Fugue in F Minor from Book II of *The Well-tempered Clavier*. Thereafter,

Goldschmidt's proceeds with an ostinato of seven bars (rather than the more usual eight) that touches all twelve notes of the octave. Despite this nod to Schoenberg's serial system, which is gaining currency at the time, Goldschmidt prefers his own rich chromatic harmonies, poignant counterthemes, and obsessive rhythmic patterns. In no less than nineteen repetitions of the ostinato, he explores a panorama of colouristic effects, from pianissimo flutes, cor anglais, harp and plucked bass, to triple-forte brass fanfares. The mood of his *Passacaglia* is similarly diverse, veering from menacing, deep bass ostinatos to high, sarcastic trumpet fanfares, occasionally relieved by lyrical violin and clarinet exchanges. In the two last repetitions, Goldschmidt pits the lower instruments against the upper ones in a strict canon one beat apart; only then does he proceed to a climactic conclusion.

CHRONICA, 1938 & 1958

Goldschmidt's predilection for the passacaglia format is borne out in the score for the ballet *Chronica* that he writes for the German choreographer Kurt Jooss, who, like the composer, has by this time fled the Nazis and was living in England. Originally conceived for two pianos and only orchestrated some twenty years later, *Chronica* consists of seven movements that range from tragedy to satire, beginning with a powerful passacaglia set in a prison yard. While Goldschmidt here reverts to the more usual eight-bar ostinato pattern, his step-like theme evoking marching prisoners is disturbingly irregular, creating an atmosphere of threat as the strings and brass enter one after another.

PAUL HINDEMITH (1895–1963)

In his later years, this German composer expressed his admiration for Bach, whose music "must always serve as a supreme beacon".[117] It is a Back to Bach journey that dates to an early work for solo viola, an instrument that Hindemith plays professionally, as well as to an orchestral work that cheekily quotes Bach as part of a rebellion against the romantic symphonic tradition. Bachian traits are also evident in his *Kammermusik* series, while his later *Trauermusik* is built around a Bach chorale.

In addition to his performing career and compositional activity, in 1937 Hindemith authors *The Craft of Musical Composition*, in which he proposes ranking equally all twelve notes of the octave and all possible intervals, thereby avoiding any tonal centre. Melodies no longer need to conform to traditional major or minor modes, and chords are classified according to their dissonances. To demonstrate his new approach to harmony to students at Yale University, where he was teaching during the 1940s, Hindemith composes *Ludus Tonalis* based on *The Well-tempered Clavier*.

SONATA FOR SOLO VIOLA NO. 1, 1919

Bach's unaccompanied Sonatas and Partitas for Solo Violin inspire Hindemith to write his four Sonatas for Solo Viola for him to perform in concert, the first of these concludes with a movement marked "In Form and Time as a Passacaglia". Like Bach's Chaconne in the Partita No. 2, this is based on an eight-bar theme in triple metre with accents on the second beat, followed by variations that explore a range of thematic potentialities and technical resources. Though written in his own musical language, Hindemith's Passacaglia follows Bach with its tranquil middle section and final variations that gain in intensity and speed until the theme reappears in its original form.

RAGTIME (WELL-TEMPERED), 1921

As a junior string player needing to earn a living, Hindemith joins dance bands and becomes familiar with jazz idioms, like those he incorporates into *Ragtime*, his first substantial orchestral composition. This bombastic, jaunty work is punctuated by sarcastic brass quotations of the opening bars of the Fugue in C Minor from Book I of *The Well-tempered Clavier*. To ensure his listeners would recognise the allusion, Hindemith adds the subtitle "Well-Tempered". He probably hoped that they would agree that this how Bach might have composed in a popular, twentieth-century idiom.

KAMMERMUSIK NOS 5, 6 & 7, 1927–8

The instrumental clarity and colouristic juxtapositions of the Brandenburg Concertos inspire Hindemith to write a series of eight concerto grosso-like works that he calls *Kammermusik* (*Chamber Music*). Like Bach, he devises these for contrasting instrumental ensembles, though there are only incidental musical connections. *Kammermusik No. 5* for small orchestra and viola, intended for Hindemith himself to play in 1927, for instance, is built almost entirely from boisterous pairs of short notes followed by pairs of longer notes, a pattern that is found, for example, in Brandenburg No. 3. In *Kammermusik No. 6*, which he wrote a year later, Hindemith revives the baroque viola d'amore, which Bach occasionally employed, as in the Mass in B Minor. Following Bach, Hindemith exploits the instrument's mournful tone.

For Brandenburg No. 6, Bach confined himself to lower strings, beginning with extended passages with overlapping phrases that create a continuous musical fabric. Hindemith devises something similar in his *Kammermusik No. 7*, commissioned to inaugurate the new organ at Frankfurt Radio Station in 1928. Its slow and calm central movement begins with an eloquent rising theme in two-part canon on the organ manuals, which is then taken up by the solo woodwind and brass players, also in canon. By compressing the thematic overlaps from two bars to single beats, Hindemith replicates Bach's interlocking lines.

TRAUERMUSIK, 1936

Travelling to London at the beginning of 1936 to premiere the viola concerto written the previous year, Hindemith learns the concert is cancelled because of the death of King George V on 20 January. To provide suitable music for the radio broadcast scheduled for two days later, Hindemith set to work at top speed to write his *Funeral Music* for strings and solo viola. Barely eight minutes long, the work consists of four short movements, the last built around "Vor deinen Thron" ("Before your throne") (BWV 668). Hindemith harmonises the melody of Bach's "Deathbed Chorale" in a gentle, atonal manner, with pauses on conventional chords at the end of each phrase, leaving gaps to be filled by himself playing newly composed, sorrowful phrases. The free, lyrical manner of these solo viola interventions contrasts with the chorale's steady triple metre. If British listeners did not recognise the funerary association of "Vor deinen Thron", they could at least appreciate its suitably solemn mood. In later years, Hindemith railed against dressing up the music of "defenceless J.S. Bach" with "fashionable trimmings",[118] but did not think to condemn his reworking of "Vor deinen Thron".

BALLET SCORE FOR *NOBILISSIMA VISIONE*, 1938

In 1937, Hindemith was approached by the dancer Léonide Massine to compose music for what is intended as "a dramatic and choreographic representation of the life of St Francis".[119] For the ballet's last scene, in which the saint receives the stigmata on La Verna, Hindemith provides a solemn passacaglia of majestic proportions inspired by Bach's organ exemplar. This is based on a six-bar ostinato in triple time that incorporates two upward and two downward steps. He announces his Bachian-derived theme in the brass, after which the strings enter to adorn it with meandering melodies that gain in rhythmic certainty. A quieter set of variations depicting St Francis in the act of contemplation have unsupported woodwinds playing the theme, eventually joined by gentle string figurations. In the third section of the Passacaglia, which serves as a final proclamation, Hindemith steers the variations towards fortissimo trills in the woodwinds and strings, flinging fragments of the ostinato back and forward between the brass instruments. Not since Bach has any composer invested a passacaglia with such monumental affirmation.

LUDUS TONALIS, 1942

In *The Craft of Musical Composition*, Hindemith declares that "no longer are we the prisoners of the key".[120] However, in this work, he reverts to writing fugues in twelve of the major and minor keys as a modernist counterpart to *The Well-tempered Clavier*, adding the explanation, "Counterpoint, Tonal and Technical Studies for the Piano". Despite the textbook seriousness implied by the Latin titles of the movements ("Fuga prima", "Fuga seconda", and so on) and the absence of homophonic melodies or chords, Hindemith's music is never abrasively discordant.

Hindemith begins *Ludus Tonalis* with a "Preludium", consisting of rapid passages, a reflective Andante and a series of chorale-like chords, all of which are then repeated in retrograde and inversion in a concluding "Postludium", thereby investing the work with an overall, strictly symmetrical structure. In between each fugue, Hindemith provides "Interludiums" in different styles, in recognition of the range of genres that Bach had incorporated into *The Well-tempered Clavier*. They include baroque dances and wistful waltzes, one in quintuple time; baroque-style fantasias, toccatas and ariosos; and lilting melodies in a quasi-romantic idiom. Pianistic textures are mostly transparent, especially in the clearly articulated voices of the fugues. Hindemith's contrapuntal dexterity is also often on display: "Fuga tertia" is divided into two parts, the second a mirror image of the first; in "Fuga decima" the main theme is inverted when repeated; "Fuga undecima", meanwhile, takes the form of a two-voice canon. To ensure rhythmic variety and musical momentum, Hindemith employs jagged rhythms followed by clusters of rapid passages, flowing triplets, grace notes and trills – all familiar from Bach's keyboard writing. Allusions to *The Well-tempered Clavier* include the oscillations in Hindemith's "Fuga nona" that resemble those in those in the Prelude in C Minor in Book I, while the gigue-like, rapid notes in Hindemith's "Baroque toccata" Interludium recall those in Bach's Fugue in A Major in the same book. With such strategies, Hindemith confirms a Back to Bach journey that aims at reconciling Bach's counterpoint with his new tonal language.[121]

KAIKHOSRU SHAPURJI SORABJI (1892–1988)

For much of his long life, this eccentric composer of part Parsi–Indian descent secluded himself in the village of Corfe Castle in England's Dorset, where he produced an enormous quantity of music, including piano works of excruciating difficulty and unrealistic length. These reflect Sorabji's delight in Indian ragas and medieval plainchant, as well as atonal melodies, dissonant harmonies, modernist polyrhythms, and rapid changes of texture and mood. Into this eclectic musical vista, Sorabji's injects an anthology of Bachian preludes, toccatas, fugues, chorales and arias. Nowhere is his approach better displayed than in what, at the time, was the longest continuous piano piece ever written.

OPUS CLAVICEMBALISTICUM, 1930

Lasting more than four hours, this work is divided into movements that include an Interludium, Prelude and Fuga. The ninth movement is a Toccata with a jangle of dissonant rapid notes leaping fearlessly across the keyboard, which Sorabji marks to be played "fast, always without delay or rush". It is followed by an Adagio and Passacaglia with no less than eighty-one variations! Despite these titles, the music owes little to Bach. Nonetheless, the presence of such movements, as well as in those in Sorabji's later solo piano pieces, like his *Toccata Seconda* of 1934, with its Preludio, Toccata, Corale, Aria, Ostinato and Fuga, reveals a lifelong fascination with Bachian formats. They are still present in *Toccata Quarta*, completed in 1967, when the composer is seventy-five.

ALFREDO CASELLA (1883–1947)

A leading representative of neoclassic music in Italy, Casella enjoys a career as a prolific composer as well as an active conductor, teacher and editor, and host of the International Festival for Contemporary Music in Venice in 1930. At the same time, Casella promotes the music of the past, especially that of Antonio Vivaldi, which is hardly known at the time, as well as that of Bach, arranging the celebrated Chaconne for large orchestra in 1935. In this transcription, Casella begins with the violins reproducing the ringing string sound of Bach's first bars, before the lower strings join in. Focusing on colouristic effects, he pits woodwinds against strings and then brings in the brass section to intensify the instrumental sonority. Casella's dedication to Bach continues into later years. In 1946, he brings out an edition of *The Well-tempered Clavier*, adding a preface outlining the historical background to the work and advising on performance practice. The following year he publishes *J.S. Bach: 23 Easy Pieces*, with an assemblage of keyboard works. Casella's Back to Bach journey also reveals itself in the baroque spirit of his own compositions, but only in a pair of modest piano works does he specifically reference the master.

2 RICERCARI SUL NOME B-A-C-H, 1932

Though his homage to Bach takes its name from the six-part Ricercar in the *Musical Offering*, each of Casella's two ricercars is built on the signature motif from *Art of Fugue*. The first, entitled "Funebre", consists of the B-A-C-H semitones on alternating longer and shorter notes, developed into a three-voice fugue. This leads to a dirge-like episode with an expressive melody carried on repeated B-A-C-H notes, ending with the four semitones sounded simultaneously. (This final dissonance anticipates how another Italian composer, Luciano Berio, almost seventy years later, concluded his funerary tribute for the conductor Giuseppe Sinopoli in *Contrapunctus XIX*, an orchestral arrangement of the last fugue in *Art of Fugue*.) Casella's second ricercar, marked "Ostinato", is a witty dance-like piece, with B-A-C-H in rapid hopping notes cunningly concealed in chords and scale-like passages.

PERCY GRAINGER (1882–1961) & WILLIAM WALTON (1902–83)

On at least one occasion, the Australian-born, British-based pianist and composer Percy Grainger embarked upon a Back to Bach journey by dissolving a Bach aria into a gentle, quasi-English folk song, like the ones he was collecting at the time. For the English composer William Walton, Bach's music was a repository of ideas to be translated into his own orchestral language.

BLITHE BELLS, 1931

Charmed by the chorale-like, soprano aria "Sheep may safely graze" from the "Hunt Cantata" (BWV 208), Percy Grainger arranges it for the piano, calling it *Blithe Bells*, since he conceives the piece as a countryside "ramble" that picks up distant sheep bells. Soon after, he makes a version for an orchestra supplemented with a piano, xylophone and chimes. The great instrumental swells that he calls for may have been encouraged by the lush score of the same aria made by Stokowski, who in

about 1930 translated Bach's melody into resonant strings, while
retaining Bach's warbling flutes.

BALLET SCORE FOR *THE WISE VIRGINS*, 1940

It was not long before Wiliam Walton sourced the same aria when
responding to a commission from Constant Lambert, director of
Vic-Wells Ballet in London, for a work based on the Parable of the
Ten Virgins in the New Testament. For the score, Lambert chooses
movements from Bach's cantatas, inviting Walton to provide the
necessary orchestrations. For the ballet's opening scene, which
is choreographed to "Sleepers Awake", Walton's arrangement
accords with Bach's chordal harmonisation, as played alternatively
in the brass, woodwinds and strings, with occasional harp
flourishes. One of the later scenes draws on "Sheep may safely
graze", in which Walton preserves Bach's flute passages but
assigns the vocal line to the cellos and then to a solo oboe, with a
violin playing a newly composed, quasi-Bachian accompaniment.

HANNS EISLER (1898–1962)

After shifting from Vienna to study with Schoenberg in Berlin, Eisler
becomes an active communist, collaborating with the German
poet and dramatist Bertolt Brecht to produce theatrical music for
agitprop events. Adapting his teacher's atonal music for working-
class audiences, Eisler discovers that Bach's music can also offer
reassurance when the Nazis come to power, forcing him and
Brecht into exile.

PRELUDE AND FUGUE ON B-A-C-H, 1934

In his choice of a fugal setting of B-A-C-H for this string trio, Eisler
expresses his concern that this should be understood as a tribute
to "the bourgeois mysticism of the workday musician".[122] He might

also have added that he found Bach comforting when writing a modest chamber work with no political purpose.

Eisler begins his Prelude with the B-A-C-H semitones as half-bar notes, at first in the correct sequence, then in retrograde. The livelier section in triple time that follows is built on repetitions of B-A-C-H on the cello. The Fugue introduces a bouncing subject that begins with the characteristic four semitones, which Eisler extends chromatically, developing a theme with drooping pairs of notes that recalls the Fugue in B Minor in Book I of *The Well-tempered Clavier*. As the music develops, Eisler gives evidence of his contrapuntal skills by introducing B-A-C-H in longer notes arranged in stretto overlaps, many of them in retrograde.

AN ANTI-HITLER SYMPHONY, 1936 (DEUTSCHE SINFONIE, 1957)

The advance of Nazism provokes Eisler and Brecht to collaborate on a two-movement orchestral work, subtitled "An Anti Hitler Symphony", which they submit to the jury of the International Society for Contemporary Music in March 1936, who agree to premiere it during the World Exposition in Paris the following year. Due to Brecht's anti-fascist text, the Society fears intervention by the Nazi regime, suggesting that Eisler substitute a saxophone solo for the vocal parts. He refuses, and only after more than twenty years is the music incorporated into an expanded cantata for soloists, chorus and orchestra, renamed *Deutsche Sinfonie*.

Though committed to Schoenberg's twelve-tone system, Eisler here references the music of Germany's past. The first movement, which he marks "Präludium", begins and ends with a mournful contrapuntal section for strings built on a twelve-tone row that concentrates on adjacent semitones. In the central section, the choir sings Brecht's "O Deutschland, bleiche Mutter" ("Oh Germany, pale mother") vigorously supported by the full orchestra.

The second movement of *Deutsche Sinfonie* is devoted "To the fighters in the concentration camps", a poem that refers to the imprisonment of political dissidents. Eisler sets Brecht's defiant words as a passacaglia built on an ostinato of eight bars, each with two pairs of notes followed by a rest, in a triple-pulse pattern that mimics the ostinato in Bach's organ exemplar. Eisler's theme obsesses around the adjacent semitones of D, making a discrete salute to the B-A-C-H semitones. Repeated throughout in the lower strings as a steady march, the ostinato supports a twelve-tone melody played in turn on the clarinet, flute and horn, and then sung by the alto soloist to the words of Brecht's text. The melody's jagged, bouncing contour expresses the valiant spirit of the fighters, while the relentless progress of the theme beneath suggests their imprisonment. The section ends with rhythmic figurations marked "eroico", to remind the performers of the fighters' bravery. In the passacaglia's central section, the choir enters with more confident declamations. At the end, however, Eisler abruptly interrupts these, suggesting that no complete (optimistic?) conclusion is possible.

DAS VORBILD, 1952

Following ten years of exile in America, Eisler returns to Berlin in 1948, where he is taken up with reclaiming highlights of German culture for the newly founded German Democratic Republic. For the beginning of *Das Vorbild* (*The Example*), written for a small orchestra and solo singer, Eisler adapts the Fugue in G Minor from Book I of *The Well-tempered Clavier*, extending Bach's theme and reducing its four voices to three. The result is an emotive piece that serves as a prelude to a pair of poems by Goethe. The first, "Göttliche" ("On the Divine"), is an alto aria beginning with the words "Man should be noble, generous and good" embedded in transparent woodwinds and strings. In the second poem,

"Symbolum", Eisler partly recasts Goethe's text so that it becomes "Man's steadfast walk resembles life". He sets the words in a folkish musical style with triple repeated notes in the bottom strings to portray the "steadfast walk". The movement ends with a short, eloquent oboe passage resembling one of Bach's obligato solos.

ALBAN BERG (1885–1935)

One of the most significant exponents of Schoenberg's twelve-tone system, Berg infuses his atonal compositions with individual lyricism and drama, especially in his two operas, *Wozzeck* (1922) and *Lulu*, the latter left unfinished at his death in December 1935. Berg's commitment to serialism is paralleled by a fascination with musical forms of the past. Two scenes in *Wozzek* are based on a passacaglia and a two-part fugue, one of the first instances of Bachian formats imported into a twentieth-century stage work. The interlude in Act II of *Lulu*, which occurs at the precise midpoint in the opera, takes the form of a palindrome that mirrors the narrative on the stage. In adhering to restrictive structures like the passacaglia, fugue and palindrome, Berg makes no direct reference to Bach. This had to wait for a concerto conceived as a memorial for a beloved young friend.

VIOLIN CONCERTO, 1935

Berg would have been familiar with Schoenberg's orchestration of "Schmücke dich...", in which the plaintive chorale melody is played by a solo cello. This sets an example for Berg to assign another Bach chorale to solo string instrument, as in the Violin Concerto, for which Berg sources "Es ist genug" ("It is enough") from Bach's cantata *O Ewigkeit, du Donnerwort* (*Oh eternity, you word of thunder*) (BWV 60). Early in 1935, Berg receives a commission for a concerto from Louis Krasner, an American violinist of Russian origin. At the time, Berg is friendly with Alma

Mahler and her daughter Manon Gropius, for whom he develops a particular fondness. Learning of her tragic death at the age of eighteen after contracting polio, Berg interrupts work on *Lulu* to write the concerto for Krasner, dedicating it to "The memory of an angel". He himself dies at the end of that same year.

In choosing "Es ist genug", Berg recognises that the chorale's spirit of lamentation would be appropriate for a work that is more in the nature of a requiem than a showpiece for a virtuoso soloist. Berg must also have realised that Bach's setting was compatible with his own exploratory, atonal language. The opening phrase of "Es ist genug" ascends in a scale of three consecutive whole-tone intervals, a unique progression, which Bach harmonises in a surprisingly daring way, beginning in A major and ending on a chord in the distant key of G-sharp major; when repeated, Bach has the phrase end on a chord in D-sharp minor, another remote key.

Berg introduces Bach's chorale in the Adagio section of the concerto's second movement. After a somewhat violent tutti climax, the chorale theme is taken up by the soloist, with the words inscribed over the notes in the score. Each of the chorale's phrases is then repeated in the woodwinds in Bach's four-part harmonisation, with an additional "religioso" marking. The exchanges between the soloist and orchestra conclude with delicate, arpeggiated chords on the violin while the woodwinds linger over the chorale's last four notes. From here, Berg quotes fragments of the chorale in the cellos and harp, one bar apart, then in mournful trombones. Listeners familiar with the chorale will easily make out its rising first phrase, though perhaps not when Berg gives the notes in inversion and retrograde. Such contrapuntal manipulations do not impede the soloist, who soars effortlessly over the orchestra. Berg then has the horns play the chorale's first four notes in retrograde while the soloist rises ever higher in a transcendental conclusion.

JOHANN NEPOMUK DAVID (1895–1977)

Known for the music he provides for Protestant church services, this German composer frequently resorts to Bach chorales and the B-A-C-H motif, as in the two works noticed here.

VARIATIONS ON A THEME OF J.S. BACH, 1942

As a teacher of composition during the war years at the Conservatorium of Leipzig, it is perhaps unsurprising that David should base an extensive orchestral work on the four-voice chorale "Was bist du doch, o Seele, so betrübet?" ("Why, oh soul, are thou so cast down?") (BWV 424). After announcing Bach's phrases in the strings and woodwinds, David writes variations that range from rapid, high string passages or pizzicatos and staccato woodwind figurations to eloquent melodies on the lower strings and oboe. The longest variation is partly fugal, its theme being a dance-like version of the chorale's opening phrase, mostly assigned to the strings. After a brief pause, David offers a stately variation with the chorale in the strings against a slower augmented version in the woodwinds that brings the work to a despondent conclusion.

ORGAN PARTITA ON B-A-C-H, 1964

Conceived in the spirit of *Art of Fugue*, this work consists of eight variations that demonstrate David's treatment of B-A-C-H in all possible serial and contrapuntal incarnations, unified by a constant, four-square pulse. In the five fugal variations that follow, David employs stretto, diminution, augmentation and invertible counterpoint, while in the other two variations he chooses an ostinato scheme. The seventh movement is a single-voice improvisation on the previous melodies that offers a welcome diversion. The last variation, which is the longest of the set and the only one in canonic form, presents a simple thematic development of B-A-C-H, concluding with a contrapuntal five-voice setting.

CHARLES KOECHLIN (1867–1950)

An individual musician with heterogenous interests ranging from astronomy and photography to Rudyard Kipling and Hollywood film stars, the Paris-born Koechlin is a prolific composer, especially of symphonic poems and chamber music. He is also an influential teacher of harmony and counterpoint, and author of a masterly treatise on orchestration. Spanning more than fifty years, his compositions are written in a mixture of atonal and polytonal styles, inspired by an assortment of traditions – the mysterious Orient; French folksong; Bach's fugues and chorales. As he discloses in his unpublished autobiography: "Perhaps it is necessary to love Bach in order to understand Koechlin".[123]

It is to Bach that Koechlin turns to during World War II, devising *Offrande Musicale* as a monumental, hopefully consoling, Back to Bach journey. He has already passed his seventy-fifth birthday when he begins, taking a further four years to complete the orchestration. Lasting some fifty minutes, the work is scored for a huge orchestra, including an organ and piano, as well as the ondes martenot, an early electronic instrument with weird, oscillating tones. *Offrande Musicale* is not premiered until 1973, more than twenty years after Koechlin's death.

OFFRANDE MUSICALE SUR LE NOM DE BACH, 1942–6

Like the *Musical Offering*, Koechlin's *Offrande* consists of a set of polyphonic pieces embracing the entire art of counterpoint – in this instance, all based on the four semitones of B-A-C-H from *Art of Fugue*. The master's signature is omnipresent throughout *Offrande*'s sections, both in its original form, as well as in inversion, retrograde, augmentation and diminution. Unlike the twelve-tone rows that included B-A-C-H employed by Schoenberg and his followers, Koechlin ensures that the theme is always audible in steadily rising or descending notes. This is true even when he extends the two pairs of adjacent semitones to three or four pairs to create an ever-expanding theme. But Koechlin's music is no mere mathematics – throughout, he invests his counterpoint with spirited energy.

Following Bach, Koechlin provides his *Offrande Musicale* with a rigorous structure. Between an opening chorale on B-A-C-H carried on swelling counterthemes and a resounding, triumphant finale, Koechlin offers an inventive catalogue of canons, fugues and free contrapuntal exercises. These are performed by full orchestral forces, as well as by smaller groups of strings or winds. Some are exploratory, such as Nos 8 and 9, imitating harmony lessons and contrapuntal schools, while No. 10 investigates fugal writing in four, five and then six voices, all based on B-A-C-H. The "symmetrical fugue" in No. 11, reserved for woodwinds alone, employs a theme that turns back onto itself before being repeated upside down. Other exercises reprise standard baroque formats like the passacaglia of No. 4. In No. 7, which Koechlin calls an "Album Sheet", a solo pianist plays a beguiling, romantically inflected rhapsody on B-A-C-H that offers temporary respite from this exhaustive inventory of Bachian strategies.

BÉLA BARTÓK (1881–1945)

In the courses on piano that he offers at the Academy of Music in Budapest between 1907 and 1934, Bartók ensures that his students are well versed in Bach. To introduce them to the master's music, he arranges several preludes and fugues from *The Well-tempered Clavier* as well as thirteen pieces from the *Notebook for Anna Magdalena Bach*. While Bartók's versions pay respect to Bach, they reflect ideas about musical education and performance, and are more detailed and elaborate than other editions of the period. To back up his piano instructions, Bartók composes his own series of pedagogical studies, notably the

Mikrokosmos, which he eventually publishes in six volumes in 1940. Ranging from modest and easy to complex and demanding, these more than 150 miniature pieces span a huge range of musical genres and styles. No. 79 in E Major, for instance, which bears the title "Homage to J.S.B.", is written in the manner of one of Bach's *Inventions*, with simple figurations shared equally between the two hands.

That Bartók's Back to Bach journey extends to his own compositions is evident from the contrapuntal nature of much of his writing, even when this is infused with the melodies, rhythms and harmonies gleaned from his ethnomusicological research in Hungary and the Balkans. This is especially true of the brooding fugal episode at the beginning of his *Music for Strings, Percussion and Celesta* (1936) and the concerto grosso format of his *Divertimento for String Orchestra* (1939) modelled on the Brandenburg Concertos Nos 3 and 6. However, only in a work for solo violin does Bartok seek a specific identification.

SONATA FOR SOLO VIOLIN, 1944

When living in New York, worried about money and declining health, Bartók accepts a commission from Yehudi Menuhin to write a solo work for the violin, treating it as an opportunity to reach back to Bach's exemplars, while at the same time continuing to explore his individual atonal manner. Bartók clearly has Bach's Chaconne in mind since he marks the opening movement of his Sonata as "Tempo di ciaccona", exactly as in Bach's heading. At the same time, Bartók references another solo violin work, the Sonata No. 1 in G Minor (BWV 1001), for he writes his sonata in the same G minor key and, like Bach, includes a "Fuga" second movement. Even so, he begins like the Chaconne, in a triple metre, with opening chords that stress the second beats of the bar. Thereafter, he continues in a Bachian manner, exploring a diversity of violin figurations to display Menuhin's virtuoso abilities: they include discordant melodic lines and jagged rhythms derived from Balkan musical traditions. As in Bach's Fuga, Bartók requires considerable agility on the part of the player to execute the three contrapuntal voices built on an abruptly fragmented theme, occasionally interrupted by freely composed episodes.

For the Adagio Melodia third movement of his Sonata, Bartók writes a lament that recalls Arab music, which he evokes through "exotic" glissandos and tremolando harmonics. (Bartók had visited Algeria in 1913 and consults his field book when it comes to composing this movement.) Bartók concludes with a Presto in rondo form, in which rustling, rapid sections alternate with a rustic rhythmic dance. A swiftly ascending scale brings the sonata to a close with a forceful G major chord.

ERNÖ (ERNST VON) DOHNÁNYI (1877–1960)

Like Bartók, Dohnányi also serves on the faculty of the Academy of Music in Budapest; however, he remains in Hungary for most of the war, continuing to compose, eventually relocating to Austria, where he finds sufficient peace to write his Symphony No. 2, taking comfort in a sacred song of Bach.

SYMPHONY NO. 2, 1944, 1949

Given the circumstance of this work's composition, it is understandable that Dohnányi should invest it with an apprehensive mood, submerging its rhapsodic melodies in abrasive, atonal dissonances. In the symphony's central two movements, he pits a lyrical, pastoral-like Adagio against a fast moving, Hungarian style "Burla", punctuated by sarcastic brass outbursts. The final Variazione movement is built on "Komm, süsser Tod, komm selge Ruh" ("Come, sweet death, come blessed rest") (BWV 478), which he would have found in Schemelli's

Musicalisches Gesang-Buch. As the Allies were bombing Budapest, the song's message must have seemed particularly apt.

Dohnányi may have got the idea of orchestrating "Komm, süsser Tod" from Leopold Stokowski, who in 1933 had arranged the song for the Philadelphia Orchestra. In Stokowski's version, Bach's sorrowful melody is heard on expressive cellos embedded in halo of upper strings before shifting to the woodwinds and a solo trumpet. Dohnányi takes a darker approach by beginning with ominous brass phrases relieved by an almost playful high duet for two solo violins. Then comes Bach's song in Dohnányi's own harmonisation, with its two dejected, downward phrases realised in resonant strings with the chorale words indicated in the score. Five variations follow: in the first, the theme is dissolved in "sobbing" figurations passing between the woodwinds and strings; in the second, it is animated with strident brass fanfares; eloquent, slower versions of the theme can be made out in the third and fifth variations, after which Dohnányi progresses to a fugue in the strings, with the chorale's opening phrase in forceful outbursts serving as the principal theme. A gloomy Adagio followed by a march-like Coda concludes with radiant outburst in E major that seems to express Dohnányi's wish for a better life after the war. This hope is realised five years later when the composer settles in Florida and begins revising the symphony.

PASSACAGLIA FOR FLUTE SOLO, 1959

In this piece, composed a year before he dies at the age of eighty-three, Dohnányi juxtaposes baroque polyphony with twelve-tone serialism. The work is written for the flautist Ellie Baker, daughter of the President of Ohio University in Athens, where Dohnányi teaches when he first arrives in America. In his Passacaglia, Dohnányi turns his back on the set of four stylised dances in Bach's Partita for Solo Flute (BWV 1013) to embrace the format of the Chaconne for Solo Violin. Following Bach, Dohnányi conforms to a traditional Sarabande, with repeated, second-beat stresses; in contrast, his eight-bar theme incorporates all twelve notes of the scale, yet begins and ends in A minor – the same key as in Bach's flute work. Again, like Bach, Dohnányi writes variations that range from tranquil and lyrical to animated and rapid. Some have patterns that recall Bach's cross-string violin figurations; one is even marked "in two voices". Dohnányi temporarily steers the variations into the major key before reprising the main theme and concluding with a brilliant Coda in A major – surely an optimistic gesture saluting his new life in America.

LUIGI DALLAPICCOLA (1904–75)

It is in a set of piano pieces dedicated to his young daughter, later transcribed for orchestra, that this Italian composer reconciles a Back to Bach journey with his highly individual, twelve-tone system.

QUADERNO MUSICALE DI ANNALIBERA, 1952, & VARIATIONS FOR ORCHESTRA, 1954

That Dallapiccola imbues *Quaderno* with the spirit of Bach is immediately apparent from its title, *Musical Notebook of Annalibera*, obviously modelled on the *Notebook for Anna Magdalena* that Bach presented to his second wife. Dallapiccola's format is also indebted to the *Notebook*, since *Quaderno* also consists of short pieces only; in this case, a theme, marked "Simbolo" ("Sign") followed by ten variations, none hardly longer than two minutes.

Quaderno's musical connection with Bach is confirmed by Dallapiccola's use of B-A-C-H in the permutations of the twelve-tone rows that regulate each piece. Beginning on B-flat, Dallapiccola announces B-A-C-H as in the original, before proceeding with diverse combinations of the four semitones to signify the master's signature, which he then applies in prime, inversion, retrograde and retrograde inversion, as well as in vertical chordal structures and even in scrambled forms. In "Simbolo", B-A-C-H is heard as full-bar notes, beginning each time on a different note of the octave against a sombre pulse interspersed with free episodes. In the variations that follow, however, the motif is concealed in complex musical manipulations. Three variations take the form of canons, which Dallapiccola marks "Contrapunctus", following Bach in *Art of Fugue*. Variation No. 3 is in two voices, to which Dallapiccola adds a third voice in inversion; No. 5 is a canon entirely in inversion; No. 7 is a canon to be played against itself in reverse. These contrapuntal ingenuities contrast with other variations that vary from rapid and rhythmic to slow and lyrical, as suggested by imaginative titles like "Accenti", "Colore", "Ombre", "Quartina", and so on. One feature of *Quaderno* is Dallapiccola's occasional use of familiar triads and chords to create music that occasionally sounds tonal.

In the *Variations for Orchestra*, completed two years later, the B-A-C-H motif in *Quaderno* benefits from colouristic emphasis achieved by contrasts of instrumental textures, fluctuating from jagged brass outbursts to quieter moments for winds, solo violin and celesta.

CANTI DI LIBERAZIONE, 1955

In this work written for chorus and orchestra to celebrate Italy's liberation from fascism at the end of World War II, Dallapiccola uses the same twelve-tone row with its embedded B-A-C-H motif that regulates *Quaderno* and the *Variations for Orchestra*. Yet he only discloses this row in the second movement of the *Canti*, which is based on an extract from the Latin version of the Book of Exodus. Dallapiccola selects this as a suitable text for the movement's dedicatee, the German novelist Thomas Mann, who spent his last years in exile, dying in Zurich earlier that year. The movement ends with the chorus invoking "Nomen eius"

("His [i.e. God's] Name") on the four B-A-C-H semitones, at first in retrograde, then in the correct sequence, ending with the note B (that is, H, the last letter of Bach's surname), while the upper voices sustain an F-sharp. The "liberating" effect of this interval of a perfect fifth (B to F-sharp), however, is subverted by the dissonance of the supporting orchestral chord, which forcefully sounds the other ten notes of the octave.

DMITRI SHOSTAKOVICH (1906–75)

With its clarity of line and rhythm expressing emotions ranging from humour and irony to lyricism and bitter suffering, Shostakovich's musical language has always exhibited affinities with Bach. That this was not always acceptable to the Soviet authorities was demonstrated in 1936 when his opera *Lady Macbeth of Mtsensk*, with its Bach-inspired passacaglia interlude, was withdrawn from performance, and then again in 1946, when he was officially denounced for "formalism". Despite these humiliations, which led to financial troubles, Shostakovich resumed his Back to Bach journey in his Piano Trio No. 2 and Violin Concerto No. 1. But it is with his 24 Preludes and Fugues for the piano that he offers his most substantial homage.

While exploring Bachian counterpoint and passacaglia forms, Shostakovich forges another Bach connection with a musical signature modelled on B-A-C-H. He achieves this by abbreviating his name to D(mitri) Sch(ostakovich), as realised in German notation and pronunciation as D, Es (E-flat), C and H (B-natural) (the last two semitones coincide with those of B-A-C-H). At first, Shostakovich hesitates to use D-S-C-H from fear of being deported to the gulags, like so many of his friends and colleagues. Only after Stalin dies on 5 March 1953 does he feel sufficiently emboldened to proclaim D-S-C-H publicly in his Symphony No. 10 and "autobiographical" String Quartet No. 8.

PASSACAGLIA IN *LADY MACBETH OF MTSENSK*, 1934

Responding to the obsessive structure of Bach's organ exemplar, Shostakovich inserts a menacing passacaglia interlude into this, his greatest operatic drama. The most brutal moment in *Lady Macbeth* occurs in Act II, during which the heroine Katerina poisons her lecherous father-in-law. As the curtain drops, the audience is subjected to violent triple-forte chords. These introduce a seven-minute-long passacaglia that begins with the ostinato played pianissimo in the lower strings. As in Bach's Passacaglia, Shostakovich's theme is in triple time, with alternating long and short notes in stepped formation; furthermore, it is in a recognisable minor key (D), ending with a clear cadence, but via the leading note (C-sharp) to the tonic (D). As the passacaglia unfolds through twelve repetitions of the ostinato, Shostakovich piles on layer after layer of melodic and rhythmic figurations, first in the strings, then in the woodwinds, and finally in the brass. After a devastating climax, he concludes in a tranquil manner, anticipating the scene in which Katerina is united with her lover, hoping for happiness.

Though *Lady Macbeth* was banned in Russia, it was presented in concert in London in March 1936, where the twenty-three-year-old Benjamin Britten heard it, remarking on the "terrific music in the entr'actes".[124] When planning his first full-scale opera, *Peter Grimes*, which premieres in 1945, Britten followed Shostakovich by inserting a passacaglia "entr'acte" at a crucial moment in the story. As in the *Lady Macbeth* interlude, this too is imbued with an ominous atmosphere: in this instance, anticipating the tragedy to come.

PASSACAGLIA IN THE PIANO TRIO NO. 2 IN E MINOR, 1944

It is possible that Shostakovich got the idea of including a passacaglia in a chamber trio from Maurice Ravel, who in 1914, as World War I broke out, incorporated an emotive passacaglia movement into his Piano Trio in A Minor. Shostakovich's ostinato is based on a scale descending through five chromatic notes from F to B, much like the chromatically descending bass line in the Crucifixus chorus of Bach's Mass in B Minor, a work that Shostakovich knows well. He supports his Bachian-derived chromatic theme on a funereal progression of eight richly scored chords on the piano, beginning in B-flat minor, between which he writes an impassioned duet for the violin and cello. With these three instruments, Shostakovich portrays a grief-stricken world, but only as an introduction to an Allegretto finale recalling a frenzied Jewish dance. According to his friend and biographer Dimitri Rabinovich, who was at the trio's first performance in Leningrad, the word "Majdanek" (the notorious Nazi death camp in Poland) "was on the lips of many people".[125] They well understood that the trio's passacaglia dirge and dance-like finale was a lament for Jewish victims.

PASSACAGLIA IN THE VIOLIN CONCERTO NO. 1, 1948

That Shostakovich never forgot Bach's Passacaglia is clear from the Andante that serves as the emotional core of this concerto. The movement consists of nine variations, demanding considerable expressiveness on the part of the soloist. While the concerto's passacaglia replicates Bach's triple-time signature and minor key (though in F minor), Shostakovich divides his theme into six unequal phrases of 2 + 2 + 2 + 4 + 4 + 3 bars, each ending in two repeated notes. This unsymmetrical pattern creates a sense of unease that pervades the whole movement, especially when first heard in the lower strings against menacing horn calls and drumbeats. After the theme appears in the woodwinds, the solo violin enters with a melancholy melody supported on the passacaglia theme in the lower strings. The violin continues to develop its own line independently, taking little notice of the orchestra until the seventh variation, when the soloist takes up the passacaglia theme in assertive, fortissimo octaves. The movement's dark mood lessens somewhat in the last two variations, before fading away to permit the violin to embark upon a long solo cadenza that leads directly into the light-hearted, burlesque finale.

24 PRELUDES AND FUGUES, 1951

In 1950, a music festival was staged in Leipzig, then part of the Soviet bloc, to mark the bicentennial of Bach's death. The event included an international piano competition, to which Shostakovich was invited as one of the judges. So impressed was he with Tatiana Nikolayeva from Moscow playing *The Well-tempered Clavier* that he not only recommends that she be awarded the gold medal, but immediately sets about composing his own set of preludes and fugues with her in mind. The following year, he performs part of his cycle for the Union of Soviet Composers, who consider his use of fugue archaic, and therefore unacceptably "bourgeois". Despite their disapproval, Shostakovich completes the work, and it is first heard in Leningrad in 1952 played by Nikolayeva, to whom it is dedicated. As in his earlier 24 Preludes of 1933, which are "character" pieces devoid of Bach allusions, Shostakovich sequences his 1951 set in pairs of major and relative minor keys progressing through intervals of ascending fifths. Like Chopin and others, he considers this arrangement more conducive to performing the preludes and fugues in groups, or even as an entire cycle.

In his preludes and fugues, Shostakovich makes frequent references to *The Well-tempered Clavier*: the chords of the calm C major prelude combine all the notes of Bach's arpeggio opening of the prelude in the same key in Book I; the comic theme of the A minor fugue imitates the jerky rhythm of the Fugue in C Minor in Book I; the jagged rhythms in the manner of a baroque French overture in the B minor prelude are like those in the Prelude in G Minor in Book II; the groups of running triplets in the A major prelude recall those in the Prelude in D Major in Book II; the broken figurations passing from one hand to the other in the C-sharp minor prelude begin like those in the Prelude in E-flat Major in Bach's Book I. However, the Bachian-inspired passacaglia in Shostakovich's prelude in G-sharp minor finds no counterpart in *The Well-tempered Clavier*.

Shostakovich invests his preludes and fugues with maximum harmonic and rhythmic variety. The theme in his C major fugue encompass almost all the notes of the octave, avoiding accidentals, unlike the D-flat major fugue, which employs a rapidly descending theme using eleven of the twelve semitones, together with equally enharmonic counterthemes. Major triads alone form the ingredients of the three voices of the A major fugue, lending it a mellifluous quality entirely free of dissonance. Modulations into unrelated, remote keys occur repeatedly: the triplets in the A major prelude are directed through B-flat, D-flat and C major; the E-flat minor fugue briefly visits the distant key of E (natural) minor; the A-flat major fugue modulates into G major before returning to the home key; and so on. Shostakovich often employs triple and quadruple rhythms but dislocates his regular patterns by introducing abrupt counterthemes (as in the C minor fugue) or sudden breaks (as in the G-sharp minor fugue, where the counterthemes are fragmented before being recombined). Asymmetrical rhythms are frequently used, like the 7/4 time signature of the E-flat minor prelude; the gently humorous theme in 5/4 in the A-flat major fugue; and the cluster of close chromatic notes in the same rhythm in the E-flat major fugue.

These contrasts of harmony and dissonance are well suited to counterpoint, for which the preludes and fugues exhibit Shostakovich's abundance of invention, as in his frequent use of augmentation for both themes and counterthemes. These often appear simultaneously in both original and expanded form, as well as in canonic imitation and stretto overlap, especially towards the end of the fugues. The E minor fugue may be singled out for it employs two themes, one a version of the other to begin with, soon followed by two additional themes, all four of which are then subjected to diminution, augmentation and even retrograde distortions.

Majestic chords contrasting with eloquent passages with greater movement characterise the final prelude in D minor. The accompanying fugue begins with a long theme of more than seven bars exploring the D minor triad, with a countertheme covering the adjacent notes. Shostakovich then introduces a new theme with continuous running notes that is developed independently and at a speedier tempo. Both themes are then superimposed, developing in intensity with forceful chords to bring the whole cycle to a powerful conclusion.

SYMPHONY NO. 10 IN E MINOR, 1953

Though he begins working on this symphony as early as 1946, only in December 1953 does Shostakovich complete the score and sanction its premiere with the Leningrad Philharmonic Orchestra. The music signifies the composer's emancipation, since here for the first time he prominently declares his musical signature. In the symphony's Allegretto third movement, D-S-C-H is first heard as a "tentative" flute solo, and then in the strings, which repeat it "defiantly" against interruptions in the brass and woodwind. Even more strident are the D-S-C-H brass outbursts at one of the climactic moments of the fourth movement, and again in repetitions in the bottom strings to support frantic figurations above, immediately before the symphony's final bars.

STRING QUARTETS NO. 6 IN G MAJOR, 1956,
& NO. 8 IN C MINOR, 1960

Shostakovich must have found his D-S-C-H symphonic utterances liberating, since he now begins using his signature in more intimate, small-scale compositions. At the end of each of the four movements in his String Quartet No. 6, for example, he "signs off" by instructing the instrumentalists to play simultaneously the D-S-C-H notes, though in each case resolving the dissonance into the work's prevailing G major key. The quartet's slow movement, which functions as a reflective moment, is a passacaglia. Its ten-bar, B-flat minor ostinato, which meanders between adjacent notes, ends with the four semitones of D-S-C-H.

Shostakovich returns to D-S-C-H with greater purpose in his String Quartet No. 8, written at a time he is contemplating suicide. Permeated with a doom-laden atmosphere, which Shostakovich calls a "pseudo-tragedy",[126] the work is dotted with quotations from his martyred opera *Lady Macbeth*, the Cello Concerto No. 1, and several of his symphonies. Shostakovich sets his autobiographical summaries in five concise, connected movements, each "signed" D-S-C-H. The motif is heard throughout the quartet, especially in the fugal themes in the opening and concluding movements, both marked Lento. In the latter, Shostakovich integrates D-S-C-H into the counterpoint that accompanies a theme taken from the last scene of *Lady Macbeth*, which depicts "a convoy of prisoners en route to Siberia",[127] surely a reference to something that Shostakovich had always dreaded. The quartet resolves on a downward pianissimo motif (C, G, A-flat and G), which Shostakovich marks "morendo" ("dying away"). Recognised as a personal epitaph, the quartet is played at the composer's funeral on 9 August 1975, together with movements from Bach's Sonatas for Violin and Harpsichord.[128]

RONALD STEVENSON (1928–2015)

In his more than one-hour-long tribute to Shostakovich, this Scottish pianist composer also discovers ways of saluting Bach.

PASSACAGLIA ON DSCH, 1962

Stevenson bases his work on an unsymmetrical, seven-bar ostinato created from the four semitones of Shostakovich's musical signature, which are repeated twice with varying rhythms and sequences. The variations that follow present a kaleidoscope of musical influences and extra-musical ideas. They begin with a conventional sonata before proceeding to a suite of Sarabande, Minuet and Gavotte dances, as well as a Sottish highland melody. Then comes "Emergent Africa", a section involving angry percussive "protests" to be executed directly on the piano strings. This is followed by an "uplifting" section resounding to the Bolshevik slogan "Peace, Bread and Land". There is even a transcription of a Dies Irae chant inscribed "In memoriam the six million", a reference to the victims of the Holocaust.

Bach makes an appearance in a double fugue, in which B-A-C-H is combined with D-S-C-H, permitting Stevenson to hail both composers simultaneously. There is even a "Tribute to Bach" Adagio, with dotted rhythms typical of Bach's French overture movements. Elsewhere, the pianistic exuberance recalls that of Busoni, whose music Stevenson is promoting, and about whom he is preparing a television documentary at the time.

HEITOR VILLA-LOBOS (1887–1959)

Throughout his life, the Brazilian composer Villa-Lobos pursues a Back to Bach journey that aims at reconciling Bach with the rich folk traditions of his native land.

BACHIANAS BRASILEIRAS, 1930–45

In these nine colourful works composed over some fifteen years, Villa-Lobos fuses Bach's harmonic and contrapuntal language with Brazilian rhythms and melodies. To preserve this dual identity, Villa-Lobos supplies double titles for each movement: one derived from Bach, the other referring to a Brazilian dance or song – thus, Introdução/Embolada, Prelúdio/Modinha and Fuga/Conversa in *Bachianas Brasileiras No. 1*. The most obvious Bachian-influenced movements in these works are the fugues that combine baroque counterpoint with Brazilian dance-like syncopations. Elsewhere, Villa-Lobos writes imposing Preludes and Toccatas, though the music owes nothing to Bach; two of the Toccatas even offer brilliant musical portraits of a steam train and a tropical bird!

In *Bachianas Brasileiras No. 1*, scored for an orchestra of cellos, Villa-Lobos delights in contrasts between vivid rhythms and lyrical melodies. In the Fuga, these elements are presented in a Bachian manner with a dance-like theme and contrasting, strident countertheme interacting in conventional counterpoint. In the Prelúdio of *Bachianas Brasileiras No. 4*, written as a piano piece in 1930, then orchestrated in 1942, Villa-Lobos employs a motif with the three ascending notes of the B minor triad, leading to a sixth above (B, D, F-sharp and G), recalling the opening of the Thema Regium from the *Musical Offering*. He then repeats this motif with slight alterations in four-bar phrases, above a supporting, steadily descending phrase in a passacaglia-like manner. The last movement of *No. 4* is based on a Miudinho, a local samba-like dance, its incessant, rapid patterns recalling Bach's keyboard writing. *Bachianas Brasileiras No. 5* (1945) is renowned for its baroque-style soprano Ária (Cantilena) floating high above a cello ensemble.

Villa-Lobos supplies fugal finales for his *Bachianas Brasileiras Nos 7, 8* and *9*. The Fuga (Conversa) of *No. 7* employs an eloquent theme in triple time that begins with a D minor triad trending upwards to B-flat and then plunging downwards to C-sharp, in another reference to the *Musical Offering*. Thereafter, Villa-Lobos develops his theme in alternating regular and syncopated notes, directing his two-bar idea through a variety of keys – first in the strings, then in the woodwinds and brass. The fugue of *No. 8* opens with rhythmically lively figurations before lyrical Brazilian melodies are introduced, with which they are then combined. With its unusual 5 + 6 patterns, Villa-Lobos conceives the fugue of *No. 9* as a skipping dance, which somehow recalls Bach's instrumental gigues.

AFTERLIVES

THE ST MATTHEW PASSION & ST JOHN PASSION

In the Passion music he provides for Good Friday services in Leipzig's churches, Bach follows a long-established German tradition of soloists singing the roles of a storyteller (called an Evangelist), as well those of Jesus, Peter and Pilate, with the chorus taking the part of the crowd. In his portrayals of the events leading up to the Crucifixion, Bach interrupts the biblical story with recitatives and arias set to newly composed verses with secular instrumental accompaniments. For the St John Passion, Bach assembles a text from diverse sources that include the popular Passion poem written in 1712 by Barthold Heinrich Brockes, which had already been set to music by Handel and Telemann. For the St Mathew, Bach commissions a new text from the Leipzig poet Christian Friedrich Henrici, known as Picander. For this work, Bach develops an ambitious scheme intended for the wooden galleries either side of the organ loft in St Thomas's, each of which is to accommodate a group of singers and instrumentalists. This arrangement allows Bach to take an antiphonal approach, with choruses rebounding across the nave. Ranging from vivid drama to deeply felt emotion, the music of Bach's Passions contrasts the narrative of the last days of Jesus, set to the words of the Gospel, with an inner world of personal contemplation, as expressed through recitatives and arias. Among the most heart-wrenching of these are the alto arias "Erbarme dich, mein Gott" ("Have mercy, my God") wreathed in solo violin elaborations in the St Matthew (No. 39), and "Es ist vollbracht" ("It is fulfilled") accompanied by a viola da gamba in the St John (No. 30).

Into these musical tableaux Bach inserts Lutheran chorales to be sung by members of the congregation, offering them opportunities to engage directly with the suffering of Jesus, as in, for instance, "O Haupt voll Blut und Wunden" ("Oh sacred head, bloodied and wounded"). Often referred to as the "Passion Chorale", it repeated no less than five times in the St Matthew, each time to a successive verse of the original seventeenth-century hymn on a different harmonic support. And in the majestic opening double chorus of this work welcoming Christ as the "Bridegroom", calling to each other "See Him, Where?", Bach finds a place for the stirring Lutheran hymn "O Lamm Gottes, unschuldig" ("Oh lamb of God, innocent"). To conclude both Passions, Bach has the chorus reassure the congregation with majestic Sarabande lullabies to the words "Wir setzen uns mit Tränen nieder" ("We sit down with tears") in the St Matthew, and "Ruht wohl" ("Rest gently") in the St John.

Bach's Passions are hardly ever performed after his death. As elsewhere in Germany, Leipzig's congregation prefers sacred music with newly composed poetical texts, rather than biblical quotations. From 1755, Carl Heinrich Graun's *Der Tod Jesu* becomes the most frequently performed Passion work. Thanks to Mendelssohn, Bach's Passions are revived, to influence newly composed sacred oratorios. More recently, pop musicians have extracted chorales from the Passions.

1807 Carl Friedrich Zelter begins rehearsing portions of the St Matthew Passion with the Berlin Singakademie.

1829 Felix Mendelssohn's epoch-making revival of the St Matthew Passion for the Singakademie.

1830 Publication of the St Matthew Passion in Berlin.

1836 In his oratorio *Paulus* (*St Paul*), Mendelssohn introduces an Evangelist narrator as well as several chorales used by Bach.

1841 Mendelssohn reintroduces the St Matthew Passion to the congregation of St Thomas's in Leipzig.

1846 Mendelssohn models arias in *Elijah* on those in Bach's Passions.

1851 Robert Schumann presents the St John Passion in Düsseldorf.

1854 William Sterndale Bennett directs the St Matthew Passion for the newly founded Bach Society in London.

1882 The Good Friday Spell, from the last act of Wagner's *Parsifal*, bears comparison with Bach's Passions.

1957 Leonard Bernstein presents the *St Matthew Passion* on Omnibus, the American television arts programme.

1965 "O Haupt voll Blut und Wunden" forms the basis for Peter, Paul and Mary's "Because all Men are Brothers".

1969 For his mystical oratorio *La Transfiguration de notre Seigneur Jésus-Christ*, Olivier Messiaen employs a tenor Evangelist and chorale-like choruses.

1973 In "American Tune", Paul Simon sources "O Haupt voll Blut und Wundun".

1985 Maricio Kagel refers to Bach's life story for his *Sankt-Bach-Passion*.

1993 *Lambarena Bach to Africa* opens with Gabonese percussionists improvising to the opening chorus of the St John Passion.

1998 Together with four other composers, Paul Grabowsky presents jazz responses to the St Matthew Passion.

2000 Helmuth Rilling of the Bachakademie in Stuttgart commissions new Easter music based on all four canonical Gospels from Wolfgang Rihm, Sofia Gubaidulina, Osvaldo Golijov and Tan Dun.

2007 David Lang sources Picander's libretto for the St Matthew Passion for *The Little Match Girl Passion*.

2009 The *Arabian Passion According to J.S. Bach*, based on the St Matthew Passion, is performed by Vladimir Ivanoff's Ensemble Saraband.

2010 Peter Sellars and Simon Rattle stage the St Matthew Passion in the Berliner Philharmonie.

2020 Nikolaus Matthes provides a Bachian-style score for his *Markus Passion* based on Picander's text, for which Bach's music is lost.

7.

BACH POPULARISED

FROM JOHN LEWIS & JACQUES LOUSSIER TO THE BEATLES & LADY GAGA

Relating Bach to popular musical cultures was anticipated by the American composer Virgil Thomson. In 1940, he observed that: "The closer the performing conditions of Sebastian Bach's music are approximated to those of eighteenth-century provincial Germany, the more the music sounds like twentieth-century American swing".[129] Three years before, the violinists Stéphane Grappelli and Eddie South had teamed up with the Romani–French guitarist Django Reinhardt in an exhilarating jazz interpretation of Bach's Concerto for Two Violins. Since then, numerous musicians have extemporised jazz on Bach's works and themes, while rock musicians and pop singers hijacked the toccatas and chorales.

JOHN LEWIS (1920–2001)

Soon after forming the Modern Jazz Quartet in New York in 1952, together with Milt Jackson on vibraphone, this pianist sets off on a jazz-inspired Back to Bach journey that is to span more than thirty years.[130] While composing his own Bachian pieces, Lewis contrives inventive jazz interpretations of Bach's keyboard preludes and fugues, a canon from the Musical Offering, and a mischievous rethink of the Goldberg Variations.

CONCORDE, 1955

In this album – one of three named after Parisian locales – Lewis offers extemporisations with imitative voices that result in light-hearted contrapuntal music. Following Bach, Lewis's fugato themes generally begin with static first statements followed by flowing second statements that lead to exhilarating rapid passages on both piano and vibraphone.

One track on *Concorde*, "Softly as in a Morning Sunrise", is an improvisation on a theme from the operetta *The New Moon*, written almost thirty years before by Sigmund Romberg. In its Modern Jazz Quartet incarnation, "Softly" is rhythmically animated, thereby losing something of its original, bittersweet yearning. Before plunging into the song, however, Lewis quotes one of Bach's canons from the *Musical Offering*. The Thema Regium is heard on lightly plucked bass, with the two imitative parts above shared between Lewis and Jackson. Each of these parts begins with two off-beat notes dropping an interval of a fourth (from C to G), before setting off on rapid runs, one chasing the other. Romberg's song starts with the same drop of a fourth, which helps explain how Lewis and Jackson can effortlessly morph Bach's canon into Romberg's wistful phrase.

PLACE VENDÔME, 1966

That in *Concorde* Lewis could source a canon from the *Musical Offering*, which was at the time little performed and barely recorded, testifies to his intense scrutiny of this work. It must have exercised a special appeal, for in *Place Vendôme* Lewis offers an arrangement of the Ricercar for his group and the Swingle Singers, sharing Bach's interweaving six lines between piano, vibraphone and plucked bass, and upper and lower voices. As the Ricercar progresses, the Swingles gain in strength, imbuing Bach's lines with an emotive richness that prevails over the drier sounds of the piano and vibraphone. Other than the plucked bass and faint percussion, such mingling of instrumental and vocal sonorities would have been familiar to Bach.

BLUES ON BACH, 1973

In this recording, Lewis takes an indirect approach to *Art of Fugue* by alternating Bach arrangements with new pieces. For the five Bach works that he transcribes for the Modern Jazz Quartet he allots imaginative labels, such as "Rise Up in the Morning", from the chorale prelude "Sleepers Awake"; "Precious Joy", from "Jesu, Joy of Man's Desiring"; and "Tears From the Children", from the Prelude in E-flat Minor from Book I of *The Well-tempered Clavier.* Between these and the two other arrangements, Lewis inserts jazz pieces of his own invention that he performs in keys that spell Bach's musical signature: thus, Blues in B-flat Major (= B), A Minor, C Minor, and B-natural (= H). Bearing no musical relationship to Bach, these pieces share with the arrangements the same transparent scoring and calm disposition.

THE WELL-TEMPERED CLAVIER, 1984–2014

Lewis issues all the preludes and fugues of *The Well-tempered Clavier* in several discs, though not always according to Bach's sequence. While he performs the preludes alone on the piano, when it comes to the fugues, he distributes Bach's contrapuntal voices among his vibraphonist, string bassist and percussionist, as well as one or more string players, adding their sonorities to his clearly articulated piano playing. Though many of the preludes and fugues are little more than inventive arrangements, Lewis cloaks Bach in a rhythmically alert jazz idiom executed with considerable delicacy. One of his strategies is to play the preludes almost the whole way through and then, just before the end, abandon Bach for a short excursion of his own, returning to Bach only in the final bars. (Bach may have understood.) At the end of the Prelude in F Major in Book I, for example, Lewis breaks up Bach's rapid notes to create a dreamy, floating melody of his own, while in the accompanying fugue he injects Bach's dancing, triple groups of notes with incessant drive. The abrupt but gentle rhythms of the Prelude in F-sharp Major in the same Book offer Lewis opportunities to infuse the music with his own jazz-like lilt.

THE CHESS GAME, 1986–7

In these twin discs, Lewis ushers the Goldberg Variations into the unlikely world of chess. With him on the piano and his wife, Mirjana, on the harpsichord, the duo performs versions of Bach's variations, between which they insert their own improvisations identified as chess moves, beginning with King's Gambit (Aria) and ending with Checkmate (Aria da capo). For the most part, regularly pulsing chords in the harpsichord support an upper piano line that reduces Bach's patterns to rhythmic fragments; meanwhile, the counterpoint is replaced by simple melodic contours that tease out the salient features of each variation. In Pawn to King 5 (Bach's No. 7), for instance, Lewis translates Bach's Sicilienne-style, triple figurations into a relaxed, sweet lyric.

THE SWINGLE SINGERS & SLIXS

Founded in Paris in 1962 by the American musician Ward Swingle, who gives his name to the group, this ensemble of eight singers gains considerable renown for their joyous vocalisations of baroque instrumental music, especially that of Bach. Accompanied by light percussion and faint string bass, their virtuoso performances are executed in the scat style of jazz singing that the Swingles have perfected as backing for pop groups. That their dexterous vocalisations turn out to be ideal vehicles for Bach's intricate instrumental writing is nowhere better demonstrated than in the astounding vocalisation by the lead soprano Christiane Legrand of the Badinerie flute solo from the Orchestral Suite No. 2 on their 1964 *Going Baroque* album. It remains one of the group's "signature pieces", repeated through the years by one nimble soprano after another.

JAZZ SÉBASTIEN BACH, 1963 & 1968

It was with these identically titled twin albums that the Swingle Singers first proclaim their Back to Bach journey, much to the delight of their listeners. Among the works that the group records is an arrangement of the ever-popular Air on the G String, an obvious choice given its inherent lyrical quality. Then there are vocalisations of preludes and fugues from *The Well-tempered Clavier* executed with a virtuosity that would surely have impressed Bach, as when two soloists navigate at a hectic pace the tricky chromatic passages in the two-voice Fugue in E Minor from Book I. In the preceding prelude, a solo tenor reveals the soulful lyricism of Bach's treble line floating over sustained vocal harmonies, with Bach's left-hand running notes faintly executed on plucked string bass. For the Prelude in C Major from the same book, the Swingles share Bach's arpeggios between the different voices to achieve a uniform vocal texture, while in the accompanying fugue, the voices are clearly divided into four, with the counterpoint boosted by the bass and percussion. An equal facility in vocalising Bach's fugal writing is heard in their arrangement of the Organ Fugue in G Minor (BWV 542).

If *Art of Fugue* does not seem to offer jazz musicians the range of rhythmic and melodic patterns to be found in Bach's keyboard works, the Swingles find a place for Contrapunctus 9, executing at breathtaking speed Bach's triplets weaving around the full-bar notes of the work's principal theme.

QUER BACH 2 & 3, 2018 & 2024

Of the many successors to the Swingle Singers, the German jazz group SLIXS are to be singled out for the astonishing agility of the six unaccompanied singers, as showcased in their *Quer Bach* (*Cross-over Bach*) albums featuring a medley of Bach's music, including the Goldberg Variations. While their sung versions of the variations help distinguish Bach's musical lines, they are also reminders of the vocal origins of Bach's polyphony. In the Aria, which one of the group converts into a wistful lyric floating in a delicate wash of vocal support, SLIXS shows that Bach was thinking of the human voice (hence the name he gives to his melody). The imitative patterns of Variations Nos 2 and 4, for instance, gain in clarity when sung rather than played, while the dance-like rhythms of Nos 1 and 7 benefit from vocal panache and charm. Throughout, SLIXS vocalise sounds that are devoid of meaning: even when they perform the Quodlibet, they ignore the actual words of Bach's popular songs.

DAVE BRUBECK (1920–2012)

In his early compositions, this American jazz performer often has Bach in mind, as in *Two-Part Contention* (1956) and *Points on Jazz* (1958). The first of these two piano works is built from a pair of independent voices that light-heartedly mimics one of Bach's Two-part Inventions, while in *Points on Jazz*, Brubeck brackets a prelude and fugue with a blues and a rag movement. It is, however, in a later composition, to which he adds "Inspired by J.S. Bach", that Brubeck truly reveals his Back to Bach journey.

CHROMATIC FANTASY SONATA, 1988

In this work, Brubeck expands the two movements of Bach's Chromatic Fantasia and Fugue by adding a chorale and a chaconne to present a panorama of formats that would constitute a comprehensive Bach tribute. Brubeck writes his Sonata for piano, oboe and string trio, but it is later transcribed by John Salmon for solo piano, in which form it is now most often heard.

Brubeck begins his Sonata with an Allegro molto that quotes the opening flourishes of Bach's *Fantasia*, before developing his own improvisatory ideas. In the Chorale that follows, Brubeck alludes to Bach's sacred music, but only in the chromatic theme of his Fugue does he make a direct reference, in this case to the Fugue in F Minor from Book I of *The Well-tempered Clavier*. The concluding Chaconne features oscillating keyboard configurations derived from Bach's organ toccatas, interspersed with a twelve-note theme incorporating B-A-C-H. By this time, it would seem, Brubeck has developed an interest serialist music.

JACQUES LOUSSIER (1934–2019)

Together with a string bassist and percussionist, this French pianist embarks upon a four-decade Back to Bach journey in the conviction that Bach's music offers abundant opportunities for jazz improvisation. Many of Loussier's recordings focus on familiar movements from the keyboard music, with occasional excursions into the chorales and instrumental works. Only in later years does he venture as far afield as the Goldberg Variations.

PLAY BACH, 1959–67

In these five albums bearing the same title, issued and reissued over some eighteen years, Loussier propels his trio to worldwide fame with sales reaching in the millions. Throughout his arrangements, especially of the preludes and fugues from *The Well-tempered Clavier*, Loussier never loses sight of Bach's rhythmic and melodic patterns, even if he interrupts these with his own improvisations. In his treatment of the Prelude and Fugue in G Minor from Book I, for instance, Loussier assigns the bottom line to the plucked bass and the upper lines to the piano to highlight Bach's interlocking voices, while in his high-speed, manic rendition of Bach's repetitive rapid notes in the Prelude in C Minor from Book I, he adds a supplementary line on the plucked bass that creates an extra supporting voice. When this prelude is repeated, he reduces the music to a soft bass solo with faint Bachian chords in the background. For the Prelude in D Major from the same book, Loussier focuses on Bach's jagged rhythms and rapid figurations, detaching them from the counterpoint to achieve a jaunty piece. Here, as elsewhere, Loussier delights in transparent textures that draw attention to Bach's independent voice writing.

Among the other pieces that feature on the *Play Bach* albums is a version of the Andante in Bach's organ Pastorale in C Minor (BWV 590). Here Loussier converts Bach's dreamy meanderings into an urgent pulse and expands what was a miniature piece into an extended improvisation, ending with a double bass solo. In the Air on the G String, Loussier adorns Bach's familiar melody with rhythmically displaced, delicate ornamentation. The version achieves fame after being appropriated by commercial television. In the advertising campaign that Benson & Hedges runs for more than twenty-five years from 1966 for their new brand of cigars, Bach's Air is heard in a series of hilarious, short skits. As protagonists seek relief from humiliating situations, they light up a cigar to the slogan "Happiness is a Cigar called Hamlet" as the opening bars of Loussier's soothing rendition are heard in the background.

JAZZ LOVES BACH, 1969

In this recording of the Brandenburg Concerto No. 5 with the Royal Philharmonic Orchestra, Loussier juxtaposes Bach's solo violin and flute parts with his own jazz flourishes on the piano. When the strings play their tutti sections, for example, Loussier gently subverts Bach's predictable rhythms with syncopated chords.

At times, he interrupts Bach's pulse with his own solos, and for Bach's keyboard cadenza, he proposes a jazz-type one of his own. And into the bouncing figurations of the gigue-like final movement, Loussier inserts cheeky interventions, perfectly in keeping with Bach's high spirits.

VARIACIONES GOLDBERG, 1999

In this recording, Loussier demonstrates how the thirty-two-bar structure of the melody in the Goldberg Variations is ideally suited to jazz extemporisations. Beginning with an exquisite rendition of Bach's Aria, Loussier progresses to the variations, often assigning Bach's bottom line to the delicately plucked bass to preserve the transparency of the upper part (Nos 4 and 8). Elsewhere, he accelerates the tempo to produce high-spirited, bouncing effects (Nos 5 and 20), adding his own jazz-inflected, floating rhythms (No. 6), or suggesting an alternative pace to Bach's lilting triple pulse (No. 7). At the end, Loussier collapses the boisterous street songs in Bach's Quodlibet (No. 30) into a single lyrical refrain, thereby returning to the mood of the opening Aria.

FRIEDRICH GULDA (1930–2000)

Bridging the classical and jazz fields, this Austrian pianist often presents Bach's keyboard works on the baroque clavichord, while at the same time composing a work that constitutes a Back to Bach journey translated into swing.

PRELUDE AND FUGUE IN E-FLAT MINOR, 1965

Gulda begins with arpeggios that recall those in the Prelude in C Major in Bach's Book I, though distorted by jazz rhythms and harmonies. Pausing on strikingly dissonant chords, Gulda proceeds to the fugue, which he builds on an asymmetrical, broken theme. After developing the counterpoint in four voices, Gulda introduces a countertheme with a downward chromatic scale, something Bach would have been familiar with, which he eventually combines with the original. Without letting up on the momentum, Gulda drives the fugue to a final B-flat seventh chord, after which he instructs the player to abandon the score and improvise freely.

Gulda's *Prelude and Fugue* attracts Keith Emerson, keyboard player with progressive English rock group The Nice, with whom he often performs the piece. This inspires him in 1967 to invent his own *High Level Fugue*.

EUGEN CICERO (1940–97)

This Romanian–German artist established a reputation as one of the chief exponents of the classic-swing style of jazz, in which he infuses the music of the past with his own "sparkling ideas, pearly runs, and phenomenal feel for rhythm".[131] Cicero's performances must be counted as among the most effervescent of all jazz-inspired Back to Bach pianistic journeys.

UND BACH?, 1965

Taking the Prelude in C Minor in Book I from *The Well-tempered Clavier*, Cicero begins by playing Bach's notes at a frantic pace, propelled by string bass and percussion. A series of forceful chords announces an excursion into Cicero's own realm, with new themes, syncopated rhythms and jazz harmonies, some vaguely recalling Bach's chordal progressions. Cicero reprises Bach at the end, and for the prelude's improvisatory final flourish, offers one of his own that almost approaches a virtuoso cadenza.

JAZZ BACH, 1985

In this medley of several of Bach's best-known keyboard pieces, Cicero is often heard together with a harpsichord player, as in "Bach Goes Latin", based on the incessant figurations of the

Prelude in C Major in Book I of *The Well-tempered Clavier*, into which he introduces his own syncopated beats and rhythmic distortions. For "Jesu, Joy of Man's Desiring", Cicero has an organist play the chorale theme, leaving him free to improvise on Bach's triplets, for a time converting them into what sounds like a romantic ballad. In the Siciliano from the Sonata for Flute in E-flat Major (BWV 1031), Cicero and a harpsichordist take turns in playing Bach's tender melody and gentle accompaniment, leaving Cicero free to add his own decorations and rhapsodic passages suspended above faint percussion.

SWINGING BACH, 1989

In the video of this ecstatic version of the Badinerie from the Orchestral Suite No. 2, Cicero adds trills and other embellishments that infuse Bach's solo flute writing with mischievous syncopations. In the repeats of the two sections, he teases out Bach's patterns, transforming them into his own jazz-inflected phrases, some recalling pop song refrains. Throughout, Cicero is encouraged by the bassist and percussionist, both of whom finds opportunities for their own solos. And at the end, Cicero signals respect by returning to the master.

NIKOLAI KAPUSTIN (1937–2020)

Despite his career as a virtuoso jazz pianist, this Russian composer evinces a lifelong commitment to Bach, seeking ways to reconcile baroque discipline with contemporary freedom. Nowhere is this better heard and seen than in the 1964 video of Kapustin playing his amazing Toccata together with the Moscow-based, Oleg Lundstrem's Big Band, one of the first such ensembles to emerge in the Soviet Union after the death of Stalin. However, it is in his later sets of preludes and fugues that Kapustin reveals his true mastery of a jazz-informed Bach idiom.

24 *PRELUDES IN JAZZ STYLES*, 1988

Sequencing his pieces in pairs of major keys and relative minor keys through cycles of fifths, a practice dating back to Chopin, Kapustin proclaims ebullient spontaneity in a variety of jazz styles, ranging from blues and swing to ballad and waltz. In the five-beat Prelude in G-flat Major, he even makes a nod to Dave Brubeck's "Take Five".

24 *PRELUDES AND FUGUES*, 1997

In a radical departure from Bach and Chopin, Kapustin pairs his preludes and fugues in two complimentary downward cycles of fifths: C, F, B-flat, etc. for the major keys, alternating with G-sharp, C-sharp, F-sharp, etc. for the minor keys, an arrangement he believes is related to the harmonic relationships he finds in jazz. Other links with jazz are the springy, syncopated rhythms, colourful expressive melodies, and startling harmonic progressions; indeed, much of the writing evokes improvisation.

If Kapustin's music communicates little audible connection with Bach, the master is present in the sheer variety and contrapuntal dexterity. The preludes range in mood from dreamy (Prelude in E Minor) and lyrically wistful in a slow blues manner (Prelude in C Major) to manic, and even cheeky (Prelude in B Flat). Regular patterns familiar in Bach's keyboard writing "dissolve" into a jazz waltz (Fugue in D Minor), manic propulsion (Fugue in C Minor) or quintuple hop (Fugue in E Minor). By importing ideas from the preludes into the fugues, often with one running the other, Kapustin forges relationships that Bach never thought of. That the master is present is evident from the preponderance of three- and four-voice fugues, except for one in two voices and another in five voices, a scheme that replicates that in Book I of *The Well-tempered Clavier*. Then there is the constant manipulation of fugal themes in augmentation and diminution, and, wherever possible, stretto overlays. Learning from Bach, Kapustin injects musical individuality into his fugal themes and counterthemes, infusing the counterpoint with infectious delight.

NINO ROTA (1911–79)
& ENNIO MORRICONE (1928–2020)

Renowned for the scores they provide over some fifty years for romances, crime stories, action thrillers and cowboy Westerns, these two Italian film composers occasionally reference Bach. Nino Rota, famous for his collaboration with Frederico Fellini and later with Francis Ford Coppola, also produces much instrumental music, including two striking B-A-C-H works for the piano. Ennio Morricone takes a step further by incorporating the B-A-C-H semitones into one of his film scores.

VARIATIONS AND FUGUE ON THE NAME BACH, 1950

Despite its crashing chords, vigorous arpeggios and soulful melodies, Nino Rota offers a virtuoso piano work that explores with Italian wit and charm the unpredictable harmonic twists of the four semitones of Bach's name. Beginning with B-A-C-H sheathed in brilliant arpeggios, the variations explore contrasting realms: a hopping, tarantella-like dance; a wistful melody that might have been borrowed from one of Fellini's steamy romantic scenes; a quasi-chorale prelude; and a Chopin-type nocturne. Rota juxtaposes his sensitive expositions with ones to be executed at the greatest speed interspersed with thunderous chords, during which B-A-C-H is always audible. For the Fugue, Rota extends the four semitones to create an expressive theme, against which he juxtaposes an oscillating countertheme. Racking up the counterpoint, Rota concludes with chordal climaxes worthy of his predecessors.

TWO WALTZES ON THE NAME BACH, 1975

Twenty-five years after his *Variations and Fugue*, Rota revisits Bach's musical signature by issuing these two works for the piano, to which he added the subtitles "Circus Waltz" and "Waltz Carillon". With its delicate yet rapid repeated notes on the four semitones, the first waltz suggests a light-hearted circus procession, while the second waltz dissolves the semitones into a demented dance caricature with bell-like tones suggesting a carillon. At the time of their composition, Fellini was working on *Casanova*, which is how the *Two Waltzes* found their way into the film's soundtrack.

THE SICILIAN CLAN, 1969

A no-less-prolific film composer than Rota, Ennio Morricone also finds moments to source Bach. When working on *The Sicilian Clan*, which gleefully follows the escapades of a global crime cartel, Morricone admits he "derived [its principal theme] from J.S. Bach's Fugue in A minor [BWV 543]. In search of originality, I found myself trapped in one of my deepest loves [of Bach]".[132] Indeed, the descending, repeated arpeggios of Morricone's melody recall those of Bach's organ configurations. Their gentle, slightly wistful character serves as a striking contrast with the violent twists in the movie's plot.

SUR LE NOM DE BACH, 1981

The same be said of the theme that Morricone invents for the French criminal thriller *Le Professionnel*. So obviously does he quote the B-A-C-H semitones that it comes to be known as *Sur le nom de Bach*, under which name it is issued on a separate album. Here, Morricone extends the four semitones of B-A-C-H into a chromatic melody that drifts sadly downwards from B-flat (the original first note of B-A-C-H) to D-flat. Supported on a similarly descending bass pulse, the melody is realised electronically in searing woodwinds and slithering strings, accentuated by trilling flutes. Heard in scenes where the movie's protagonist, played by Jean-Paul Belmondo, reflects on his inner conflict, Morricone's reimagination of B-A-C-H directs the audience to the hero's inner realm, distant from outer intrigues.

JIMI HENDRIX (1942–70) & JACO PASTORIUS (1951–87)

For some rock guitarists, Bach's keyboard improvisations act as magnets, attracting music greats like Hendrix and Pastorius.

RIFF ON THE PASSACAGLIA, c. 1968

Despite his violent, revolutionary and almost experimental playing, Jimi Hendrix was by no means ignorant of past traditions: as he was to complain: "I don't want anybody to stick a psychedelic label around my neck. Sooner Bach and Beethoven".[133] And in fact, Bach does make an appearance in a breathtaking extemporisation on the ostinato theme of the organ Passacaglia. As recorded in "Lift Off" on the album *Jimi Hendrix at His Best*, issued three years after the guitarist's death in 1970, Hendrix accelerates Bach's triple-beat pulse into a four-beat melody, injecting it with demonic power. After repeating it twice, he progresses to one of his frenzied riffs.

RIFF ON THE CHROMATIC FANTASIA, 1981

Hendrix sets an example for Jaco Pastorius, bass guitarist with the American jazz fusion band Weather Report. In the album *Word of Mouth*, Pastorius executes the opening passages of Bach's Chromatic Fantasia with astonishing virtuosity before the band enters, propelling Bach into pure rock energy.

THE BEATLES

During their decade-long career in the 1960s, this most famous of all English rock bands cheerfully appropriate music of the past, including Bach. The English composer and television presenter Howard Goodall even went so far as comparing the Beatles to Bach, commenting that: "like Bach [they] borrowed here and there with unabashed enthusiasm and made it all their own".[134] The Beatles were never coy about their Back to Bach journey: in later years, Paul McCartney confessed that "Bach was always one of our favourite composers; we felt we had a lot in common with him … and we latched onto him amazingly quickly".[135] In this, the group was encouraged by the classically trained George Martin, their producer from 1962, who is credited with introducing Bach to the Beatles and even arranging some of the Bachian quotations used in their songs.

"In My Life", a song they record in 1965, George Martin plays a mock-Bachian interlude on a piano speeded up to sound like a harpsichord. Two years later, the Beatles revert to similar Bachian nostalgia in "Penny Lane", into which they insert a piccolo (high) trumpet solo. McCartney apparently gets the idea after seeing a television broadcast of Brandenburg Concerto No. 2 with David Mason as soloist. He promptly summons Mason to join him in the recording studio.

"ALL YOU NEED IS LOVE", 1967

The simple message of this song, which resonates so profoundly with audiences of the day, is mostly conveyed on a simple succession of three chords. The music proceeds in this predictable fashion until it shifts into a high gear, propelled by David Mason playing high-pitched trumpet snatches lifted from Bach's keyboard Invention No. 8 in F Major (BWV 779). These balance an assortment of other quotations, such as the first phrases of "La Marseillaise", with which the song opens. By setting the words and melody of "All You Need Is Love" within this musical miscellany, the Beatles seem to proclaim the universality of their message. Most of their listeners would have agreed.

"BLACKBIRD", 1968

For the music of this song, written in response to the racial tensions in America at the time, McCartney admits plagiarising the beginning of "a well-known piece by Bach"; only later does he remember that it is the Bourrée from Lute Suite in E Minor (BWV 996), which he probably came across when learning the guitar. McCartney utilises Bach's opening chord progression, altering the phrases and harmonies to accommodate his concluding refrain: "You were only waiting for this moment to arise".

McCartney is not the only rock musician to source Bach's Bourrée. In his 1969 album *Stand Up*, Ian Anderson of Jethro Tull, the British progressive band, proposes a rock-flute version that displaces Bach's lilting rhythms with jerky but stylish syncopations.

PROCOL HARUM & MOTT THE HOOPLE

Bach must have been in the air when the Beatles issued "All You Need Is Love", for in that same year, and then a little later, two other English rock groups independently sought out the master.

"A WHITER SHADE OF PALE", 1967

Procol Harum has colossal success with an album that includes "A Whiter Shade of Pale". As the rock group's songwriter Gary Brooker later explains: "it does a bar or two of Bach's 'Air on a G String' before it veers off".[136] Sounded on the electric organ with a string bass plucking the descending octaves, Bach's Air launches the haunting melody and hallucinatory lyrics that make the group famous with what has been described as "the best British pop song of all time".[137]

"REPENT WALPURGIS", 1967

Another track on the same Procol Harum album is a wordless song built on repetitive sequences of four-bar chords supporting guitar and keyboard improvisations. The somewhat angst-ridden music is interrupted by Brooker playing the tranquil arpeggios of the Prelude in C Major from Book I of *The Well-tempered Clavier* on the piano, as if to suggest the peace of Walpurgis's repentance. After barely ten bars, the electric instruments return to steer the song back to its original anguish.

"REST IN PEACE", 1974

Inspired by Procol Harum, English rock band Mott the Hoople sources the same C major prelude from *The Well-tempered Clavier*, not for an interlude, but as an introduction to their song "Rest in Peace". This begins with a calm piano rendition of Bach's prelude, with Gounod's *Ave Maria* (based on the same C major prelude) heard faintly on electric keyboard in the background. About halfway through, the prelude dissolves into un-Bachian arpeggios and the song begins with the soulful words "Oh if the wheel could take another turn and if my life replaced itself again".

PETER, PAUL AND MARY & PAUL SIMON (1941–)

Some writers of pop songs seek out chorales of suffering that Bach includes in his Passion music to support their own poignant messages.

"BECAUSE ALL MEN ARE BROTHERS", 1965

In their quest to merge music with social commentary, the American vocal group Peter, Paul and Mary choose "O Haupt voll Blut und Wunden", which Bach has used in the St Matthew Passion, for a song on their album *See What Tomorrow Brings*. By vocalising Tom Glazer's words, "Because all men are brothers wherever men may be" to Bach's chorale melody, the group substitutes Bach's reflection on the suffering of Christ with lyrics that call for justice and unity.

"AMERICAN TUNE", 1973

The expressive phrases of "O Haupt voll Blut" also entice the American songwriter Paul Simon. In "American Tune", Simon's words, "I've often felt forsaken and certainly misused", sung to Bach's melody, resonate with the words "Oh head full of blood…". The remainder of the lyrics are a reflection on personal grief, before proceeding their own way. The song ends with Simon's affecting words, "That's all I'm trying to get some rest", a yearning for peace that permeates so many pious texts that Bach himself set to music.

KEITH EMERSON

Though drawn to Bach's keyboard works, pop groups tend to avoid his instrumental music. An exception to this is The Nice, the progressive English rock band, which during the 1960s fuses rock with the Brandenburg Concertos, thanks to Keith Emerson's astonishing keyboard antics.

BRANDENBURGER, 1968

With its irreverent label, this disc features Emerson playing a keyboard arrangement of the instrumental opening of Concerto No. 3, propelled by percussive accents that highlight Bach's rhythmic patterns. After spiking Bach's pulse with blues and jazz syncopations, Emerson returns to the master, interspersing the music with his own showy flourishes.

"COUNTRY PIE" 1969

Emerson's facility in navigating between pop and Bach is demonstrated with even greater panache in The Nice's arrangement of Bob Dylan's 1969 song "Country Pie", in which the band morphs effortlessly into the figurations of Brandenburg Concerto No. 6. In between Dylan's verses, which he renders in a light, folksy manner, Emerson plays an arrangement of Bach's string work on the harmonium, animated with percussion solos, keyboard "cadenzas", and vocal exclamations.

APOLLO 100 & THE BEACH BOYS

Because Myra Hess's arrangement of "Jesu, Joy of Man's Desiring" is practiced by just about all piano students, including those who become pop and rock musicians, it is only a matter of time before it is "highjacked". Among the first to do so is Apollo 100, the short-lived British rock band, followed by the Californian pop group The Beach Boys.

"JOY", 1972

Apollo 100 simply called their Bach-inspired track "Joy", which means that probably not many of their fans made the connection with "Jesu, Joy". In their take on the chorale, Apollo 100 strips Bach's triplets of their pastorale-like quality by spiking them with the manic energy of electric guitars and keyboards, fuelled by insistent percussion. Though "Joy" hardly sounds like Bach, the band uses triplet accompaniments as interludes between the phrases of the chorale sounded on the guitar and upper keyboard, thereby preserving Bach's original scheme.

"LADY LYNDA", 1979

Al Jardine, chief songwriter for the Beach Boys, takes a different approach to the same chorale. His song "Lady Lynda" begins with an instrumental rendition of Bach's noble triplets before progressing to his newly invented song. With their mention of "green canyon meadows [where] we'll hear the birds sing in the spring", Jardine's lyrics suggest an idyllic landscape attuned to Bach's music.

JON LORD (1941–2012)

Co-founder of the English rock band Deep Purple, this keyboard player becomes celebrated for his ecstatic performances on an amplified Hammond organ. Lord is classically trained, so it is no surprise to discover Bach's presence in a cross-over collaboration with the Munich Chamber Orchestra, and then later in an exploration of Bach's most celebrated organ work.

CONTINUO ON BACH, 1973

Into this richly scored, almost Stokowski-like orchestral transcription of the last, unfinished contrapuntal exemplar in *Art of Fugue*, Lord is heard playing several of the fugal themes on the organ. At the point where Bach's writing abruptly breaks off, Lord and his Deep Purple fellow musicians launch into an energetic improvisation based on snatches of Bach's themes, supported by orchestral players. This progresses to an extended percussion solo, with phrases ending on forceful B-A-C-H notes leading to the violent conclusion that startled the audience in Munich's Hercules Hall in June 1974.

BACH ONTO THIS, 1982

On this occasion, Lord turns to the Toccata and Fugue in D Minor, harnessing the Hammond organ for Bach's opening flourishes before summoning electric guitars and percussion to play an extended, animated interlude loosely based on Bach's harmonic progressions. About halfway through, the band returns to Bach, with Lord converting the oscillating passages from the Fugue into dance-like rhythms animated by drums and cymbals. For the final Coda, Lord offers a spirited extemporisation inspired by Bach's original.

SKY

Deep Purple is not the only rock group to seek out the Toccata and Fugue in D Minor. Two years earlier, this British group, known for their creative blend of classical music, rock and jazz, accessed the same work.

TOCCATA, 1980

Sky's interpretation on their album *Sky2* was to prove immensely popular when released separately, leading to the group performing *Toccata* on the British television show Top of the Pops. With their arsenal of electronic keyboards, amplified guitars and percussion, Sky injects Bach's figurations with strident sound and overpowering momentum. The rapid, repeated triplets are heard in the keyboard and guitars punctuated by drums and cymbals, while the diminished minor chords on electronic keyboards take on a menacing power.

DISMEMBER

As translated into the sonorities of this Swedish "death metal" band, Bach's sacred song, "Komm, süsser Tod, komm selge Ruh" (BWV 478) serves as an antidote for violence and personal grief.

"LIFE – ANOTHER SHAPE OF SORROW", 1995

In this song on the album *Massive Killing Capacity*, Dismember's lead guitarist, David Blomqvist, plays the opening sorrowful phrases of Bach's sacred song before revving up the tension with obsessive percussion and amplified guitars, into which he shouts rather than sings. As the song progresses, accelerated fragments of "Komm, süsser Tod" can be made out, engulfed in aggressive music that accompanies Blomquist's angry lyrics. Peace eventually returns with electric keyboards playing organ-like chords that offer a soothing background to Blomqvist reciting (in English) the song's original words, "Come, sweet death, come blessed rest".

TINA HARRIS (1975–) & JEM (1975–)

For the lyrics of their songs, these two female pop singers sought the reassurance of Bach's music.

"EVERYTHING'S GONNA BE ALRIGHT", 1997

It is with the German-based group Sweetbox that the American singer Tina Harris records this song, accompanied by a plucked string bass replicating the descending line of Bach's Air on the G String. As the song progresses, the Air's melody is heard in the background played on an oboe, before being picked up by the violins to create the tranquil mood that contributes to the song's comforting message.

"THEY", 2004

When the Welsh singer and songwriter Jemma Griffith, better known as Jem, wished to protest social injustice, she turned to Bach. In the song she simply calls "They" on her debut album, *Finally Woken*, Jem repurposes the Prelude in F Minor from Book II of *The Well-tempered Clavier*, not as Bach wrote it, for the keyboard, but in the bubbling vocalisation by the Swingle Singers borrowed from their 1963 *Jazz Sébastien Bach* album. Jem's lyrics, especially the refrains "I'm sorry, so sorry", "Who are they, where are they?" and "Do you see, what I see?", merge seamlessly with Bach's pairs of drooping motifs.

LADY GAGA (1986–) & GIOVANNI DETTORI (1975–)

In a sensational career specialising in electropop, the American singer and songwriter known as Lady Gaga has little use for Bach. Even so, on one notable occasion, she (or perhaps her producer) briefly quotes the master. No explanation is offered.

"BAD ROMANCE", 2009

In the video of this song, which sells more than twelve million copies worldwide, Lady Gaga appears in futuristic scenes bracketed by the opening bars of the Fugue in B Minor from Book I of *The Well-tempered Clavier*. Lady Gaga portrays a drugged sex slave who, after singing and dancing her way through a sequence of weird settings, eventually immolates her kidnapper. Such a gruesome scenario may seem an altogether inappropriate destination for a Bach fugue, yet when played on a tinny harpsichord at top speed, the first bars of its chromatic theme take on a demonic character in keeping with the song's vengeful spirit.

LADY GAGA FUGUE, 2009

"Bad Romance" does not exhaust the connection with a Bach fugue. Soon after the video is released, the Italian composer Giovanni Dettori, known for his efforts to reconcile pop music with Bachian counterpoint, devises *Lady Gaga Fugue*. In this joyous work, he repurposes the song's jaunty "Rah, Rah, Ah-Ah-Ah" opening refrain as the theme for a three-voice, Bachian-style fugue. When performed by the Croatian pianist Dejan Lazić at London's Royal Albert Hall in September 2011, the audience instantly recognised the "Bad Romance" refrain and proceeded to relish the witty Bachian parody. Since then, *Lady Gaga Fugue* has sprouted numerous arrangements for string ensemble and brass band and wind groups.

BOBBY MCFERRIN & THE TURTLE ISLAND QUARTET

The Swinging Bach concert staged in Leipzig's marketplace in July 2000 to commemorate the 250th anniversary of Bach's death featured eminent classical, jazz, pop and rock musicians. The impressive line-up of performers was hosted by the American singer Bobby McFerrin, who inaugurated the event with a fluent vocal rendition of the Air on the G String. This was followed by a string quartet version of the Air by the San Francisco based ensemble, inspired by the 1963 album *Seven Steps to Heaven* by the acclaimed jazz trumpeter Miles Davis.

SEVEN STEPS TO BACH, 2000

The quartet begins according to Bach, but soon morphs into jazz terrain, with slithering strings recalling Davis's high-voltage trumpet solos, and the cello acting as both bass and percussion by plucking the strings and tapping the belly. Meanwhile, snatches of the Air and syncopated chords from *Seven Steps to Heaven* can be made out, submerged in fragments of Bach's Air.

FALK & SONS

Like the Bachs in their day, the German rock group Falk & Sons demonstrates that making music can still be a family business. With Dieter, the pianist father, and Max and Paul, the two sons playing electric guitar and percussion, the group presents numerous arrangements of Bach's music, animated with the frenzied antics that their audiences expect. Not content to merely quote Bach, the Falk family also devises entirely new instrumental pieces, recasting Bach's melodic and harmonic patterns into rock rhythms and jazz chords. They justify their use of amplified instruments by claiming that if Bach would be living today, "he would be using state-of-the-art computers and keyboards". As they explain to their audience, "Bach's music not only has tempo, groove and sophistication … but also soul, depth and melancholy, the same as real life".[138]

TOCCATA, 2013

One of Falk & Sons' most dynamic encounters with Bach is an outdoor performance in Hamburg simply called *Toccata*, in reference to Bach's celebrated organ work. The video of this event features the group performing Bach's oscillations on electric keyboards backed by incessant percussive pulses. Apart from the rhythmic dislocations and strident sounds, their version is faithful, except for the reprise of the opening proclamations at the end, something that Bach did not think to do.

CHARL DU PLESSIS (1977–)

Throughout his arrangements of baroque masters, this South African pianist and his fellow musicians aim at a rhythmic clarity and instrumental transparency that is well suited to Bach.

BAROQUESWING, 2013–19

For his version of the organ Toccata on the first of these four identically labelled albums, du Plessis on the piano substitutes perky, jazz syncopations for Bach's triplets, animating the cascading passages with nimble percussive touches. The Fugue mostly benefits from crystalline playing, except for the concluding arpeggios and grandiose chords that recall the piano writing of the romantic era.

Other Bach works featured on the *Baroqueswing* albums include the Preludes in C Major and C Minor from Book I of *The Well-tempered Clavier*, the Capriccio from the keyboard Partita No. 1 in B-flat Major, the slow movement from the Concerto for Two Violins, and the Preludio from the Partita No. 3 in E Major for Solo Violin. Never losing sight of Bach's contrapuntal precision, du Plessis adds his own jazz syncopations and figurations, sharing his improvisations with the plucked bass and percussion.

ILLIA BONDARENKO

Most pop musicians avoided the solo violin Chaconne, perhaps in the belief that Bach's variations left them too little room to extemporise. Judging from a video of a private performance, this Ukrainian violinist disagrees.

CHACONNE, 2017

Bondarenko begins by converting the Chaconne into a lively, jazz-tango work for himself and three fellow musicians. After giving Bach's first eight bars, albeit with a slight jerk that breaks up the triple rhythm, the piano becomes fixated on a minor flourish in Bach's first two variations, which is then picked up by Bondarenko and his fellow violinist. After obsessing with this motif, Bondarenko guides his ensemble through versions of a harmonically rich, tango-like theme derived from this fragment. After six enjoyable minutes, Bondarenko pauses on an unresolved chord before playing eight of the variations exactly as Bach has written them. A brief reprise of the tango brings this creative homage to an end.

BACH IN JAZZ, 2017

In this video of Bach selections, Bondarenko appears together with the pianist Natalia Lebedeva, a second violinist, string bassist and percussionist. While subjecting the music to constant rhythmic and melodic deformations, Bondarenko retains Bach's expressive lyricism, which he captures effectively in the Air on the G String and slow movement of the Concerto for Two Violins. The same is true in his versions of the organ chorale "Ich ruf zu dir, Herr Jesu Christ" ("I call to thee, Lord Jesus Christ") and the alto aria "Erbarme dich, mein Gott" ("Have mercy, my God") from the St Matthew Passion.

BILL CUNLIFFE (1956–)

In his 2017 album *BACHanalia*, this American pianist and arranger offers a selection of Bach's music in jazz band incarnations. The album opens with "Sleepers' Awake", in which Cunliffe matches a trumpet and a female vocalist singing in a scat style to execute the buoyant countertheme of Bach's chorale prelude, while the stately melody is shared between the piano and other brass instruments. The most extensive piece on this album, however, is Cunliffe's wind band take on the Goldberg Variations.

GOLDBERG CONTRAPTION, 2017

Cunliffe begins by playing the Aria as Bach had written it, except for some discrete, jazz harmonic interventions. A solo guitar soon enters, followed by a trombone and then a saxophone, cloaking the music with a faintly sombre mood. By the time all the brass instruments join in, the Aria is charged with surging jazz rhythms. Percussion interludes lead to a series of episodes based on the Aria and several of the variations. Bach's No. 10, with its bouncing subject building up in four voices, for example, proves ideal for different band sections. For No. 15, Cunliffe begins on the piano before an elegiac solo oboe takes over. The instrumental textures gradually intensify until a trombone offers an extended solo improvisation. After several more episodes, the pianist offers a virtuoso cadenza that leads into a lushly harmonised reprise of the Aria.

JÖRG ACHIM KELLER (1966–) & BILL DOBBINS (1947–)

Some leaders of German big bands specialising in American dance music of the 1930s and 1940s are now pioneering innovative Bach arrangements. Though expressed in strident bass tones, soulful woodwind solos, and insistent percussive accents, their Back to Bach journeys in no way violate the originals.

BACH GOES BIG BAND, 2018

In this work arranged for Frankfurt Radio, Jörg Achim Keller selects four pieces from *The Well-tempered Clavier*. For the Prelude in

C Minor from Book I, Keller picks out Bach's harmonic structure in isolated notes on the piano, guitars and muted trumpets, while a string bass is faintly heard plucking the running notes beneath. Bach's concluding flourish is converted into a free cadenza for a saxophone solo. When it comes to the accompanying Fugue, Keller faithfully transcribes Bach's counterpoint for three different instruments. For the Prelude in C-sharp Minor from the same book, Keller has clarinets and saxophones transform Bach's counterpoint into continuously flowing passages, while trumpets and trombones pick out the hopping, triple rhythm. In the central section, Keller temporarily abandons Bach for improvisations on trumpet and trombone before reprising the first section.

In the Prelude in G Minor from Book I, Keller has a solo trumpet render Bach's right-hand figurations, answered on a saxophone against a background of piano and trombones. Instead of extemporising, Keller keeps close to the score to emphasise Bach's lyrical melody. Faithfulness to Bach also characterises his version of the Fugue in D Minor from Book II, with the brass cheerfully navigating Bach's flowing triplets. However, Keller abruptly interrupts these to introduce solo improvisations on clarinet, trumpet and saxophone.

THE BIG BAND GOLDBERG PROJECT, 2022

Bill Dobbins is well experienced to accept this commission from the West German Broadcasting Station (WDR) in Cologne, having already arranged Bach's Christmas Oratorio (BWV 248) for the King's Singers and the WDR Big Band in 2014. In this take on Bach's variations, Dobbins transfers Bach's intimate, intricate keyboard writing to the sonorities of trumpets, trombones, saxophones and clarinets, backed by piano, guitars, string bass and percussion. Framing instrumental solos with exuberant full-

band tuttis, Dobbins infuses the Goldberg Variations with sweet
jazz harmonies expressed through colouristic and rhythmic variety

Dobbins begins with the Aria as Bach has written it, with the
solo piano alternating with peaceful ensembles for the repeats.
In Bach's No. 2, Dobbins slightly alters Bach's pattern to achieve
a floating quality. A similar rhythmic twist of the theme in Bach's
fughetta No. 10 results in momentum as different band sections
enter one after another, until the piano offers a virtuosic solo.
Lightweight scoring characterises the "Overture" (No. 16), until the
ensemble joins in for the second part. In Nos 18 and 24, Dobbins
assigns Bach's lines to instrumental solos, while for the Adagio
(No. 25) he complements Bach's darkly emotive melody with a
doleful one of his own for the saxophone. Dobbins dispels this
somewhat sombre atmosphere with cheerful brass renditions of
the street songs in the concluding Quodlibet.

MATT HERSKOWITZ, BRAD MEHLDAU (1970–) & ADAM BIRNBAUM (1979–)

Judging from recent recordings by these North American pianists,
the preludes from *The Well-tempered Clavier* continue to attract
jazz musicians intent upon capturing the essence of Bach himself
at the keyboard.

BACH À LA JAZZ, 2011

For this video, the Montreal-based pianist Matt Herskowitz selects
the Prelude in C Minor from Book I of *The Well-tempered Clavier*,
taking delight in Bach's obsessive, rapid patterns, from which
he extracts a melodic outline by holding over some of the notes
from one bar to the next. After executing Bach's flourishes at the
end of the Prelude, Herskowitz breaks out in forceful chords and
then proceeds to the lively rhythms and showy passages of an

extended improvisation. Having invested the Prelude with his own excitement, Herskowitz returns to Bach in the final bars.

AFTER BACH, 2018

In this hybrid work, which lasts well over an hour, the American jazz pianist Brad Mehldau plays four preludes and one fugue from *The Well-tempered Clavier*, interspersing them with his own extended jazz compositions. From Bach's rhythmic Prelude in C-sharp Major in Book I, for example, Mehldau extracts a jerky pattern in quintuple time on which to base a rondo with harmonically adventurous episodes. He then borrows the triplets from the adjacent Prelude in D Minor to support a rippling improvisation. Bach's three abrupt statements in the G minor Fugue in Book II are followed by six repeated notes, which Mehldau converts into an ostinato theme on which he constructs a piece that builds in pace and complexity. Mehldau then repeats these acts of musical reconstruction in his dreamlike meditation on motifs taken from the Prelude in F Minor in Book I.

PRELUDES, 2023

Together with a string bassist and percussionist, Adam Birnbaum chooses a dozen preludes from Book I of *The Well-tempered Clavier*, infusing them with spirited rhythms and melodies derived from Latin and samba beats. In the Prelude in C Minor, for example, Birnbaum pits his own jazz harmonies against light accents in the percussion and plucked rhythmic displacements, after which he proposes a lyrical melody carried on romantic arpeggios and chords. For the Prelude in D Minor, Birnbaum removes one of Bach's notes in every second set of six to create an unsymmetrical pulse of 6 + 5, while at the same time retaining Bach's harmonic scheme. Birnbaum's predilection for lyricism is shown in his treatment of the Prelude in E Minor. Abandoning the continuous, fast-moving notes in the bass, Birnbaum concentrates on the melody above, coaxing Bach's ornamentations into an expressive melody more akin to a Chopin nocturne than a baroque aria. The same is true when he injects the contemplative chordal progressions of the Prelude in B-flat Minor with gentle blues dissonances.

MC FIOTI (1994–) & GRANDPAMINI

Bach is now exported into bizarre realms, such as that devised by the Brazilian funk rapper MC Fioti. He is even "injested" into popular "mashup" culture, which fuses music from different genres and eras, like the project concocted by the Paris-based Chilean "galactic" DJ performer known as Grandpamini.

BUM BUM TAM TAM, 2017

In the video of this Orientalist erotic fantasy, MC Fioto and his dusky attendant attempt to seduce girls by playing passages from the Partita for Solo Flute (BWV 1013). Bach's music proves irresistible.

GUESS WHO'S BACH?, 2017

By substituting "Bach" for the word "Back" and having famous pop singers and rappers perform to Bach's music, Grandpamini contrives video songs like "Get Bach" (Ludacris vs Bach), "Lean Bach" (Fat Joe vs Bach) and "Sexy Bach" (Justin Timberlake vs Bach). This makes it possible to witness eleven-year-old Michael Jackson gyrating to "I Want You Bach" against passages from the Toccata and Fugue in D Minor.

RAINER HERSCH (1962–)

With his reputation for devising humorous caricatures of classical music, this British conductor proposes an irreverent version of Bach's most famous organ work translated into the Latin dance rhythms showcased in Leonard Bernstein's 1957 score for *West Side Story*.

TOCCATA MAMBO IN D MINOR, 2018

Scored for a small instrumental group, including percussion and piano, this high-spirited incarnation of the Toccata veers between straightforward renditions of Bach's organ passages and cheeky brass and percussion outbursts in a syncopated mambo style. The shouts from the audience that punctuate the music mimic the ecstatic utterances of the dancers in the mambo scene of *West Side Story*.

JOACHIM HORSLEY

Known for the scores he provides for movies and TV series, this Los Angeles-based pianist and composer also takes time to fuse Bach with jazz harmonies, Caribbean rhythms and African percussion.

BACH'S CUBAN CONCERTO, 2024

In this adaption, Horsley transforms the first movement of Bach's Concerto for Keyboard No. 1 in D Minor (BWV 1052) into a double concerto for piano and tres, a popular Cuban three-stringed guitar, supported by a string ensemble animated with maracas, bongos, congas and drums. By inserting off-beat syncopations into Bach's opening theme, itself infused with rhythmic vigour, Horsley intensifies the momentum of Bach's instrumental writing, imbuing the tutti sections with dance-like delight. And in the solo passages that accord with those of Bach, Horsley recalls the Brandenburgs by sharing the musical ideas between two tonally distinct, solo instruments. Injecting jazz idioms into Bach's figurations and harmonic progressions, Horsley creates an infectious, high-spirited work that is both Bachian and Cuban.

AFRO BACH, 2025

On this album, Horsley reissues his Cuban Concerto with six other Bach arrangements. They open with "Afrobeats Prelude and

Amapiano Fugue" based on the Prelude in C Minor from Book I of *The Well-tempered Clavier*, in which Horsely disrupts Bach's regular four-note patterns without abandoning the harmonic structure. Despite occasional jazz-like excursions on the piano, Horsley reprieves Bach's concluding improvisatory flourish before proceeding to the Fugue, which he subjects to similar rhythmic dislocation without interfering with the counterpoint. In "Bach Boogaloo", his take on the Badinerie from the Orchestral Suite No. 2, Horsley converts Bach's skipping flute passages into virtuosic piano passages interrupted with strident, brass band snippets. The first movement of Bach's Cello Suite No.1, as reimagined in "Tropical Prelude", begins with arpeggio excerpts answered by the piano in a civilised duet, momentarily interrupted with cheeky brass inserts. Together with the three other arrangements, Horsley persuasively exports Bach into the sonic world of Latin America and South Africa.

NTT DOCOMO & LUO NI

That Bach has now entered mainstream popular culture is nowhere more evident that in the products of these two Japanese and Chinese companies.

"JESU, JOY OF MAN'S DESIRING", 2011

To promote their new mobile phone set in a cedar case, NTT Docomo constructed a gigantic, sloping xylophone out of cedar planks. When a wooden ball is set free to bounce downwards along its planks, the instrument transmits Bach's lilting triplets and chorale melody into the serenity of a Japanese cedar forest.

G MINOR BACH, 2015

For the hugely popular *Piano Tiles 2*, issued by the Beijing-based Cheetah Mobile Company, the creator of this game, Hu Wen

Zeng, commissioned several composers to provide instrumental "songs" that would be "unlocked" as rewards for players as they progress through the game's different levels. For the tenth level of *Piano Tiles 2*, the Chinese musician Luo Ni responds by selecting the C Minor Prelude in Book I of *The Well-tempered Clavier*, even though he calls it "G minor". His "song" begins with Bach's rapid note oscillations carried on a new, lively foundation. In the central section, Luo Ni converts the oscillations into an agreeable theme on simple chord progressions. Both hands are occupied with Bach's rapid notes in the final, third part of the song, in which Luo Ni emphasises the top notes to create a tender melody. In this way, Bach is processed for players of mobile phone games who have never heard his name, let alone his music.

AFTERLIVES

GOLDBERG VARIATIONS

Bach begins his longest and most technically challenging keyboard work with an expressive melody he calls an Aria, in keeping with its graceful, lyrical character. Shaped by stresses on the second beat, its stately triple rhythm conforms to a traditional sarabande, which Bach expands beyond the usual limit of two blocks of eight to create an unusually long, thirty-two-bar theme. But Bach is less interested in the Aria's elegant contour and intricate embellishments than in its supporting bass line. Its first eight bars comprise a G major scale descending through the octave to B and then rising to D, before dropping to a low G – a pattern that replicates the ostinato in a keyboard Chaconne in the same G major key published by Handel a few years earlier.[139] While Bach follows Handel to begin with, he extends the bass line to carry his expanded theme, which then serves as a harmonic support for the thirty variations that follow. These explore the broadest possible range of contrapuntal devices, melodic ideas, rhythmic patterns and keyboard textures. Unable to resist exhibiting his contrapuntal prowess, Bach inserts canons at progressively higher intervals after every three variations, beginning with one on the unison (No. 3) and ending with one on the interval of a ninth (No. 27). So subtly does he craft his canons that they never impede the musical flow.

Bach divides his Variations into two groups of fifteen, marking the middle one as an "Overture" in the strident French manner (No.16), as if to signal a new start. The chromatic expressiveness of the reflective, arioso-like variation in G minor (No. 25) contrasts markedly with the exuberant running passages, crashing chords and rushing triplets of the variations that follow. In the ebullient last "Quodlibet" variation (No. 30), Bach combines two cheerful street songs that would have been familiar to listeners of his day. Having touched on the world of everyday familiarity, Bach then writes "Aria da Capo e Fine", instructing players to return to where they had begun, thereby offering a calm destination to his musical explorations.

While Beethoven and Schumann admired the Goldbergs, only in later times are they performed publicly, inspiring musicians to make instrumental and vocal arrangements, as well as their own variation sets.

1741 Bach publishes his *Aria with Diverse Variations* as the fourth part of his Clavier-Übung series.

1804 With its fifty-seven variations, *Art of Varying* by the Czech-born Anton Reicha is the most extensive keyboard set since the Goldbergs.

1823 Beethoven references the Goldbergs in his *Diabelli Variations*.

1845 Robert Schumann's *Six Studies in Canonic Form*.

1933 & 1942 Wanda Landowska records the Goldbergs on the harpsichord, then later presents them in concert.

1938 Jósef Koffler's arrangement for chamber orchestra.

1956 In his debut album, Glenn Gould launches himself and the Goldbergs to worldwide fame.

1984 Dmitry Sitkovetsky's string trio arrangements.

1986–7 John Lewis identifies the Variations with different chess moves.

1997 *Gilded Goldbergs* by Robin Holloway.

1999 Jacques Loussier's *Variaciones Goldberg*.

2000 Uri Caine sets the Variations in a work that encompasses a vast spectrum of musical styles.

2004 Lara Downes invites thirteen composers to respond to the Goldbergs in *13 Ways of Looking at the Goldbergs*.

2004 In *Goldberg's Lullaby*, the American pianist Paul Whetstone plays variations on George Shearing's popular 1952 song "Lullaby of Birdland" that mimic the formats of the Goldbergs.

2007 United Instruments of Lucilin juxtapose performances on period instruments with new compositions in *Goldberg's Ghost*.

2008 In the science fiction film *The Day the Earth Stood Still*, the Aria serves as a beacon of hope for mankind.

2011 Dan Tepfer's jazz piano *Goldberg Variations/Variations*.

2013–15 Bach's Aria is labelled as the "Hannibal Theme" in the NBC *Hannibal* psychological-thriller series.

2013–16 Karlheinz Essl's *Gold.Berg.Werk*.

2017 *Goldberg Contraption*, Bill Cuncliffe's big band version of the Goldbergs.

2018 & 2024 In their *Quer Bach* albums, SLIXS vocalise several Variations.

2020 Bryce Messmann's *Community Goldberg Variations*.

2021 *The Big Band Goldberg Project* by Bill Dobbins for WDR in Cologne.

8.

BACH REIMAGINED

FROM SWITCHED-ON BACH & ARVO PÄRT TO MAX RICHTER & ENSEMBLE SARBAND

Bach has now been submerged in artificial soundscapes or entirely reinvented in electronic sound. Such mechanical *Back to Bach* journeys were to some extent anticipated in Gödel, Escher, Bach, the widely read (but not always understood) 1979 book by Douglas R. Hofstadter, subtitled "A Metaphorical Fugue on Minds and Machines". Composers have deconstructed Bach, rearranging his musical "shards", especially the B-A-C-H semitones, according to complicated mathematical formulas. For those writing under Soviet repression, Bach offered support; for others, his music served as an excuse for incarnations bordering on satire, or for collaborative projects that attracted responses from contemporary musicians. As the Argentinian–German composer Mauricio Kagel concluded: "although not all musicians believe in God, all believe in Bach".[140]

LA MONTE YOUNG (1935–)

While turning his back on the preludes and fugues in *The Well-tempered Clavier*, La Monte Young, one of the pioneers of American minimalist music, pays tribute to Bach by rethinking his system of keyboard tuning.

THE WELL-TUNED PIANO, 1964

In this radical work, Young replaces the firmly established, equal tuning of the modern piano with his own "just intonation" based on complicated pitch relationships between perfect fifths and harmonic sevenths. His efforts to explore new possibilities of tuning parallels that of Bach almost 250 years before, even if the music itself repudiates the past. Young's conception of *The Well-Tuned Piano* is essentially formless, being constructed entirely from improvisations and repetitions of chordal series and arpeggios. Lacking perceptible pulse or melody, the music achieves an immersive experience sustained over more than six hours! This otherworldly effect is intensified in the 1987 video showing a solo pianist against a colouristic light installation created by the composer's wife, Marian Zazeela.

WALTER/WENDY CARLOS (1939–)

In the two albums produced by this sound engineer, who transitioned during their production, Bach's music is projected beyond the realm of human voices and acoustic instruments thanks to the tones of the newly invented Moog synthesiser. In less than a decade, the discs sell more than one million copies, captivating an audience that had never listened to Bach, while at the same time introducing synthesisers to pop artists and rock groups.

SWITCHED-ON BACH, 1968 & 1973

Carlos's electronic Back to Bach journeys feature transcriptions of instrumental works that include movements from Brandenburg Concerto No. 3, two preludes and fugues from Book I of *The Well-tempered Clavier*, and the ubiquitous Air on the G String. Converted into artificial sound, Bach's complex figurations and buoyant rhythms are presented with astounding clarity. Little wonder that the first *Switched-On Bach* disc was labelled as a "cross-over album extraordinaire",[141] and hailed by the Canadian pianist Glenn Gould as one of the great feats in the history of keyboard performance.[142]

EDUARD ARTEMYEV (1937–2022), ISAO TOMITA (1932–2016) & RYUICHI SAKAMOTO (1952–2013)

Among the "hits" of Bach included in the *Switched-On Bach* discs were "Jesu, Joy of Man's Desiring" and "Sleepers Awake", which encouraged musicians working with electronic sounds to seek other Bach chorales. Notable among these figures were Eduard Artemyev, known for the film scores he provided for the Russian director Andrei Tarkovsky; Isao Tomita, one of the pioneers of Japanese electronic music; and Ryuichi Sakamoto, who also earned a reputation with his film scores.

SOUNDTRACK FOR *SOLARIS*, 1972

For Tarkovsky's brooding, science fiction movie *Solaris*, Artemyev sources "Ich ruf zu dir, Herr Jesu Christ" ("I call to thee, Lord Jesus Christ") from the *Orgel-Büchlein* (BWV 639) for the scene in which the psychologist Kris Kelvin roams pensively through the forest surrounding his childhood home. As he gazes into a pond and listens to birds singing, Bach's organ chorale is heard in the background, before dissolving into eerie, artificial sounds. The music anticipates Kelvin's departure from the earth's natural habitat, as represented by Bach's music, to the space station where the disquieting events of the story will unfold to more other-worldly music.

BACH: THE SEA NAMED SOLARIS, 1978

The "extra-terrestrial" potentiality of "Ich ruf zu dir" in Artemyev's film score so impresses Tomita that, six years later, he devises his own musical homage based on the same organ chorale, which he also imports into a disembodied, ethereal soundscape.

For additional ideas, Tomita draws on Sinfonia No. 2 in C Minor (BWV 788), not in Bach's original keyboard version, but in an arrangement for strings and voices that sound like those of the Swingle Singers. With these dismembered quotations, he creates an eerie atmosphere that portrays a remote world comparable to that experienced by Tarkovsky's hero.

SOLARIS, 2017

Tomita is not the only Japanese composer to be fascinated with Artemyev's score for *Solaris*. In the version of "Solaris" on his album *Async*, Sakamoto offers a chorale theme of his own invention on a constantly moving notes that replicate the texture of Bach's chorale prelude as played on a synthesiser submerged in a fog of electronic sound.

ARVO PÄRT (1935–)

During the rule of the Soviets in his native Estonia, Pärt avoids censure by developing his "collage" technique, in which he references the music of the past, especially that of Bach. Pärt first acknowledges Bach in a modest chamber piece and then in an ambitious allegorical choral work expressing disintegration, collapse and reawakening. After experiencing an impasse, when he altogether ceases writing, Pärt returns to composing in what he called his "tintinnabuli" style suitable for small instrumental ensembles modelled on the Brandenburg Concertos, such as the one he employs in his *Tabula Rasa*. But in *The Passion of Our Lord Jesus Christ According to John* of 1982, based on a Latin version of the Gospel, Pärt reasserts his Catholic faith and renounces Bach.

COLLAGE ON BACH, 1964

Written for chamber orchestra, Pärt's references to Bach are immediately apparent from the titles of its three movements: Toccata,

Sarabande and Ricercar. The first, for strings alone, comprises repeated, rapid note patterns with the strings playing all four semitones of B-A-C-H simultaneously to begin with, and then in combination with adjacent semitones. In his second movement, Pärt offers an instrumentation of the Sarabande from the English Suite No. 6 (BWV 811) but retains Bach's triple-time signature and D minor key. Played eloquently on the oboe, supported by a harpsichord and violins, the theme is divided into three sections separated by dense string clusters that repeat the Sarabande's theme and rhythmic pattern but introduce a mood of unrest. As in the Toccata, Pärt's last movement is also for strings alone. It begins as a fugue on the B-A-C-H motif, with the four semitones transposed, inverted and augmented, then finally played together as repeated chords, which eventually resolve into a sonorous D minor chord.

CREDO, 1968

Scored for solo piano, large chorus and full orchestra, Pärt conceives this epic religious work around two confessions of Christian faith "supported" musically and spiritually by a Bach prelude. The first words, "Credo in Jesum Christum", are taken from the Mass; the second quotation comes from the Sermon on the Mount in the New Testament: "An eye for an eye, and a tooth for a tooth, but I say unto you, do not resist injury". Pärt must have realised that these texts were futile gestures against a repressive regime. Soon after the premiere of *Credo*, the work is banned by the Soviets, leading him to embark upon eight years of compositional silence.

Pärt begins with the choir proclaiming "I believe", followed by the arpeggios of the Prelude in C Major from Book I of *The Well-tempered Clavier* signifying peace and order. The solo piano is soon overtaken with menacing drum rolls, before the choir intones "An eye for an eye …" on chords derived from Bach's harmonic structure disposed between the different orchestral sections. Aggressive brass outbursts soon intrude, with the pianist reduced to senselessly bashing the keyboard, and the choir voicing nonsense syllables and hellish shrieks in a sonic portrayal of chaos. When the choir arrives at the words "… do not resist injury", Bach's consoling arpeggios are heard once again. The prelude's harmonies are then taken up by the voices and orchestra in a richly scored, tonal interlude. A brass fanfare introduces the final voicing of "I believe", after which the piano gently touches the notes of Bach's opening chord, ending on a high pitch C, which offers a final release.

TABULA RASA, 1977

Modelled on Bach's concerto grosso format, *Tabula Rasa* is one of the first products of Pärt's "tintinnabuli" style that he develops after resuming composition. This takes its name from the Latin word for a bell, which Pärt evokes through the interweaving of two violins – one following melodic steps, the other oscillating between the notes of a major or minor triad, as in a church bell. Marked "Ludus" ("Game"), the opening movement presents static pianissimo chords alternating with expanding canonic variations. These proceed up and down the scale and triad of A minor, which Pärt overlaps to create a continuous musical web, a pattern that recalls the opening of Brandenburg Concerto No. 6.

The ethereal atmosphere of the second movement of *Tabula Rasa*, which Pärt calls "Silentium", owes much to the D minor scale played by one soloist at the slowest possible tempo, "suspended" over a regular tintinnabuli pulse played by the second soloist. Meanwhile, the orchestra executes the same minor scale, but at twice the speed if not quicker. Despite such Bachian, stretto-like overlaps, Pärt marks his movement "without motion", thereby altogether renouncing Bach's momentum. For Alex Ross, the chords "silence the noise of the self, binding the mind to an eternal present".[143]

KRZYSZTOF PENDERECKI (1933–2020)

The music that this Polish composer writes during the Soviet era, such as his *St Luke Passion*, signals political protest by expressing personal faith. Though adopting an experimental, almost revolutionary musical language, Penderecki locates his work within the Protestant tradition by following the narrative formats of Bach's two Passions and quoting the B-A-C-H motif.

ST LUKE PASSION, 1966

Penderecki scores his musical narrative for a large choir divided into separate groups, supported by an orchestra equipped with a plethora of percussion instruments and an organ. As in Bach, the events are related by a tenor Evangelist, with the words of Christ assigned to a bass soloist. Penderecki's text is eclectic, drawing on the Gospel of St Luke, the Stabat Mater and several of the Psalms. The work focuses on the last days of Jesus, with the chorus taking a central role by singing and speaking, also responding to events by shouting, hissing and mocking. The orchestral texture is mostly transparent, but there are occasional massive tutti outbursts that result in crucifix-like, horizonal-vertical-horizontal patterns in the written score.

Penderecki derives much of the musical materials in *St Luke Passion* from twelve-tone rows with clusters of adjacent semitones that incorporate B-A-C-H. He invests these semitones with expressive intensity at key moments, such as when the chorus sings "Miserere mei, Deus" (No. 12) from Psalm 55. When the same words are sung by Jesus (No. 27), Penderecki gives B-A-C-H in transposed and retrograde forms before the original sequence returns. At No. 16, the chorus and soloists perform the remonstrances of Christ with his people, while B-A-C-H serves as the basis for a passacaglia in the accompanying tympani, altos and organ. Though the musical language is unrelentingly atonal, Penderecki sets "Deus veritas", the final words of his Passion, in "pure" E major.

GERD ZACHER (1929–2014)

With his long experience of performing *Art of Fugue*, this German organist, composer and musicologist is well qualified to "interrogate" Bach in this somewhat capricious Back to Bach journey. Zacher probably feels his interventions are justified by the fact that Bach did not specify how his contrapuntal exemplars might be performed.

DIE KUNST EINER FUGE, 1968

Without altering a single note of Bach, Zacher explores the acoustic potentialities of Contrapunctus 1 in "Ten Interpretations". After announcing the fugue as in Bach's original version, Zacher subjects its four voices to sonic distortions: increasing the volume as the music progresses; bringing out the melodic possibilities of the alto line, which Bach had "underprivileged"; stressing the harmonic rather than the linear qualities of the voices; and so on. In his fifth interpretation, Zacher assigns different tone colours to different note values – the shortest notes, for example, being highlighted with a bright cymbal stop. In the next interpretation, Zacher rearranges Bach's four voices, positioning the soprano beneath and the bass on top, making the fugue sound different, but preserving the counterpoint. He then draws attention to the notes with accidentals, or those that belong to harmonic chords. In his ninth interpretation, Zacher reminds today's listeners of the hand-operated bellows of organ lofts in Bach's time. When the principal theme of the Contrapunctus appears, it is heard in full volume: as the music progresses, the pipes whistle in falsetto as the "air pressure" diminishes. Zacher concludes these somewhat humorous "deconstructions", each of which elucidates another aspect of Contrapunctus 1, with "No (-) Music", in which he reduces *Art of Fugue* to gestures derived from Japanese No drama to be performed in some way by the organist!

ALFRED SCHNITTKE (1934–98)

Like Arvo Pärt, Schnittke is another Eastern European composer who, under pressure from the Soviets in Russia, where he spent his early years, develops an individual stylistic idiom – in this case, a mingling of tonality and atonality.[144] In several of these "polystylistic" works, Schnittke discloses his Back to Bach journey by quoting B-A-C-H as part of a dissonant chord or melodic sequence.

QUASI UNA SONATA, 1968

In this duet for piano and violin, Schnittke is obsessed with adjacent semitones, both in the Sonata's connected movements and in the solo cadenza sections that test the virtuoso limits of both players. The partly tonal, pianissimo Andante, for example, begins with B-A-C-H in the top notes of piano chords, continuing with similar patterns at higher intervals on both instruments. The following Allegretto opens with two chords on the violin encompassing the B-A-C-H semitones, repeated on the piano, while in the Andantino, the violin offers retrograde versions of B-A-C-H transposed into D-flat. Continuous rapid notes on the violin in the lively Allegro are punctuated by the piano sounding the four semitones as separate notes and then as harmonised chords. A notable moment occurs when, after a long piano solo, Schnittke has the violin entering with rapid, upward glissandos reaching all the B-A-C-H notes. A cadenza leads to a calm Grave that ends with four double stops, the upper notes playing B-A-C-H, the lower ones H-C-A-B.

PIANO QUINTET, 1976

Soon after his mother dies in 1972, Schnittke begins scoring his next significant B-A-C-H work for piano and string quartet but only completes it four years later. The quintet expresses the composer's personal loss by its melancholy mood realised in spare string sonorities and delicate piano harmonies, occasionally disrupted by emotive dissonances. And in recollection of his mother's love of dance, Schnittke writes a bitter-sweet "Tempo di Valse" second movement, which begins with B-A-C-H, extended with an additional B-flat to serve as a melody in triple time. Any sense of a traditional waltz, however, is subverted by overlapping B-A-C-H semitones in the strings, supported by piano chords sounding other sets of adjacent semitones. The final Moderato Pastorale is based on a consoling, rocking motif heard in the high register of the piano, with the first violin entering with a quasi-B-A-C-H melody.

In 1978, Schnittke reveals his purpose in writing the quintet by making an orchestral version, which he calls *In Memoriam*.

CONCERTO GROSSO NO. 3, 1985

Compared with the introspective mood of his Piano Quintet, this work, which was a commission of East German Radio as part of the tercentenary of Bach's birth year, is vigorous and outgoing. Not only does it bear a baroque title that would have been familiar to Bach, its scoring, for two solo violins, harpsichord and celesta with string orchestra and piano, is eighteenth century in scope. To this ensemble, Schnittke adds four bells tuned to the B-A-C-H semitones, which are struck at various moments. Lasting more than twenty minutes, the work comprises five contrasting movements, each underpinned by a twelve-tone row incorporating B-A-C-H. The first begins with overlapping string figurations recalling those of the Brandenburg Concertos Nos 3 and 6. As one of the bells is sounded, the music dissolves into atonality, while the two solo violins play pianissimo chords, with the lowest notes moving between the B-A-C-H semitones.

Schnittke begins the third movement of his Concerto Grosso with a striking announcement of B-A-C-H in fortissimo strings leaping rapidly up and down between the semitones. Tension is only released with calming tonal passages on the solo violins and harpsichord. In the fourth Adagio movement, Schnittke has the harpsichord announce B-A-C-H before proceeding to barely audible themes extracted from the Fugues in C-sharp Minor and F Minor from Book I of *The Well-tempered Clavier*. These quotations are followed by canonic passages on the solo violins supported by tutti strings playing the B-A-C-H semitones. After bells forcefully sound the B-A-C-H notes, the soloists set off on virtuosic passages. Schnittke ends with pianissimo high strings, with his twelve-tone rows are heard faintly on the celesta in a truly transcendental conclusion.

Over the next eight years, Schnittke goes on to write three more concerto grossos. Though neither these, nor his earlier first two, betray a musical connection with Bach, the set eventually numbers six, as in the Brandenburgs.

MAURICIO KAGEL (1931–2008)
Two works of this composer manifest contradictory approaches to Bach's music: delight in distortion and total renunciation.

CHORBUCH, 1978
In this work, Kagel sources more than fifty Bach chorales, assigning the melodies to keyboards and the supporting chords to voices

singing in harmonies that are determined by a complicated system derived from geometric diagrams. Unsurprisingly, the music does not sound remotely like Bach, nor does the singing, which is often conducted through megaphones, or is reduced to shouts and mimed gestures. The result has been described as a "bizarre conglomerate of stable chords in the most unstable harmony …. a testimony to the indestructible qualities of Bach's music."[145]

SANKT-BACH-PASSION, 1985

Kagel conceives this monumental oratorio as a tribute to the format of Bach's Passions rather than the music. Written for a mixed choir and children's choir, an orchestra with celesta, harpsichord and harp, and even an organ, this approximately 90-minute-long work replaces the sufferings of Jesus based on the Gospels with the everyday tribulations of Bach himself, as revealed though contemporary documents, such as the *Nekrolog* of 1754. As narrated by an Evangelist-like, tenor soloist, Kagel punctuates the story with musical scenes, such as that portraying Bach's visit to Frederick the Great. In the other episodes from Bach's life, the role of Bach is assumed by a speaker, interspersed with reflective sung pieces that refer to well-known works of Bach, though with changes in key words: thus, the chorales "Ein feste Burg ist unser Bach" ("A mighty fortress is our Bach") and "Herzliebster Johann" ("Dear-hearted Johann"), the latter from the St Matthew Passion (No. 3). Despite the indirect references to Bach's texts, the distorted vocal writing, much of it in a *Sprechgesang* style that mingles speaking and singing, and high-pitched, wordless glissandos, Kagel offers a deeply affecting musical portrait of the composer.

SOFIA GUBAIDULINA (1931–2025)

As a devout member of the Russian Orthodox church, Gubaidulina regards her compositions as expressions of the mystic symbolism that served her as a refuge from the stifling political atmosphere of Soviet rule. To this end, she crafts an individual idiom that privileges dense chromatic harmonies, striking instrumental textures, and violent percussive effects.

OFFERTORIUM, 1980

Commissioned by the Latvian violinist Gidon Kremer, this concerto reconciles Gubaidulina's musical language with the rites of the Orthodox service. The work's title refers to the offering of bread and wine during the celebration of Mass, as well as to the offering of a musical idea – in this instance, the Thema Regium from the *Musical Offering*. At the beginning of the concerto, Gubaidulina announces Bach's theme in D minor (rather than the original C minor), sharing its notes between different brass instruments, somewhat in the manner of Anton Webern's orchestration of the six-part Ricercar from the *Musical Offering*. The last note of the Thema Regium is "sacrificed" by the violin, which enters on a violent glissando trill, and then interacts both aggressively and lyrically with the orchestra, which Gubaidulina scores in an array of astonishing tutti glissandos and tremolandos. When Bach's theme recurs, again divided between the different orchestral sections, it lacks its first note. Thereafter, only fragments of it are recognisable, such as the descending semitone scale from its second part, which is often heard in retrograde as an ascending semitone scale. As the concerto progresses, Gubaidulina gives the violin several extended, cadenza-like solos, although these are mostly disturbed by violent orchestral outbursts. Towards the end of this more than thirty-minute-long work, she creates a calmer mood in chorale-like sections that resemble the phrases of a noble hymn, as expressed by the soloist elevated on orchestral strings.

MEDITATION ON THE BACH CHORALE "VOR DEINEN THRON", 1993

In this chamber work built upon Bach's "Vor deinen Thron tret ich hiermit" ("Before your throne I now appear"), Gubaidulina is preoccupied with the sense of impending death. The composer deconstructs Bach's "Deathbed Chorale" by submerging its theme in chromatic dissonances and shimmering textures produced by a harpsichord and five string instruments. Elsewhere in *Meditation*, she engulfs the chorale in unnerving violin clusters, sonorous cello tones, pianissimo tremolandos, and whistling harmonics. Towards the end, Gubaidulina allows the theme to be "revealed" in unison strings backed by harpsichord trills, as if Bach's chorale can only be experienced after musical turbulence.

REFLECTIONS ON THE THEME B-A-C-H, 2002

Similar discomfort is experienced in this composition commissioned by the Brentano String Quartet, in which Gubaidulina responds to *Art of Fugue* with her usual wailing glissandos and tremolandos to create music of considerable intensity. Interspersing these weird string textures with Bach quotations, especially themes sourced from Contrapunctus Nos 6 and 7, and the B-A-C-H semitones, Gubaidulina offers a series of agonised reflections.

TOM JOHNSON (1939–2024)

Known for the uncompromising mathematical constructions of his compositions, this American composer and critic is credited with being the first to apply the term "minimalism" to contemporary music.[146] Over more than thirty years, Johnson produces a steady stream of works that explore notions of self-replicating melodic and rhythmic patterns, a preoccupation that he expounds in his 2014 treatise *Other Harmonies: Beyond Tonal and Atonal*.

Despite the extreme, abstract nature of his sound world, Johnson occasionally arrives at musical propositions that somehow parallel those of Bach.

RATIONAL MELODIES, 1982

Johnson writes each of this set of twenty-one short melodies in a single "voice", to be played by any acoustic or electronic instrument, or any combinations of instruments in unison or octaves. (In this respect, Johnson is following Bach's lack of performance specifications in the *Musical Offering* and *Art of Fugue*.) Most of Johnson's *Rational Melodies* are assemblages of miniature ideas that contract and expand on each repetition according to the fragmentation and re-combination of notational or rhythmic patterns. At least two examples bear comparison with Bach. The incessant double sets of triple notes in No. X are subtly altered by minimal shifts that alter the implied harmonies. The effects recall those of the Prelude in C Major in Book I of *The Well-tempered Clavier*, with its similarly, unvarying figurations with gradual changes that result in ever-evolving harmonies. In No. XV, Johnson employs a repeated fifteen-note melody, on which he superimposes an emerging, constantly changing musical figure, a device that parallels the ostinato format of Bach's organ Passacaglia. Johnson's obsession with such predetermined configurations does not preclude emotional expression, which is what Bach always insists on.

ANTHONY BURGESS (1917–93)

Reputedly written in no more than three weeks to mark the tercentenary of Bach's birth, this piano work reveals a fascination with Bach by this unusually versatile English composer, novelist and playwright.

THE BAD-TEMPERED ELECTRONIC KEYBOARD, 1985

In this cheekily titled work, Burgess draws on idioms from all periods of music history to inject his twenty-four preludes and fugues with humour and diversity. His E-flat Major Prelude, for example, begins with rippling notes that sound as if they could have been written by one of Bach's sons, while the carefree, dancing theme of the following fugue begins harmonically but soon descends into twentieth-century dissonance. The arpeggios in the A Major Prelude recall those of in a nocturne by Chopin, while the C Major Prelude seems to have been borrowed from Shostakovich, and that in F major from the world of jazz. Though some of his fugal themes vaguely resemble those of Bach, Burgess tends to avoid contrapuntal complexities. Even so, his final B Minor Fugue may be compared with the one in the same key in Book I of *The Well-tempered Clavier*. Its serious mood, however, is eventually undermined by the "cha-cha-cha" cadence that ends the cycle on a mischievous note, though hardly a "bad-tempered" one.

Burgess further honours Bach by supplementing his cycle with a "Finale. Natale 1985", which turns out to be a four-voice, spirited fugue based on the Christmas carol "Good King Wenceslas".

KNUT NYSTEDT (1915–2014)

This Norwegian composer's choice of Bach's funeral song, "Komm, süsser Tod, komm selge Ruh", is in keeping with his other works based on biblical texts and religious themes. On this occasion, however, Nystedt offers music of exceptional transcendent beauty.

IMMORTAL BACH, 1988

In this inspired realisation for unaccompanied voices, Nystedt exploits the first two phrases of the funeral song that Bach contributed to Schemelli's *Musicalisches Gesang-Buch* by converting the original soprano solo and bass line into a four-part chorale of his own invention. Dividing the voices into five separate groups, he instructs each group to sing the same chorale at different speeds, not necessarily beginning or ending together, overlapping and merging the phrases into one another. In this way, Nystedt arrives at other-worldly effects that communicate the yearning of the opening phrase, "Come, sweet death, come blessed rest". Little wonder that *Immortal Bach* is now considered a religious work to be performed in church.

TAN DUN (1957–)

That Bach's music could be integrated into an instrumental-vocal work evoking a Chinese shamanistic funerary rite is effectively demonstrated in a piece commissioned by the San Francisco-based Kronos Quartet from Tan Dun, the Chinese–American composer who was to become famous in 2000 for his film score for *Crouching Tiger, Hidden Dragon*.

GHOST OPERA, 1994

Performed together with Wu Man, who plays the pipa, a type of Chinese lute, Tan Dun has five instrumentalists singing, shrieking and striking gongs and tiny bells in a cross-cultural and cross-media performance piece. Into this almost forty-minute-long mix of unpredictable, occasionally frightening sounds, Tan Dun introduces the mournful, opening phrases of the Prelude in C-sharp Minor from Book I of *The Well-tempered Clavier*. These are first heard on the strings emerging from the sounds of a hand being dipped into a bowl of water. Then come the exhalations of a ghostly monk, a wistful Chinese folk song sung by the pipa player, and a brief, partly vocalised excerpt from Shakespeare's *The Tempest*. As the work proceeds, Tan Dun overlays Bach, the folk song and Shakespeare to create a dialogue between these distant, disparate traditions. For him, Bach's prelude acts as a "seed from which grows a new counterpoint of different ages, different sound worlds and different cultures". This facilitates the contact between different time frames and spiritual realms that characterises the Chinese "ghost opera" tradition.[147]

RON NELSON (1929–2023)

Known for the music he provides over many years for wind bands, much of it in an accessible popular style, such as "Savannah River Holiday" (1953), this American composer produces two works that reveal a committed Back to Bach journey. Both are intended to showcase the outstanding woodwind, brass and percussion sections of the United States Air Force Band

PASSACAGLIA (HOMAGE ON B-A-C-H), 1993

Taking inspiration from Bach's organ exemplar, Nelson fuses his Passacaglia with Bach's musical signature in what may be judged as perhaps the most serious tribute to the master ever conceived for wind band. That this is a celebratory work is clear from the music that progress from darkness to light, leading to a joyous climax. Nelson bases his Passacaglia on an eight-bar ostinato that accords in many respects with Bach's, beginning and ending with short-long steps in triple time, up and down the C minor triad; the only differences are the dissonant, chromatic scale-like steps along the way. Unlike Bach, Nelson does not present his theme clearly at the outset; it can only be made out in the faint tones of the deep brass and woodwind. Meanwhile, fragments of the B-A-C-H motif on the trombones and muted trumpets signal that the master is already present. As the passacaglia theme follows its unvarying course through twenty-five variations, the B-A-C-H motif is extended to take on the contour of a full melody. In three variations, it is heard as a canon between the woodwinds and horns; in another, it is picked out in the pungent tones of the alto saxophone. By adding instrumental density and rhythmic momentum, Nelson propels the work ever forward until the eighteenth variation, at which point Nelson discloses his debt to Bach by proclaiming the Passacaglia ostinato in the high woodwinds. To add to this musical complexity, Nelson inserts quotations from Contrapunctus I in *Art of Fugue*. Despite this profusion of Bach reference, Nelson's Passacaglia now enjoys a regular place in the wind band repertoire.

CHACONNE (IN MEMORIAM...), 1995

The funereal atmosphere of this later piece suggests a musical epitaph, but Nelson discloses no personal loss. In typical chaconne fashion, this elegiac work is based on an eight-bar chord progression, which is repeated throughout as a harmonic support for a series of variations. The chords eventually morph into the phrases of the chorale "O Welt, ich muss dich lassen" ("Oh world, I must now leave you"), the melody of which Bach used in both the St Matthew Passion (Nos 10 and 37) and St John Passion (No. 11). Initially heard in full brass, the chorale progresses to brighter trumpet sounds against a delicate woodwind background. Disinclined to sustain these shafts of sonorous light, Nelson has them die away, bringing the Chaconne to a quietly sad conclusion.

PETER SCHICKELE (1935–2024)

Known for his "discovery" in 1965 of the oeuvre of P.D.Q. Bach, the fictional son of the master, this American pianist, musician and humourist here pays a witty tribute to *The Well-tempered Clavier*.

THE SHORT-TEMPERED CLAVIER, 1995

Schickele's impertinence is revealed in this work's subtitle, "Preludes and Fugues in all Major and Minor Keys Except for the Really Difficult Ones", as well as in the mock nineteenth-century jacket of the score, complete with reversed dates for the composer and tongue-in-cheek musicological explanations. Unexpected sources are discovered in many of the fugal themes: "Chop Sticks" (C major) and "Pop Goes the Weasel" (D minor); the "Fate" motif from Beethoven's Symphony No. 5 (in the same C minor key as Beethoven); and the chimes of London's Big Ben (A major). Some of Schickele's preludes look further afield: the dreamy melody of the C-sharp minor Prelude turns out to be a leisurely version of "Mary Had a Little Lamb", while the chaconne-like D Minor Prelude is based on a boogie-woogie bass line. Yet Bach is not altogether abandoned. Many preludes bristle with Bachian references, enhanced with occasional flashes of atonality and jazz-like syncopations. Schickele's C major prelude, for example, imitates the arpeggios of the prelude in the same key in Book I of *The Well-tempered Clavier*, while that in G minor recalls Bach's "little" C Minor Prelude originally written for the lute (BWV 999).

HUGHES DE COURSON (1946–)
& PIERRE AKENDENGUÉ (1943–)

As a tribute to the life of the distinguished Bach organist and biographer Albert Schweitzer, a French arranger of popular music and a composer from Gabon here collaborate on a project that juxtaposes Bach's music with that of western coastal Africa, where Schweitzer served as a medical missionary. Under the name of Lambaréné, the town where Schweitzer practiced from 1913 until his death in 1965, de Courson and Akendengué offer pieces that mingle Bach's choruses, arias and instrumental works with Gabonese singing, fluting and drumming.

LAMBARENA BACH TO AFRICA, 1993

Music drawn from the St John Passion dominates this work, imbuing it with an overall sacred atmosphere. In the opening chorus, "Lasset uns den nicht zerteilen" ("Let us not divide it") (Bach's No. 27b), Bach's rhythmic counterpoint is animated with Gabonese bouncing marimba figurations and spiky percussion. The same effects are heard in the backgrounds to the majestic proclamations of "Herr, unser Herrscher" ("Lord, our Lord") (Lambarena No. 4), with which Bach introduces the Passion narrative, at first on the organ and then with voices, as well as in the mournful phrases of the concluding "Ruht wohl" ("Rest well") chorus. The devotional character of *Lambarena* is sustained with a straightforward rendition of the Agnus Dei from the Mass in B Minor, with the alto soloist embellished with violins on organ chords, as Bach had intended (No. 9). More joyous is the final chorus taken from the "Hunt Cantata" (BWV 208) (No. 13).

In between these more or less faithful quotations, de Courson and Akendengué seek further ways to locate Bach within Gabon's sonic landscape. In "Mabo Maboe" (No. 5), restless marimba passages and distant flutings offer a background to triple figurations extracted from the Gigue in the Suite No. 4 for Solo Cello (BWV 1010), while in "Pepa Nzac Gnon Ma" (No. 7), the energetic opening bars of the Prelude from the Partita No. 3 for Solo Violin (BWV 1006) set the pace for the marimba and percussion, followed by Gabonese vocalists and chorus. At one point, the violin floats high above the singers. In contrast, "Mamoudo Na Sakka Baya Boudouma Ngombi" (No. 8) begins with vocalists who gradually make way for phrases from the Prelude in F-sharp Minor from Book II of *The Well-tempered Clavier*, with the piano notes carried on gentle percussion. De Courson and Akendengué end their Bach to Africa journey with the ever-popular "Jesu, Joy of Man's Desiring" propelled by Gabonese percussion and voices (No. 13). It is a fitting conclusion to a cross-cultural project that affirms Bach's universal appeal.[148]

PAUL GRABOWSKY (1958–)

De Courson and Akendengué are not the only musicians who conduct Bach's sacred works on unexpected journeys. Together with four other "spontaneous" composers, Paul Grabowsky devises a jazz response to the St Matthew Passion for the Australian Art Orchestra. In their one-hour-long tribute, they reinterpret Bach's choruses, arias and recitatives from the perspectives of contemporary music, giving new musical life to the suffering and redemption of the Passion story as portrayed by Bach.

PASSION, 1998

Following Bach, Grabowsky begins with "Come, Daughters" [1], named after the opening chorus in the St Matthew Passion (No. 1). Here, fragments of Bach's fugal theme are heard intermittently on a saxophone, submerged in street noises mingled with jangling percussion and violin glissandos that eventually morph into a piano-violin improvisation. For "Captive" [3], the guitarist Doug de Vries translates Bach's vocal duet "Behold, my Jesus is now captured" (No. 33) into entwining solo woodwind and brass figurations. The sparse instrumentation underscores the desolate atmosphere introduced by a violin solo, into which the instruments violently intrude to suggest Bach's choral outbursts "Loose him, bind him not!". In "For Love" [5], Alister Spence begins with Bach's free-floating aria for soprano, flute and oboes (No. 58), which he gradually unwinds until finding release in a wistful jazz duet for tenor saxophone and piano. Figurations from Bach's aria return at the end, reduced to transcendental celesta and flute textures that evoke the original text "In love, will my Saviour die".

For the German born jazz drummer and composer Niko Schäuble, it is Christ's death that needs to be musically depicted. In "Crucified" [7], he takes a sequence of Bach's scenes, beginning with the alto recitative "Oh Golgotha" (No. 69), which he evokes through an atonal melody. For the accompanying aria (No. 70), Schäuble converts the vocal line into a set of violin variations, and for the Evangelist-Jesus recitative that follows he offers into a tenor saxophone–tuba duet, before introducing mocking brass outbursts to portray the outrage of the angry chorus. Relentless drum rolls evoke Christ's death, redeemed with a sorrowful trumpet solo playing the "Passion Chorale".

Into the pieces just described, Grabowsky inserts four of Bach's chorales sung by the soprano Christine Sullivan to Bach's original hymn tunes, but with Grabowsky's words. Presented in un-harmonised, static settings, the chorales function as moments of reflection within the overall musical drama. To supply *Passion* with a "Finale" [9], the violinist composer John Rodgers offers a movement based on Bach's majestic, Sarabande-like concluding chorus (No. 78), which he assigns to a trombone soloist, then a violin, trumpet and saxophone, before combining them with other instruments to create a sonic cacophony propelled on an ominous triple pulse. Rodgers ends his movement, and indeed the whole of Grabowsky's *Passion*, with a hushed, sustained unison note, which the journalist and critic John Shand interprets as a "fitting metaphor for the powerful convergence of the *St Matthew Passion* [as realised by] five modern composers, a striking singer and an orchestra of outstanding improvisers".[149]

URI CAINE (1956–)

For the 250th anniversary of Bach's death, this American classical-jazz pianist offers a two-hour work that locates Bach within a vast spectrum of musical idioms, both past and present.

THE GOLDBERG VARIATIONS, 2000

Caine begins by playing Bach's Aria and first variation on what sounds like one of the experimental fortepianos that Bach improvised on for Frederick the Great, together with a viola da gamba picking up the bass line. He then supplements Bach by inserting specially commissioned pieces that run the entire gamut from baroque instrumental ensembles to Moog-style synthesisers, and from romantic era slush to twentieth-century blues, jazz, hip-hop and slapstick. With this kaleidoscope of rhythms, melodies, and instrumental and vocal textures, as realised with the talents of jazz performers and a DJ, as well as a traditional choral group and a quartet of viols, Caine's more than fifty pieces bounce off each other in unpredictable and delightful ways. In his "Dig It" and "Hot Sixth Variations", as well as those titled "Waltz", "Stomp" and "Tango", Caine acknowledges the world of dance, updated since Bach's time, while Gothic humour is represented by the "Dr. Jekyll & Mr. Hyde" and "Nobody Knows" Variations. Music history is represented by variations bearing the names of Handel, Vivaldi, Mozart, Verdi and Rachmaninoff, while Bach himself makes a cameo appearance in a "B-A-C-H Variation", and Handel in a "Hallelujah Variation". For Bach's light-hearted concluding Quodlibet, Caine employs a group of drunken youths singing out of tune. In the opinion of one commentator, this freewheeling take on the Goldbergs is best understood as "a bold, carnivalesque celebration of Bach's enduring appeal".[150]

BRENTANO STRING QUARTET

Noted for an innovative repertoire that encompasses specially commissioned works, this New York-based ensemble celebrated their tenth anniversary by inviting ten composers to contribute companion pieces to *Art of Fugue*. The project results in a programme that gave listeners the chance to hear string quartet arrangements of Bach's fugues juxtaposed against new works.

BACH PERSPECTIVES, 2002

The broad range of engagements by contemporary composers[151] is apparent from the outset with Nicholas Maw's *Intrada*, which serves as a prelude for Bach's first fugue. Its Bachian rhythms and contrapuntal strands couched in D minor anticipate those to come, while other composers investigate new auditory territories. Sofia Gubaidulina's *Reflections on the Theme B-A-C-H*, has already been noticed. In *Bach-Shards*, Shulamit Ran seeks tensions and dissonances that present maze-like, contrapuntal patterns, which the composer describes as "a mildly deconstructed Bach". Peter Mackey is a musician with a background in rock guitar; in *Lude*, he dissolves Contrapunctus 11 into his own pop figurations and syncopated rhythms – as they gently recede, Bach emerges.

For Charles Wuorinen, the subject of Contrapunctus 9 provides the ingredients for *Alap*, an atonal piece that gradually trends towards more conventional harmonies. As in the opening section of an Indian raga, his Bachian ideas are heard at first only in fragments. Eric Zivian borrows Bach's inverted theme in Contrapunctus 4, to which he adds his own dance-like subject to construct the materials on which to build his *Double Fugue.* Though inspired by Bach, Zivian's counterpoint is dramatic, though hardly strict. Other musicians altogether opt out of Bach's contrapuntal language. The trumpeter Wynton Marsalis proposes a high-octane, jazz-inflected fugue that replicates the rhythmic pattern of Contrapunctus 12, while in *Contrapunctus Variabilis*, Chou Wen-chung altogether abandons Bach by resorting to traditional Asian musical modes.

ART OF FUGUE, 2016

As a further exploration of the work's creative potential, the Brentanos perform a staged version of Bach's last unfinished fugue accompanied by music, light and dance, in collaboration with the designer Gabriel Calatrava, son of the celebrated Spanish architect. Calatrava creates a background of continuously shifting, illuminated ropes that seem to suggest Bach's polyphonic layering. Inside Calatrava's flexible ropes, six dancers twist and rotate according to John-Mario Sevilla's choreography. By the time Bach's fugue comes to its abrupt end, the dancers have left the stage, and the ropes are stilled and raised in an arresting image.

ROBIN HOLLOWAY (1943–)

This English academic supplements his courses in composition at the University of Cambridge by using the Goldberg Variations as an eclectic survey of music history.

GILDED GOLDBERGS, 1997

In these arrangements for two pianos Holloway translates Bach's variations into what he describes as "ever-widening curves of exploration – of melodic, harmonic, polyphonic enrichment, of stylistic transformation, and pianistic techniques".[152] To help his students, Holloway specifies the styles of his re-compositions: thus, "Gigue in Antiphony" (Bach's No. 4); "Trio and Landler. Brief history of Austro-German Music in Triple Time" (No. 19); "Hazy Trills and Tremolos" (No. 28); "Toccata with Clusters. Enharmonic" (No. 29), and so on. Sometimes he specifies the composers he has in mind, such as "Vivace à la Scarlatti" (No. 5), "Homage to Grainger" (No. 9), and "Dreaming. Homage to Schubert and Brahms" (No. 11). By ushering the Goldbergs into these post-Bach futures of classicism, romanticism and modernism, Holloway offers a genuinely "gilded" tribute.

LARA DOWNES (1973–)

Known for her innovative collaborations with musicians from different backgrounds, on one occasion this American classical pianist and cultural activist turned her attention to the Goldbergs.

13 WAYS OF LOOKING AT THE GOLDBERGS, 2004

Downes invites thirteen composers to contribute a short variation of their own to complement those from the Goldbergs for her to include in a concert programme, to which she gives a title that refers to the 1917 poem "Thirteen Ways of Looking at a Blackbird" by Wallace Stevens. Most composers respond with oblique, ironic or humorous references. In his *Goldmore Variation*, for example, Lukas Foss begins with a wistful melody that recalls the Sarabande pace of Bach's Aria before proceeding to his own variations. In his high-spirited *Chasing Goldberg*, Fred Lerdahl evokes Bach's keyboard spirit in hopping figurations that conform to Bach's harmonic scheme, while in *Variation on Variation with Variation*, Ralf Gothóni presents a pastiche of Bachian passages and ornaments, in which the Aria can only vaguely be made out.

Other composers pursue more flippant approaches, with side glances to the poem's blackbird. In *Yet Another Goldberg Variation*, William Bolcom has the pianist scampering all over the keyboard with his left hand, as if chasing a bird, while rapid, detached leaps evoking bird-like chirps are heard in Derek Bermel's impudently titled *Kontraphunktus*. Following Bach, Downes concludes her programme with a reprise of the Aria.

LAIBACH

Known for their radical political views, this avant-garde Slovenian music band adopts the German historical name for their hometown Ljubljana, which, in their reimagination of *Art of Fugue*, merges with Bach's name.

LAIBACHKUNSTDERFUGE, 2006

In this audio-visual extravaganza, Laibach treats Bach's contrapuntal exemplars as mathematical algorithms, feeding the music into computer programmes, which act as musical instruments. The results are electrically amplified as sounds and images projected onto gigantic screens, such as those that mesmerised the audience at the Bach Festival in Leipzig.

Laibach begins in darkness: only gradually do weird acoustic effects and images on the screens give "birth" to the outline of the D minor theme that runs through *Art of Fugue*. As expressed in Contrapunctus 1, the theme moves laboriously from note to note, with Bach's counterpoint submerged in dense electronic sound, its mathematical complexity suggested by moving mechanist imagery. By slowing down Contrapunctus 2 to a snail's pace, Laibach draws out the counterpoint for more than twenty minutes, with the fugue's four voices in ghostly tones altogether robbed of Bach's momentum. In Contrapunctus 8, the band reduces Bach's lines to vocal-metallic, aquatic plops that unexpectedly clarify the counterpoint. Similarly inappropriate effects in Contrapunctus 10 result in the counterpoint going in and out of focus. A more "faithful" electronic version of Bach is the canon in augmentation and contrary motion, in which the somewhat jerky rhythm is converted into an unvarying pulse, realised in sustained, artificial tones. With such manipulations, Laibach seems to be arguing that Bach be considered as a pioneer of techno computer music.

DAVID LANG (1957–)

For his Passion music based on Hans Christian Andersen's tender tale, this co-founder of Bang on a Can, the New York-based organization committed to contemporary classical music, was awarded the Pulitzer Prize in 2008.

THE LITTLE MATCH GIRL PASSION, 2007

In his retelling of Andersen's *Little Match Girl*, Lang sources the contribution of Bach's librettist for the St Matthew Passion, who wrote under the name of Picander. The heartfelt suffering described in the story is underscored by Lang's use of English translations of Picander's German texts, such as the opening chorus "Come daughter, help me cry" (No. 1); the narrative "From the sixth hour there was darkness…" (No. 11); and the final chorus "Rest gently…" (No. 15). These quotations compare the sufferings of Andersen's tragic heroine to those of Jesus, justifying Lang's decision to add "Passion" to the work's title.

Despite Lang's references to the St Matthew Passion, his minimalist score owes nothing to Bach. Lang writes his music for a small choir, unaccompanied except for glockenspiel and chimes, the bell-like tones of which imbue Andersen's story with pathos. The spare writing results in a bittersweet melancholy, which helps explain how *The Little Match Girl Passion* has found appreciative audiences, especially when performed in a church.

NIKOLAUS MATTHES (1981–)

David Lang is not the only musician to resort to Picander when writing Passion music. For his Markus Passion, this German-born conductor and composer sources the poet's libretto for the 1731 Good Friday service in St Thomas's. While Picander's text survives, the music that Bach provided is lost. Rather than speculating on what music Bach might have composed, or repurposed, as Ton Koopman and Robert Koolstra have suggested in their "reconstructions", Matthes devises a "brand new St Mark Passion that often feels as old as Bach, but simultaneously fresh and vital".[153]

MARKUS PASSION, 2020

Having absorbed Bach's Passion format into his own neo-baroque idiom, as realised with the same vocal forces and instrumental ensemble, Matthes writes choruses, chorales and recitatives, as well as solo arias with instrumental embellishments, that communicate the narrative of the last days of Jesus. The music recalls Bach but does not imitate Bach; instead, Matthes offers his own noble harmonisations in the chorales and expressive melodies in the arias. Even so, there are occasions when he evokes Bach, as in the viola da gambas that accompany the alto in the aria "Mein Tröster ist nicht mehr bey mir" ("My comforter is no longer with me"); these recall the dark tones and entwining figurations of the twin viola d'amores in the tenor aria "Erwäge" ("Ponder") in Bach's St John Passion (no. 20). When it comes to the final chorus "Bey deinem Grab" ("At your grave"), Matthes follows Bach in his two Passions by resorting to a noble sarabande, though infusing it with a lilting rhythmic pulse. If Matthes only rarely approaches the emotional intensity that underscores Bach's biblical dramas, his Back to Bach journey cannot be dismissed as mere musical nostalgia.

UNITED INSTRUMENTS OF LUCILIN

By fusing performances on period instruments with techniques of improvisation and reworking, this Luxembourg-based ensemble has earned a reputation for its creative approach to the music of the past that includes their reworkings of the Goldberg Variations.

GOLDBERG'S GHOST, 2007

In this recording, United Instruments begin by playing Bach's Aria, canons and Quodlibet in the 1984 string trio arrangements by the Soviet–American violinist Dmitry Sitkovetsky. The group intersperses these with new pieces rendered on the harpsichord, viola d'amore and baroque violin, as well as on the flute, clarinet, saxophone and percussion, steering fragments of Bach's harmonies and keyboard patterns into glissandos, string harmonics and woodwind flutterings. The intentionality of these and other eerie effects, as expressed in titles like "Hotberg Stories", "Desert/Forest" and "Metamorphosis", justifies the name that the group gives to their album.

CHRISTOPH POPPEN (1956–)
& LAWRENCE POWER (1977–)

The manuscript of Bach's Chaconne for Solo Violin dates from 1720, but when exactly in that year is not specified. This uncertainty has not deterred the German musicologist Helga Thoene who believes that Bach wrote the Chaconne only after his first wife, Maria Barbara, died in July 1720, and that he conceived the work as a musical epitaph, or "tombeau".[154] In support of her argument, Thoene draws attention to the chorale melodies referring to death "concealed" in the violin's chords, arpeggios and running passages. While Thoene's propositions can be no more than sheer speculation, musicians find them stimulating. They include the German violinist Christoph Poppen, who invited the Hilliard Ensemble, the English male vocal quartet specialising in early music, to collaborate on a project he calls *Morimur*, from "In Christo Morimur" ("In Christ we die").

MORIMUR, 2010

Following Thoene's "tombeau" suggestion, Poppen plays the Chaconne according to Bach's score while the Hilliards intone the chorales that Thoene claims to have discovered in the music. Devoid of harmonic support, the melodies are sung in overlapping phrases that create a vocal backdrop to the solo violin. They include the chorale from *Christ lag in Todesbanden* (*Christ lay in the bonds of death*) (BWV 4), and the soprano-alto duet from the same cantata, "Den Tod niemand zwingen kunnt" ("No one could defeat death"). As sung by the Hilliards, these and other doleful texts merge seamlessly with the Chaconne's harmonic scheme, shrouding the violin passages in liturgical messages of death. By combining the dynamic violin writing with static choral melodies, Poppen presents a Back to Bach journey of unusual pathos.

64 VARIATIONS, 2021

Eleven years after Poppen and the Hilliards record *Morimur*, the English violist Lawrence Power creates *64 Variations*, a title that refers to the number of variations in the Chaconne. In a video recorded during the Covid epidemic, Power plays Bach's violin work in the darker, lower tones of the viola, while in the second half of the Chaconne, the soprano Héloïse Werner sings Thoene's chorale melodies. Before long, the dancer Sharia Johnson appears, converting the chorale texts on death into bodily twists and flying hands that give physical expression to grief. This partnership of instrumentalist, vocalist and dancer takes place in the bleak, stripped-down interior of London's riverside Barge House.

KARLHEINZ ESSL (1960–)

As a pioneer of algorithmic compositions using computer programmes to create new musical structures, often in real time, this Austrian composer also finds an opportunity for a creative Back to Bach journey.

GOLD.BERG.WERK, 2013–16

For Essl, Bach's separate propositions in the Goldberg Variations present ideal opportunities for merging live performance with electronic improvisation. In the videos he issues of this work, Essl has three string players performing a selection of the variations in Sitkovetsky's trio arrangements, which he intersperses with electronic interludes improvised on a computer set up next to the musicians. These interventions convert Bach's harmonic structures and interweaving figurations into artificial soundscapes with suspended and slithering tones robbed of any definite pitch or rhythmic pulse. The result is a disembodied music that may be considered as a personal response to Bach far removed from demands of the concert stage. In this sense, Essl's reflections of the Goldbergs constitute meditations rather than variations.

MAX RICHTER (1966–)

The musical deconstructions and reinterpretations of this German-born British composer sometimes involve Back to Bach journeys of astounding originality. Never hesitant about declaring his debt, Richter admits that: "Talking about Bach is a like talking about the force of gravity – we don't have an opinion about it, there's nothing to say, it just is. For a musician, there's Bach and then there's everything else".[155] While Richter often blends his instrumental writings with ambient electronics to achieve a meditative, minimalist idiom, he specifically references Bach on at least two occasions.

"THE DEPARTURE", 2014

In the signature theme that he provides for the multi-episode HBO series *The Leftovers*, Richter offers solace to broken-hearted families, amplifying their struggles and encouraging them to continue living. He achieves the desired poignancy by consulting the familiar Prelude in C Major from Book I of *The Well-tempered Clavier*. Replicating its incessant, eight-note arpeggios, Richter aims at simpler figurations and harmonies but soon introduces a rudimentary melody reduced to detached pairs of downward notes. The intense expressivity of this simplest of themes recalls the lyrical quality of Charles Gounod's *Ave Maria*, floating naturally over the arpeggios of the same prelude, written some 160 years before.

BACH STUDY, 2016

If Richter recalls Bach only distantly in "The Departure", he directly quotes the master in this less-than-five-minute work for electronics and piano. Richter begins with bell-like, rhythmic pulses embedded in a mysterious wash of artificial sound. After a short time, the notes of a piano gradually emerge, playing at the slowest possible tempo a dozen bars or so from the Prelude in E-flat Major from Book I of *The Well-tempered Clavier*. Without tampering with the original, Richter allows Bach's reassuring polyphonic progressions to gradually displace the electronics, in a gesture that salutes the persuasion of Bach's art.

CHAD LAWSON (1975–)

This American pianist has earned a reputation for combining music with life experiences and meditation techniques. So it comes as no surprise that his Back to Bach journey should focus on the chorales as springboards for personal introspection.

BACH INTERPRETED, 2016

Lawson arranges ten of Bach's four-voice chorales for the piano, transforming them through musical subtraction: reducing the supporting harmonies to the faintest background; omitting the final notes of the chorale phrases; suppressing the rhythmic momentum that propels the fervent prayers. With such distillations, he creates an atmosphere akin to private meditation.

For "Christus, der uns selig macht" ("Christ who makes us blessed"), with which the second part of the St John Passion begins (No. 15), for example, Lawson maintains Bach's repeated, two-bar phrases, though with additional notes, but withholds the final pause notes, thereby avoiding the chorale's stirring proclamation. Other discontinuities with Bach are Lawson's supporting arpeggiated chords that owe little to Bach's harmonic progressions. Though Lawson takes a similar approach with "Herr Jesu Christ, meins Lebens Licht" ("Lord Jesus Christ, light of my life") (BWV 335), the chorale's floating melody can still be made out by listeners as they delve deep into the music. In his more continuous treatment of the melody of "Es stehn vor Gottes

Throne" ("I stand before God's throne") (BWV 309), Lawson arrives at a transcendental, reflective language far removed from Bach's Protestant affirmations.

MATT HAIMOVITZ (1970–) & PETER GREGSON (1987–)

As exponents of the Suites for Solo Cello, these two instrumentalists embark upon contrasting Back to Bach journeys. For the Israeli-born American Matt Haimovitz, the Suites offer opportunities to commission new works from contemporary composers that would complement him playing each of Bach's six works.[156] In contrast, the English cellist Peter Gregson substantially reworks Bach's movements, and together with an ensemble of fellow players, performs what are in essence entirely new works.

OVERTURES TO BACH, 2016

With his *Overture*, Philip Glass prepares listeners for Suite No. 1 by creating an eloquent, calm frame of mind. For No. 2, Du Yun creates a heartbreaking quilt of cries in *The Veronica*, mingling a Russian Orthodox prayer for the dead with Central European, gypsy fiddle music. In *Run*, Vijay Iyer reacts to the steady pulse of the Prelude in No. 3 with infectious rhythms that celebrate the natural resonance of the instrument as well as the composer's jazz roots.

In *La memoria*, Roberto Sierra evokes the intense, recitative passages in the Prelude of Bach's Suite No. 4 through intense tremolandos and pizzicato Caribbean rhythms. *Es War*, David Sanford's response to No. 5, opens with a tour de force of pizzicato effects and then cloaks Bach's epic cello fugue with saxophone-like wails. For No. 6, Luna Pearl Woolf proposes a Hawaiian chant, taking advantage of the virtuosic possibilities of the piccolo cello, the five-stringed instrument, for which Bach wrote his last suite.

BACH RECOMPOSED, 2018

Gregson's approach to the Suites involves repeating fragments extracted from the various movements, which he subjects to harmonic and rhythmic interferences. These "recompositions" vary from lush, interweaving arpeggios in the Prelude from Suite No. 1, and the darker, expressive phrases from the Prelude in No. 5, to the bouncing triple pulse against a tremolando background derived from the Minuets in No. 2, and the playfully leaping figurations with echoing open strings from the Gigue in No. 6. Along the way, Gregson offers brief but eloquent quotations, as in the Minuets from Suite No. 1, the Sarabande from No. 3, and the Prelude from No. 4.

WILLIAM WHITEHEAD (1970–)

One of the most ambitious collaborative Back to Bach projects is that which aimed at completing the 118 unfinished chorales in the *Orgel-Büchlein*. Posing the question: "How might Bach have written these were he alive today?",[157] this English organist, who spearheaded the project, sought responses from a host of contemporary musicians.

ORGELBÜCHLEIN PROJECT, 2017–22

Most of Whitehead's contributors announce the chorale melody clearly on the keyboards or pedals but make no attempt to replicate Bach's harmonic schemes, concentrating instead on the ornamental figurations and contrapuntal devices. In "Weltlich Ehr und zeitlich Gut" ("Worldly honour and transient good"), for example, the American composer Nico Muhly shifts the melody around the registers of the organ, embellishing it with dissonant chords, rippling five-note arpeggios, jagged figurations, and running fast notes.

Other composers conjure up musical realms unknown to Bach. Christian von Bohn converts the melody of "Ach Gott, erhör mein Seufzen und Wehklagen" ("Oh God, hear my sighs and lamentations") into a sweet, Brahmsian intermezzo, while Franz Josef Stoiber elevates the melody of "O heiliger Geist, o heileger Gott" ("Oh holy spirit, Oh holy God") on sweeping arpeggios and insistent bass steps that recall the late romantic idiom of Charles-Marie Widor. A more "exotic" approach is taken by Zsigmund Szathmáry, who proposes a Hungarian folk song version of "Mag ich Unglück nicht widerstahn" ("May I misfortune no further endure") animated by vernacular rhythms. In her minimalist rendition of "Warum betrübst du dich, mein Herz" ("Why are you so afflicted, my heart"), the Lithuanian-born composer Juste Janulyte dismembers the chorale melody; only towards the end does she give it in an almost complete form, supported on Bachian chords. Roderick Williams, the British baritone and composer, conveys Bach into a quasi-electronic world by setting the theme of "Ich weiss ein Blümlein hübsch und fein" ("I know a blossom pretty and fine") between warblings in the pedals and the highest register.

VIKINGUR ÓLAFSSON (1984–)

Throughout his performances and recordings, this Icelandic pianist explores ways of merging Bach with contemporary music, some of it artificially produced. His commitment to Bach is borne out in his determination to perform the Goldberg Variations at eighty-eight concert venues worldwide, a project that concluded in Germany in June 2024.

J.S. BACH – WORKS & REWORKS, 2018

On the first of this pair of discs, Ólafsson plays several of Bach's shorter keyboard works, including several of Busoni's piano transcriptions. On the companion disc, he progresses to new Bach arrangements that locate the piano in unfamiliar electronic sounds. In a track labelled "And at the Hour of Death", Ólafsson conducts the arpeggios in the Prelude in C Major from Book I of *The Well-tempered Clavier* into echoing piano acoustics, a strategy he also deploys for "Prelude in G major" from the Suite for Solo Cello No. 1. In "Above and Below", Ólafsson introduces faint voices and electronic distortions to enhance Alexander Siloti's Prelude in B Minor, itself a "rework" of a practice piece that Bach intended for his first son, while in "Il Adagio", he offers a mysterious, otherworldly version of the Adagio from Alessandro Marcello's Oboe Concerto in D Minor, which Bach himself had rescored for solo keyboard (BWV 974).

MARC ROMBOY (1966–) & DAN TEPFER (1982–)

These two musicians conduct Bach into imaginative worlds that enhance live performances with electronic manipulations.

RECONSTRUCTING BACH, 2019

In this video, the German DJ Marc Romboy collaborates with the violinist Miki Kekenj and other instrumentalists to offer a version of Bach's Badinerie that blends acoustic instruments with the tones of a synthesiser set against colouristic back projections. Romboy begins with throbbing electronic pulses and percussion to introduce fragments of Bach's leaping figurations, at first on the flute, as in the original movement from the Orchestral Suite No. 2, then more humorously on a bowed double bass. By introducing a string quartet as well as a harpsichord, Romboy makes a gesture towards Bach's sonic world, while at the same time justifying his electronic update: "when you look at his old compositions, you realize how open-minded he was when it comes to his own music".[158]

BACHUPSIDEDOWN, 2020

The French-born American jazz pianist Dan Tepfer has long been fascinated with Bach, and in 2011 devised a series of improvisations that he calls *Goldberg Variations/Variations*. However, when the Covid pandemic interrupted his concert schedule, he embarked upon an experiment with this same work that he could do at home. By feeding recordings of his performances into a computer triggered to a programme that would instruct his electrically equipped piano to reproduce Bach's musical lines upside down, Tepfer produces musical inversions that preserve the original contrapuntal patterns but obliterate the harmonic logic. The result is Back to Bach journey that is both familiar and unfamiliar.

BRYCE MESSMANN

Essl is not the only software electronics specialist to source the Goldbergs. This American-trained German engineer also turns to this work for an innovative collaborative project.

COMMUNITY GOLDBERG VARIATIONS, 2020

To persuade a raft of young musicians working in electronic media to supply new variations incorporating Bach's theme, Messmann begins by providing the first four bars of the Aria's bass line. This "theme" is heard in fifteen new variations (half the number of Bach's) in various disguises: as a bass support, a figure of repeated semiquavers; a chorale-like melody, part of a complex chord, and so on. Some composers respond by choosing baroque formats, like Andy K in his two-part canon; Stefano Paparozzi in his choral-prelude-like variation; and Messman himself in an extended, concluding fugue recalling Bach's great organ exemplars. A more classical approach is taken by Messmann in a Beethovian "All marcia" variation, and in the Scherzo and Trio variation by Sires. Then there are the romantic rhapsodies by Scriabin is my Dog and by Cmaj7, and the Debussy-like harmonies in Andy K's Adagio. Such Back to Bach journeys conduct the Goldbergs through musical landscapes expressed in artificial sounds.

NIKLAS LIEPE (1990–)

As he observed pianists and even big bands reimagining the Goldbergs, this German violinist yearned to play the work himself. The result is a project in which he presents arrangements of the Aria and thirteen of the variations for a solo violin and a baroque ensemble of strings and harpsichord, juxtaposed with new versions of the Aria by eleven contemporary composers.

GOLDBERGREFLECTIONS, 2020

Andreas N. Tarkmann, who is responsible for the arrangements, often directs Liepe to execute Bach's complicated patterns in combination with a solo viola and/or cello and harpsichord, as in the dance-like duet of Variation No. 7, the overlapping passages in No. 8, the canonic voices in Variations in Nos 9 and 21, and even the hopping, virtuosic interchanges that Bach had devised for two hands in No. 29. In No. 19, Tarkmann mingles pizzicatos with bowings to highlight Bach's shifting ideas, while in No. 16, he harnesses all the strings to recall the orchestral French overtures that Bach replicates on the harpsichord in No. 16. For the G minor Adagio (No. 25), Tarkmann instructs Liepe to convert Bach's lyrical passages into a heart-rendering solo.

Having paid homage to the original variations, Liepe then ushers the Goldbergs into the present day by playing new works that explore the potential of Bach's Aria. He begins with Rolf Rudin's *Dialog mit Bach*, which has the soloist dancing over Bach's bass line in exciting rhythmic patterns as well as in wispy pizzicatos. Sidney Corbett's *Goldberg Hallucination Remix* presents disembodied, haunting fragments of the Aria, robbed of Bach's momentum to suggest a dreamlike state. In *Sleepless After J.S. Bach*, Dominik Johannes Dieterle summons string tremolandos based on fragments of the Aria to portray Count Keyerslingk's insomnia. Pizzicatos ratchet up to the tension until the unaccompanied solo violin ushers in a tranquil interlude, presumably representing welcome rest. In *Sleepless (Goldberg Goes Crazy)*, Tobias Rokahr promises relief by pitting agitated solo violin passages against aggressive strings that eventually morph into suspended solo harmonics and soft glissandos, a peaceful realm that is eventually subverted by an abruptly frenetic ending.

For his *Goldberg Reflections Aria*, Wolf Kerschek has the soloist injecting the Aria with jazz rhythms, supported on a piano playing blues chords, while Friedrich Heinrich Kern resorts to the tuned glass tubes of a verrophone to create an eerie, meditative background for the Aria in *Reflections on a Dream*. An earthier realm is portrayed in *GoldBergHain* by Stephan Koncz, who draws on Bach's everyday street songs for his version of the Quodlibet (No. 30). And to end, Liepe plays the Aria Da Capo, according to Bach instructions.

THOMAS ENHCO (1988–)
& VASSILENA SERAFIMOVA (1985–)

In their shared Back to Bach journey, this French jazz and classical pianist and Bulgarian virtuoso marimba player team up to import Bach's music into idioms that veer from classical and romantic to gentle jazz and pop. On the way, the duo achieves intriguing contrasts of dynamism and suspended calm.

BACH MIRROR, 2021

Several of the thirteen tracks on this album are straightforward arrangements, with little alteration of Bach's writing other than sharing the music between the piano and the hammered wooden slats of the marimba. It is a combination that achieves a heightened clarity, as in the Vivace from the Organ Sonata No. 3 in D Minor (BWV 527) and "Jesu, Joy of Man's Desiring" in the Myra Hess version. Elsewhere, Enhco and Serafimova unpick

Bach's rhythmic patterns, while retaining the underlying harmonic structures. The results can be exquisite, especially when they slow down the tempo and reduce Bach's arpeggio-like passages to single notes floating in a sea of faint marimba oscillations, as in "Silence", based on the Prelude from the Suite No. 4 for Solo Cello (BWV 1010). In "Reflets", Enhco and Serafimova convert Bach's eight-note arpeggios in the Prelude in C Major from Book I of *The Well-tempered Clavier* into mesmeric cascades, while in "Avalanche", based on the Prelude in C Minor from the same Book, the duo recasts Bach's eight-note patterns into filigrees of unsymmetrical seven notes. After reaching the prelude's midpoint, they set off on their own solos that explore Latin jazz rhythms. When it comes to the Air on the G String, Enhco transforms Bach's eloquent melody into a meditative ballad, supported on a faint wash of marimba support. Entirely new is his composition "Sur la Route", based on the four semitones of B-A-C-H, which Enhco embeds in rhapsodic jazz improvisations.

VLADIMIR IVANOFF (1957–)

In 1986, this German-based Bulgarian musicologist and composer founded *Ensemble Saraband* to forge links between European music and the traditions of the Orthodox Christian and Arabic worlds. By presenting the St Matthew Passion in the language and acoustic of the Middle East, Ivanoff seems to be suggesting that the tragedy this region is experiencing today may be compared with the sufferings of Jesus.

THE ARABIAN PASSION ACCORDING TO J.S. BACH, 2019

In his rethink of Bach's Passion, Ivanoff merges baroque precision and complexity with the spontaneity of classical Arab music and American jazz, as played on a Middle Eastern flute, violin, oud and percussion, as well as a clarinet and western flute. For the heart-wrenching, Arabic-language renditions of "Erbarme dich, mein Gott" ("Have mercy on me, my God") (No. 39) and "Können Tränen meiner Wangen" ("If the tears on my cheeks") (No. 52) sung by the Lebanese contralto Fadia El-Hage, Ivanoff recasts Bach's obligato accompaniments into the plaintive tones of an oboe or Arabic violin embellished with gentle plucking lutes. In "Geduld, Geduld!" ("Patience, patience!") (No. 33), originally a tenor aria, El-Hage is supported on Bach's jagged cello line, while percussion instruments emphasise the singer's anguish, which continues when a zither sets off on an extended improvisation. In another highpoint, Ivanoff focuses on the words, "… und weinete bitterlich" (".... and wept bitterly") sung by the Evangelist when describing Peter's third denial of Jesus (No. 38c). Accompanied by Middle Eastern woodwinds, Ivanoff invests Bach's vocal line with an Oriental acoustic and rhythmic pulse, continuing with a jazz-like improvisation on the clarinet.

Ivanoff's Back to Bach journey transcends histories and cultures. As one listener imagined on hearing *The Arabian Passion*: "Bach rose from his pew and sat on a prayer rug … the sense of the prayers remained the same … a sounding plea for toleration and peace".[159]

ANDREA AGOSTINI (1970–) & DANIELE GHISI (1984–)

In the present age of computer-aided music, Bach is now summoned as a guiding spirit, as in this website created by these two Italian musicians.

BACH: AUTOMATED COMPOSER'S HELPER, 2013

Offering a collection of tools for graphic music to assist composers to script, edit and modify new scores, this website showcases techniques that Bach himself would have been familiar with, except that the music is routed through a computer. Agostini and

Ghisi simulate Bach's idiom by focusing on musical representation, analysis and composition, without, so far, producing convincing replicas. The same is true of other sites like *BachGPT* or *DeepBach*, which aim at emulating, even replicating, the polyphonic logic and harmonic structure of Bach's art.

AFTERLIVES

ART OF FUGUE & B-A-C-H

In this his last, unfinished work, Bach investigates all the possibilities of manipulating a single musical idea confined mainly to the notes of the D minor triad (D, A, F and D, ending on F). On this modest theme, Bach constructs fourteen fugues and four canons of unsurpassed variety and contrapuntal inventiveness. As his exemplars progress, each of which he labels "Contrapunctus", except for the last "fugue in 3 voices", Bach modifies the rhythmic contour of his theme by inversion, augmentation, diminution and stretto. He even devises two mirror fugues that can be played either the right way up or upside down! Throughout, Bach offers expressive counterthemes that take on a life of their own. Sometimes he begins with the countertheme and only later introduces the principal theme; this seems to have been his intention in the last fugue.

Bach gives no indication how his fugues and canons might be played; he is more concerned with their construction than how they might sound. Even so, he must have considered the *Art of Fugue* as a personal statement, for he "signs off" with the B-A-C-H semitones in the work's last and longest fugue. Up to the point when he begins to integrate the B-A-C-H motif with the fugue's two earlier ideas, the principal D minor theme running through *Art of Fugue* has not appeared, leading Bach's followers to wonder whether this last fugue belonged to the work at all. Their doubts were only later cleared up by Gustav Nottebohm, a Vienna-based scholar who had laboured for many years deciphering Beethoven's cryptic notebooks. Having dispensed with Beethoven, Nottebohm redirected his sleuthing skills to Bach, and in 1880 showed that the principal D minor theme in *Art of Fugue* is compatible with

B-A-C-H as well as the other themes in the last fugue, and that all these ideas can be combined in different vertical combinations in four-voice "invertible" counterpoint. Such dizzying configurations would have served as a fitting climax to Bach's ultimate journey.

Though until recently Bach's exemplars were not listened to as music, the B-A-C-H motif has a vigorous afterlife as an independent idea to be contrapuntally manipulated, or as a motif regulating a larger musical structure. The fact that the four semitones have no inherent harmonic implication, explains how B-A-C-H came to be incorporated into so many atonal works.

c. 1760 Johann Christian Bach's Organ Fugue on B-A-C-H.

1782 Mozart transcribes Contrapunctus 8 for string trio.

c. 1819 Beethoven considers using B-A-C-H in the Agnus Dei chorus in his Missa Solemnis.

1825–26 Themes resembling the B-A-C-H semitones in Beethoven's last string quartets.

1825 Beethoven conceives his *Grosse Fuge* in the shadow of *Art of Fugue*.

1845 Robert Schumann's *Six Fugues on B-A-C-H*.

1855 Franz Liszt's *Fantasy and Fugue on the Theme B-A-C-H*.

1865 For themes in his Cello Sonata No. 1, Johannes Brahms consults *Art of Fugue*.

1878 *Six Variations on the Theme B-A-C-H* by Nikolai Rimsky-Korsakov.

1910–22 Ferruccio Busoni conceives his *Fantasia Contrappuntistica* in the spirit of *Art of Fugue*.

1927 Wolfgang Graeser's orchestration of *Art of Fugue*.

1928 Arnold Schoenberg integrates B-A-C-H into his *Variations for Orchestra*.

1929 *Prelude and Fugue on the Theme B-A-C-H* by Leopold Godowsky.

1932 *Valse-improvisation sur le nom de B-A-C-H* by Francis Poulenc.

1932 Arthur Honegger's *Prélude, arioso et fughette sur le nom de B-A-C-H*.

1934 *Prelude and Fugue* on B-A-C-H by Hanns Eisler.

1938 Anton Webern uses a twelve-tone series based on B-A-C-H in his String Quartet.

1942–6 *Offrande musicale sur le nom* de B-A-C-H by Charles Koechlin.

1947 Alberto Ginastera's *Toccata, Villancico and Fugue on B-A-C-H* for organ.

1950 & 1975 *Variations and Fugue on the Name B-A-C-H* and *Two Waltzes on the Name B A-C-H for piano* by Nino Rota.

1952 The B-A-C-H semitones appear in Luigi Dallapiccola's *Quaderno Musicale di Annalibera*.

1953 Learning from B-A-C-H, Dmitri Shostakovich devises D-S-C-H as his own musical signature, proclaiming it first in his Symphony No. 10.

1964 B-A-C-H is heard in Arvo Pärt's *Collage on Bach*.

1968 Alfred Schnittke finds places for B-A-C-H in his *Quasi una Sonata*.

1968 Gerd Zacher's *Die Kunst einer Fuge* for the organ.

1973 In *Blues on Bach*, John Lewis offers four new jazz pieces in the keys of B-flat, A, C and B-natural.

1973 *Continuo on BACH* by Jon Lord.

1981 Ennio Morricone's "Sur le nom de Bach" in the film *Le Professionnel*.

2001 *Contrapunctus XIX* by Luciano Berio is an orchestration of Bach's last exemplar.

2002 The Brentano Quartet invites ten composers to contribute pieces to complement their string renditions from *Art of Fugue*. Sofia Gubaidulina responds with *Reflections on the Theme B-A-C-H*.

2006 Techno-visual extravaganza *Laibachkunstderfuge*.

9.

INEXHAUSTIBLE BACH

FINAL REFLECTIONS

I have now described more than 300 moments or stories that link composers, performers and passionate advocates to the extraordinary creativity of Johann Sebastian Bach. These Back to Bach journeys bear witness to his influence through a succession of musical eras – late baroque, classical and romantic; neoclassical, serialist and minimalist; jazz, pop and rock; experimental, techno and now even digital realms. It seems no age can resist Bach's magnetism, as one generation after another comes to view the composer as a creative resource. George Bernard Shaw, who began his career as a concert critic, intuited Bach's persistent appeal when he remarked: "Bach belongs not to the past, but to the future".[160] Paying homage, if only by quoting the B-A-C-H semitones, was a way of identifying with Bach's unsurpassed mastery; hopefully, it would prove beneficial. Debussy counselled fellow musicians to consider Bach as "a benevolent God to whom [they] should pray to guard themselves from mediocrity".[161]

As they peruse my chapters, readers will find no notice of Handel or Haydn, two crucial figures in eighteenth-century music. Handel never evinced interest in the output of his exact contemporary and avoided meeting Bach whenever he visited his hometown of Halle, barely a day's journey from Leipzig.

Haydn, on the other hand, obtained a score of the Mass in B Minor, but when it came to his late oratorios, referenced Handel, not Bach.[162] Nor will readers come across the names of Berlioz, Bruckner, Tchaikovsky, Sibelius or Richard Strauss, who were similarly unmotivated to absorb Bach's art into their own in any obvious way. I consider them exceptions to the greater number of composers and musicians who did.

But what is there about the music that has propelled this multitude of Back to Bach journeys through the 275 years or so since his death? Schumann thought the question was pointless: as he wrote in 1840 to a fellow critic, "to my mind Bach is unapproachable – he is unfathomable."[163] (This did not inhibit him from writing Bachian-style fugues and canons.) Disregarding Schumann, I take courage and address those features which I believe to be fundamental to Bach's art in the hope that, considered together, they may contribute to an overall explanation. At first, these appear to yield contradictory results: the free, improvisatory spirit of Bach's fantasias and toccatas when compared with the mathematical ingenuities of the fugues and canons; the mighty architectural logic of the musical structures versus the intense emotionality of the choruses and arias; the devoutly Lutheran content of the chorales in the cantatas and Passions as against the joyous courtly dances in the keyboard and instrumental suites that also "infiltrate" the sacred works. Bach fuses all these elements into a unified musical domain that satisfies in so many ways – whether we seek rhythmic energy, intellectual engagement, spiritual inspiration, inner peace or simply sheer beauty. This, then, is the miracle of Bach.

EXEMPLARY BACH

Bach's art is grounded in teaching and learning a wide range of practical and theoretical skills by example. Today's instrumentalists and singers, like those in the past, strive to capture the essence of Bach's music through precise renditions of his complex contrapuntal passages, chromatic harmonies, and intricate ornamentations, together with his phrasings and expressions, and improvisations based on them. Though Bach wrote many works to instruct his sons and other students, he invested these with contrapuntal sophistication and expressive intensity, as in the "emotional fervency" of the Sinfonia No. 9 in F Minor.[164] After settling in Leipzig, Bach attracted pupils from all over Germany, providing music that would train them to improve their technical and interpretive abilities. By this time, he had completed the first set of fugues in *The Well-tempered Clavier*, which required students to play three or more independent voices with all ten fingers, while the accompanying preludes often focused on specific mechanical problems – arpeggios, rapid scales, chord clusters, wide leaps, and so on. Such was the demand for these pedagogical exemplars that twenty years later, Bach issued a second set of preludes and fugues under the same title. In the Goldberg Variations, published around this same time, Bach presented players with a veritable catalogue of keyboard challenges. As the Icelandic pianist Vikingur Ólafsson recently demonstrated, much to adulation of audiences worldwide, a flawless performance still constitutes a virtuoso feat.

Bach's masterpieces for the organ have never been surpassed for their exploitation of pedals, keyboards and pipes to achieve majestic effects on this greatest of all instruments. Violinists, cellists and flautists continue to struggle with the musical and technical complexities that Bach proposes for their instruments, notably in the Chaconne for Solo Violin, one of his longest, most brilliant showpieces. The chorales and choruses exploit the vocal resources of the singers that Bach himself rehearsed, as do the expressive arias that he incorporated into his Passions and cantatas. (That this church music was written for professionally trained boys and young men is today ignored by choral groups with female singers.)

In addition to the technical and interpretive difficulties to be overcome when rehearsing and performing Bach, the music itself serves as a limitless resource for compositional method. Unlike several of his pupils,[165] Bach never authored a manual on counterpoint and harmony; instead, he demonstrated what could be done and how. In his organ and harpsichord fugues and canons, as well as in his grandly conceived, choral-instrumental cantatas and Passions, Bach brought the long-standing European tradition of polyphony to unsurpassed perfection. Those wishing to learn how to write independent voices in all possible configurations only had to scrutinise *The Well-tempered Clavier*, *Musical Offering* and *Art of Fugue*. When it came to mastering the art of harmony, the preludes and fugues written in the major and minor keys on all twelve semitones of the octave pointed the way forward to the chromatically inflected music of later times, and from there to atonality. Despite the noble melodies of the Protestant chorales that Bach inherited, his settings offered invaluable lessons in chordal invention. Probably this is what Beethoven had in mind when he declared Bach to be "the progenitor of harmony."[166] As they departed from long-established conventions, later composers often turned to Bach. When, in 1878, Wagner wished to explain the source of his revolutionary musical language, he called attention to one of Bach's keyboard fugues. Some forty years later, Schoenberg set about orchestrating three of Bach's organ works at the same time he was refining his radical, twelve-tone system. Thanks to the timeless quality of the music, Bach could always be consulted. As Debussy explained: "Bach was the only one who saw ahead to the truth".[167]

ADAPTABLE BACH

No matter how his music is translated into later idioms and acoustics, Bach is always present. Little wonder that one commentator characterises him as "Bach the Inexhaustible",[168] a title I appropriate here. When it came to borrowing, Bach himself showed the way, shuffling pieces back and forth between his courtly and ecclesiastical commissions as need arose. To complete his Mass in B Minor, he sourced choruses and arias from earlier church cantatas, while for the introduction to his Christmas Oratorio, he adapted a chorus with festive drums and trumpets written to celebrate the birthday of Queen Maria Josepha, wife of Augustus II, Elector of Saxony (BWV 214). Bach also transcribed works by his Italian contemporaries, arranging for the organ several violin concertos by Antonio Vivaldi, reinforced with his own polyphonic rigour. In later years, he prepared Giovanni Battista Pergolesi's Stabat Mater for performance, expanding the instrumentation and substituting a German text for the Latin original (BWV 1083).

By repurposing his own music as well as that of others (a common practice at the time), Bach set a path for future composers: Mozart recast Bach's harpsichord fugues for string trio; Liszt and Busoni removed his toccatas, fantasias and chorale preludes from the organ loft to the grand piano on the stage; Stokowski submerged Bach in a dense web of symphonic sonorities in the concert hall, as in his version of the organ Toccata and Fugue in D Minor. For Webern, the six-part Ricercar in the *Musical Offering* presented an opportunity to explore a modernist kaleidoscope of fragmented instrumental colours. John Lewis of the Modern Jazz Quartet recorded the same Ricercar, interweaving the piano and marimba lines with the voices of the Swingle Singers. Bach survives these and other such transpositions in settings that vary from thick, romantic harmonies to minimalist, atonal dissonances, from jazz syncopations to frenetic rock dislocations.

How were such transformations possible? One explanation is that Bach's art is largely independent from any specific sound; it exists "absolutely", which means it can function in any audible context. In Albert Schweitzer's opinion, Bach "conceived everything for an ideal instrument".[169] This is true even when Bach investigates the technical possibilities of the solo violin in the Chaconne, the double-keyboard harpsichord in the Goldberg Variations, or the pedals and pipes of an organ in the Toccata and Fugue in D Minor. On occasions, Bach seems altogether unconcerned as to how his music might sound. He writes *Art of Fugue* in open score, giving no indication of the instrument (or instruments) on which its contrapuntal elaborations might be played.

Time and again, Bach shares his ideas between different instruments, and even between instruments and voices, as in the many cantatas and Passion arias. It is a strategy that enables the importation of Bach's music into instruments he could never have known, like the modern piano, saxophone or vibraphone. It is true even when his music is translated into electronic sound, whether produced in a recording studio or blasted live into a rock concert stadium. This adaptability helps explain the vigorous afterlives of so many of his musical genres. It is important to remember that Bach was not the first to couple his preludes, toccatas and fantasias with fugues; nor did he invent the passacaglia and chaconne, or even the concerto grosso. But by bringing these long-standing formats to a peak of matchless excellence, Bach offered paradigms that promised further possibilities. Composers from Chopin to Shostakovich honoured *The Well-tempered Clavier* by devising their own sets of twenty-four piano preludes in all the major and minor keys. The ostinato theme in Bach's great organ Passacaglia proved irresistible to Goldschmidt and Britten when writing their own orchestral passacaglias. As for the Brandenburg Concertos, now Bach's most familiar instrumental works, these served Elgar, Hindemith, Bartók, Stravinsky and Schnittke as models for their own concerto-grosso-type works.

IMPROVISATORY BACH

Not only is Bach's music adaptable, but much of it also seems to be a transcript of an improvisation. This is hardly surprising. During his lifetime, Bach was best known for his extemporisations in churches all over Germany on the numerous occasions he was invited to advise on repairing old organs and testing the pedals and pipes of new ones. In 1720, Bach travelled to Hamburg to play for Reincken. The seventy-seven-year-old organist declared that up to then he believed the art of improvisation was dead: "I see it still lives in you," he enthused.[170] Indeed, much of Bach's music seems to be written-down versions of impromptu keyboard performances, as in the "spontaneous freshness of invention"[171] of the opening flourishes of the Toccata and Fugue in D Minor or Chromatic Fantasia and Fugue, and the cadenza-like solo in Brandenburg Concerto No. 5. Stimulated by such writings, later composers invented their own freely composed preludes and fantasias, while jazz pianists morphed Bach's extemporisations into their own. As Jacques Loussier once put it: "Bach's music is ideal for jazz improvisation. So many of the structures … are very similar".[172]

Throughout his music, Bach extends his melodies, rhythmic patterns, and harmonic progressions to create continuously evolving structures. These reveal all the possibilities contained within a single idea, no matter how simple. It is a compositional method sometimes described as *fortspinnung* (spinning forth), a term unknown in Bach's day, but which is useful here. Bach's "spinning forth" resonated with later musicians, who acknowledged the debt by using Bach's melodic or rhythmic ingredients as springboards for their own creative efforts. By extracting these "nuggets" from Bach, they discovered that these could serve as building blocks for entirely new works. Nowhere is this better shown than in the ever-accumulating responses to the preludes and fugues in *The Well-tempered Clavier*, whether they be cheeky quotations of the Fugue in C Minor from Book I in Hindemith's orchestral *Ragtime (Well-Tempered)*, or pianistic antics on the accompanying prelude by Eugen Cicero, propelled by plucked string bass and persistent percussion. Even rock performers could be energised by Bach, as Jimi Hendrix demonstrated in his unforgettable electric bass guitar riff on the organ Passacaglia.

MATHEMATICAL BACH

Complementing Bach's improvisatory art is the mathematical logic that underpins his music – from the grand instrumental-choral edifices of his Passions and cantatas to the intimate fugues in *The Well-tempered Clavier* or *Art of Fugue* and canons in the Goldberg Variations, and even the buoyant bourrées and gigues in the keyboard suites. Whether writing for a single voice or multiple voices in his instrumental and vocal works, Bach constructs his music contrapuntally with supporting bass lines, sometimes supplied with "figures" indicating the harmonies to be fleshed out.

Despite the constraints of strict counterpoint, Bach never produces what his son Carl Philipp Emanuel called "dry mathematical stuff".[173] To the contrary, he imbues his fugal themes and counterthemes with musical individuality. In his greatest organ works, Bach achieves drama by intensifying the contrapuntal tension. He pits two contrasting themes against one another in the fugal section of the Passacaglia, injecting the counterpoint with relentless energy until it climaxes on a startling melodramatic chord. Nowhere is the poetic fire of Bach's counterpoint more evident than in the astounding performance of the Chromatic Fantasia and Fugue on the harpsichord by Wanda Landowska in her 1935 recording. Significantly, many of these works are in A, C,

D or E minor – keys that Bach considered especially amenable to polyphonic spectacle. That the idea of counterpoint as drama had later repercussions is clear from the fugal episodes (usually called fugatos) that contribute excitement to movements in classical symphonies, as in the Adagio "Marcia funebre" of Beethoven's Symphony No. 3 ("Eroica").

In addition to contrapuntal drama, Bach engages players and listeners with seemingly limitless mathematical ingenuity, combining his themes in canonic overlaps, turning them upside down or back to front, doubling or halving their time spans, and combining them in dizzying vertical combinations. While these devices are found throughout his music, Bach crafts the *Musical Offering* and *Art of Fugue* as special vehicles for his contrapuntal wizardry. No matter how much they admired Bach's ingenuities, later composers were rarely equipped to match these contrapuntal exemplars, a notable exception being Mozart in the polyphonic pyrotechnics of the finale of his Symphony No. 41 ("Jupiter"). Judging from recent fugal writing, the fascination with Bach's counterpoint is by no means exhausted, even if this takes light-hearted turns, as in Giovanni Dettori's *Lady Gaga Fugue*. Meanwhile, engineers fuse mathematics with the technicalities of the computer age in an attempt to generate Bachian fugues.

RHYTHMIC BACH

Bach anchors all his music in rhythmic momentum. For John Eliot Gardiner, "the essential fluidity of its movement and underlying rhythm" count as much as "its sharpness of contour [and] its harmonic depth".[174] Bach's music progresses inexorably with a perceptible pulse, often in accordance with the popular dance patterns of his day, as in the suites of English, French and German dances for keyboard, and the stylised dance movements in the Brandenburg Concertos and Orchestral Suites. One commentator even characterises Bach's Suites for Solo Cello as "an apotheosis of the dance".[175] Dance rhythms also make an appearance in Bach's sacred music, as in the grieving, Sarabande-like chorus that brings the St Matthew Passion to a close. When it comes to his keyboard preludes and fugues, Bach fixes on specific rhythmic patterns that dictate the counterpoint, as in the dance-like theme of the Fugue in G Major in Book I of *The Well-tempered Clavier*. Even the unvarying arpeggios in the Prelude in C Major from Book I press continuously onwards, while the intertwining themes in the six-part Ricercar of the *Musical Offering* never lose momentum. A comparable forward movement infuses even the slowest, most expressive pieces, like the eloquent G minor "arioso" in the Goldberg Variations (No. 25), seemingly suspended outside time. When providing chorales for his Passion and cantata movements or his organ preludes, Bach animates the static melodies with inner voices that are constantly moving to achieve varying degrees of tension and relaxation.

Learning from the momentum in Bach's counterpoint, Beethoven imbues his fugal movements with powerful wilfulness, as in the jagged, often violently interlocking rhythms in his *Grosse Fuge* for string quartet. That Stravinsky is more attracted to Bach's rhythms than his counterpoint is confirmed in the Concerto in E-flat ("Dumbarton Oaks"), modelled on the hopping figurations in the Brandenburg Concertos. Jazz pianists and rock guitarists are equally attracted to Bach's persistent rhythms, which they absorb into their own idioms. As he listened to Bach's pulsating patterns, the legendary American jazz saxophonist Coleman Hawkins is supposed to have exclaimed, "man, it's all there!"[176]

For the musicologist Wilfrid Mellers, Bach's rhythms are rooted instinctively in the human body, moving in harmony with nature around the speed of the human pulse. In what Mellers calls the "dance of God", Bach's polyphonies sing and soar, sometimes transcending or counterposed to this "earth-beat". The music is attuned to a regular rhythm that is "as unremittent as the turning earth, as continuous as the surging sea".[177]

ESOTERIC BACH

Fascination with Bach extends beyond mathematics and rhythms to the extra-musical dimensions of his art. Throughout his works, Bach inscribed his scores with the words "Soli Deo Gloria" or the letters "SDG".[178] Dissatisfied with these outer manifestations of steadfast Christian faith, musical sleuths have turned to the symbolism they believe underlies the composer's musical schemes.[179] Having suggested that the three sections in each of the Kyrie and Credo movements in the Mass in B Minor represent God the Almighty, Jesus Christ, and the Holy Spirit, they recognise the same Trinitarian allegory in the central role of the key of E-flat (with three flats) and the three-part fugue in the Prelude and Fugue in E-flat Major ("St Anne") for organ.[180] When it comes to the Goldberg Variations, one interpreter is sufficiently inspired to imagine that Bach's canons on the nine ascending notes of the scale represent "an ascent through the nine spheres of Ptolemaic cosmology", notably the Earth, the Moon, Mercury, Venus, the Sun, Mars, Jupiter, Saturn and the "Fixed Stars".[181]

Number symbolism has proved particularly tempting to some scholars, despite the lack of evidence that Bach ever absorbed such obscure meanings into his music, other than inventing canonical puzzles with cryptic instructions like those in the *Musical Offering*. Among the number alphabet systems current in Germany during Bach's lifetime is the one in which numbers are assigned to notes in a progressive sequence: thus, A = 1, B = 2, C = 3, and so on, yielding 14 for "Bach", and 41 (the mirror image of 14) for "Johann Sebastian Bach".[182] One especially keen investigator claims to have discovered that an analysis of Bach's 1736 revision of the St Matthew Passion yields fourteen recitatives that include the name "Jesus", and forty-one separate recitatives in all, along with fourteen solo arias and fourteen chorales, which, when added to the other movements, make for a further forty-one movements! [183] Another enthusiast points out that the "Overture" (No. 16) in the Goldberg Variations consists of ninety-five bars, and, given that 9 + 5 =14, it must therefore refer to Bach himself.[184] It has even been suggested that Bach delayed joining the Society of Musical Science in Leipzig until he could be listed as the fourteenth member.[185]

Such numerological speculations contrast with the certainty of Oriental philosophy, into which Bach was inducted in 1942 by R.H. Blyth, the renowned translator of Japanese haiku poetry. On this occasion, Blyth proposed that the Passacaglia be considered an embodiment of Zen paradox – that is, the ability to comprehend two different things at the same time. According to his view, "the unchanging bass of the pedal and the ever-changing melodies of the two manuals *together* … reached the realm where the paradox of theme and variation, absolute and relative, human and divine, law and freedom, was resolved".[186] To support his argument, Blyth reproduces the first two pages of Bach's score in his *Zen in English Literature and Oriental Classics*. Bach might well have agreed that his theme and variations might reconcile the contradictions of human experience.

EXPRESSIVE BACH

Despite the complexity of his architectonic brilliance, Bach's complex counterpoint and rhythmic subtlety are never without emotional content. When combining and synthesising so many elements to such an extremely high technical and intuitive level, Bach is always expressive. Employing chromatic transitions, dissonances and modulations into distant keys, and organically matching them with diverse rhythms and fluent phrasings, Bach creates harmonic progressions that invest his music with intense purpose and feeling. Later composers recognised the emotional impact of Bach's harmonies and have been inspired to respond creatively. One such example of this is Gounod, who effortlessly floats his lyrical *Ave Maria* on the arpeggiated chords of the Prelude in C Major from Book I of *The Well-tempered Clavier*.

Bach creates themes of compelling beauty. Whether scored for voices or instruments (or for both in multiple, interlocking lines), his melodies achieve emotional intensity and satisfaction thanks to the chromatic chordal support and ornamental embellishment, as in the heart-wrenching alto aria "Erbarme Dich" with violin accompaniment from the St Matthew Passion (No. 39). That Bach's music could illustrate words and concepts was revealed by Albert Schweitzer in his pioneering study, originally published in 1905 as *J.S. Bach, le musicien-poète*. In his settings of religious texts, Bach often uses ideas that are represented graphically and perceived audibly: thus, drooping semitones for suffering; rising arpeggios for hope; rapid scales proceeding up and down for joy; gentle, meandering triplets around a single note for reassurance, and so on. Bach allots these ideas to soloists and choruses to illustrate the sacred words they sing, and shares them with supporting instruments, exploiting the plaintive tones of an oboe, the comforting elaborations of a solo violin, or the triumphant proclamations of a trumpet. He also transmits this expressive vocabulary beyond his settings of the Lutheran liturgy to imbue his non-religious works with equal emotional vibrancy. Nowhere is this better illustrated than in the enchantment of the Aria in the Goldberg Variations, to which performers and their audiences willingly respond.

For many listeners, it is the soul-searching spirituality of Bach's music that ultimately persuades. After playing "Schmücke dich, o liebe Seele" to Schumann, Mendelssohn confessed: "If life were to deprive you of hope and faith, this one [organ] chorale would bring it all back again to you".[187] The same may be said of "Ich ruf zu dir, Herr Jesu Christ", whether played on the organ as Bach had intended in the *Orgel-Büchlein,* on the piano in Busoni's profoundly sensitive transcription, in the yearning tones of the cello rendered by Pierre Fournier, or even in Stokowski's mellifluous orchestral transcription. The promise of reassurance and hope in this chorale persuaded Eduard Artemyev to select it when seeking a musical symbol of earthly peace for the score he provided for the 1972 science fiction *Solaris*. The director of the 2013 Polish film *Ida*, in which a Catholic novice discovers her tragic Jewish background, did likewise. As she returns to the convent to take her final vows, "Ich ruf zu dir" is heard in the background, offering her solace.

In the end, Bach offers solace to us all. In the words of the novelist J.M. Coetzee: "the best proof we have that life is good, and therefore that there may perhaps be a God after all, who has our welfare at heart, is that to each of us, on the day we are born, comes the music of Johann Sebastian Bach. It comes as a gift, unearned, unmerited, for free".[188]

NOTES

1 Christian Apslund, "A Body Without Organs: Three Approaches – Cage, Bach, and Messiaen", *Perspectives of New Music*, 35/2 (1997), p. 181.

2 See Ute Henseler, "Johann Sebastian Bach und der Neoklassizismus", in Michael Heinemann and Hans-Joachim Hinrichsen (eds), *Bach und die Nachwelt, Band 3: 1900–1950*, Laaber: Laaber Verlag, 2000, pp. 253–7.

3 Quoted in Robert Marshall, *The Music of Johann Sebastian Bach: The Sources, the Style, the Significance*, New York: Schirmer Books, 1989, p. 68.

4 Michael Geck, *Bach*, London: Haus Publishing, 2003, p. 14.

5 Nicholas Kenyon, *The Faber Pocket Guide to Bach*, London: Faber & Faber, 2011, p. 295.

6 As related by Gerber's son, quoted in Hans T. David and Arthur Mendel (eds), *The New Bach Reader: A Life of Johann Sebastian Bach in Letters and Documents*, revised and enlarged by Christoph Wolff, New York: W.W. Norton, 1998, p. 372.

7 Malcolm Boyd, *Bach: The Brandenburg Concertos*, Cambridge: Cambridge University Press, 1993, p. 11.

8 Errors accumulate when the strings are tuned one after another according to geometric ratios: 2:1 for an octave, 3:2 for an interval of a "perfect" fifth, 4:3 for a "perfect" fourth, and so on. See Ross W. Duffin, *How Equal Temperament Ruined Harmony (And Why You Should Care)*, New York: W.W. Norton, 2008, especially p. 25.

9 Bradley Lehman, "Bach's Extraordinary Temperament: Our Rosetta Stone", *Early Music*, 33 (2005), pp. 3–23 and 211–31.

10 Bach's inscription is given in Christoph Wolff, *Bach's Musical Universe: The Composer and His Work*, New York: W.W. Norton, 2020, p. 33.

11 David and Mendel, op. cit., p. 338.

12 See discussion in Wolff, op. cit., p. 285.

13 See a discussion of the possible performance(s) of the Missa in John Eliot Gardiner, *Music in the Castle of Heaven: A Portrait of Johann Sebastian Bach*, London: Penguin Books, 2014, pp. 483–7.

14 The goblet survives and is displayed in the Bachhaus in Eisenach. See Eric Thomas Chafe, "B-A-C-H: What's in a Name", in *Tonal Allegory in the Vocal Music of J.S. Bach*, Berkeley: University of California Press, 1991, pp. 27–63.

15 As recorded by Bach's biographer, Johann Nikolaus Forkel. See discussion by John Butt in Malcolm Boyd (ed.), *Oxford Composer Companions, J.S. Bach*, Oxford: Oxford University Press, 1999, p. 195.

16 Geck, op. cit., p. 30.

17 While the B-A-C-H notes occur from time to time in other works of Bach, they are only used in passing and are never clearly audible.

18 Geck, op. cit., p. 140.

19 In the words of Hermann Keller, quoted in Geck, op. cit., p. 22.

20 The editors of the *Bach Werke Verzeichnis, Kleine Ausgabe*, Wiesbaden: Breitkopf & Härtel, 1998, p. 324, consider the work to be an adaption or a forgery. The notable Bach scholar Christoff Wolf, however, accepts its authenticity, characterising it as "refreshingly imaginative, varied and ebullient, as it is structurally undistinguished and unmastered". See *Johann Sebastian Bach: The Learned Musician*, Oxford: Oxford University Press, 2001, pp. 169–70.

21 Albert Schweitzer, *J.S. Bach*, London: Adam & Charles Black, 1923, vol. I, p. 269.

22 Neil Minturn, *The Music of Sergei Prokofiev*, New Haven: Yale University Press, 1977, p. 40.

23 Schweitzer, op. cit., vol. I, p. 229.

24 Percy M. Young, *The Bachs, 1500–1850*, London: J.M. Dent & Sons, 1970, p. 202.

25 Alfred Einstein, *Mozart, His Character, His Work*, London: Cassell, 1961, p. 149.

26 See Wolfgang Hildesheimer, *Mozart*, London: J.M. Dent & Sons, 1985, p. 246.

27 Related by Robert W. Gutman, *Mozart, A Cultural Biography*, London: Secker & Warburg, 2000, p. 636.

28 Though Kirnberger does not identify the chorale, he notes that it was "set in three ways by the famous J.S. Bach". See David Beach and Jurgen Thymn (eds and trans), *Johann Philipp Kirnberger: The Art of Strict Musical Composition*, New Haven and London: Yale University Press, 1982, p. 231; see also Markus Rathey, "Mozart, Kirnberger and the Idea of Musical Purity", *Eighteenth-Century Music*, 13/2 (2016), pp. 235–52.

29 Neither Giesecke nor Mozart ever discover that the "pharaonic mysteries" of Sethos were invented some fifty years earlier by the Abbé Jean Terrasson, an enterprising French cleric. See discussion in Jacques Chailley, *The Magic Flute, Masonic Opera*, London: Victor Gollancz, 1972, pp. 35, 143.

30 David and Mendel, op. cit., p. 488.

31 For Wagner's remark, see Martin Gregor-Dellin and Dietrich Mack (eds), Geoffrey Skelton (trans.), *Cosima Wagner's Diaries, Vol. I, 1869–1877*, London: Collins, 1978, p. 336.

32 Johann Nikolaus Forkel, *Ueber Johann Sebastian Bachs Leben, Kunst und Kunstwerke*, Leipzig: Hoffmeister & Kühnel, 1802.

33 Joel Lester, *Bach's Works for Solo Violin: Style, Structure, Performance*, New York: Oxford University Press, 1999, p. 20.

34 Schweitzer, op. cit., vol. I, p. 240.

35 Orlando Figes, *The Europeans*, London: Penguin, 2009, p. 107.

36 According to Johann Friedrich Rochlitz, who wrote appreciative articles about Bach's music in the *Allgemeine Musikalische Zeitung*, which he edited; see Schweitzer, op. cit., vol. I, p. 237.

37 David and Mendel, op. cit., p. 490.

38 Beethoven quotes the ostinato theme of the Crucifixus in a letter of 15 October 1810 sent to the publishers Breitkopf & Härtel; see Michael Hamburger (ed. and trans), *Beethoven: Letters, Journals and Conversations*, London: Thames & Hudson, 1984, p. 94.

39 Though today played on the flute, Beethoven knew it as a violin solo, which is how it appeared in the 1845 Bach Gesellschaft edition.

40 Lewis Lockwood, *Beethoven: The Music and the Life*, New York: W. W. Norton, 2003, p. 392.

41 Donald Francis Tovey, *Essays in Musical Analysis: Chamber Music*, London: Oxford University Press, 1944, p. 124.

42 David Charlton (ed.), *E.T.A. Hoffman's Musical Writings: Kreisleriana: The Poet and the Composer: Music Criticism*, Cambridge: Cambridge University Press, 1989, p. 85.

43 See Alfred Kanwischer, *From Bach's Goldberg to Beethoven's Diabelli: Influence and Independence*, Lanham, MD: Rowman & Littlefield, 2014.

44 See Lockwood, op. cit., p. 367.

45 Warren Kirkendale, "The 'Great Fugue' Op. 133: Beethoven's 'Art of Fugue'", *Acta Musicologica*, 35/1 (1963), pp. 14–24.

46 Lockwood, op. cit., p. 463.

47 Lockwood, op. cit., p. 442.

48 Christopher H. Gibbs and Morten Solvik (eds), *Franz Schubert and His World*, Princeton: Princeton University Press, 2014, p. 283.

49 Alfred Einstein quotes Schubert's remark in *Music in the Romantic Era*, New York: W.W. Norton, 1947, p. 92.

50 The remark is by Carl Dahlhaus; see R. Larry Todd, "On Mendelssohn's Sacred Music, Real and Imaginary", in Peter Mercer-Taylor (ed.), *The Cambridge Companion to Mendelssohn*, Cambridge: Cambridge University Press, 2004, p. 181.

51 Quoted in Schweitzer, op. cit., vol. I, p. 243.

52 Quoted in Russell Stinson, *The Reception of Bach's Organ Music from Mendelssohn to Brahms*, Oxford: Oxford University Press, 2006, p. 56.

53 Discussed in Mercer-Taylor, op. cit., p. 164.

54 Jean-Jacques Eigeldinger, *Chopin: Pianist and Teacher: As Seen by his Pupils*, Cambridge: Cambridge University Press, 1986, p. 61.

55 Judith Chernaik, *Schumann, The Faces and the Masks*, New York: Alfred A. Knopf, 2018, p. 100.

56 One of the maxims that Schumann includes in his "Advice for Young Musicians: Musical Rules for Home and Life", which is appended to his *Album for the Young* published in 1850. See Chernaik, op., cit., p. 219.

57 See Georg Predota, "Fugenpassion", interlude.hk/fugenpassion-inspiration.

58 Stinson, op. cit., p. 104.

59 Wagner's comment is quoted in Geck, op. cit., p. 47.

60 Christian Thorau, "Richard Wagners Bach", in Michael Heinemann and Hans-Joachim Hinrichsen (eds), *Bach und die Nachwelt, Band 2: 1850–1900*, Laaber: Laaber Verlag, 1999, pp. 163–99.

61 Einstein, 1947, op. cit., pp. 243–4.

62 Ernest Newman, *The Wagner Operas*, New York: Alfred A. Knopf, 1984, p. 304.

63 Newman, op. cit., p. 354.

64 Newman, op. cit., p. 631.

65 See Thorau, op. cit., p. 176.

66 Newman, op. cit., p. 688.

67 Roger Scruton, *Wagner's Parsifal: The Music of Redemption*, London: Allen Lane, 2020, p. 130.

68 Robin Holloway, "Experiencing Music and Imagery in Parsifal", in *Overture Opera Guides, Parsifal*, Richmond, Surrey: Oneworld Classics, 2011, p. 39. Holloway even compares Wagner's "indefinitely extensible … musical material" to certain bars of Contrapunctus XI in Bach's *Art of Fugue*.

69 Raymond Kendall, "Brahms's Knowledge of Bach's Music", *Papers of the American Musicological Society* (1941), pp. 50–6.

70 Schweitzer, op. cit., vol. I. p. 254.

71 Ibid., vol. I, p. 222.

72 In the words of Karl Geiringer, quoted in Kendall, op. cit., p. 50.

73 Quoted in Malcolm MacDonald, *The Master Musicians, Brahms*, London: J.M. Dent & Sons, 1990, p. 197.

74 Reinhard Schäfertöns, "Johannes Brahms und die Musik von Johann Sebastian Bach", in Heinemann and Hinrichsen, 1999, op. cit., pp. 215–16.

75 Styra Avins, *Johannes Brahms, Life and Letters*, New York: Oxford University Press, 1997, p. 515.

76 In a letter quoted in Stinson, op. cit., p. 141.

77 Richard Specht, Eric Blom (trans.), *Johannes Brahms*, London: J.M. Dent, 1930, p. 270. See also Raymond Knapp, "The Finale of Brahms' Fourth Symphony: The Tale of the Subject", *19th-Century Music*, 13/1 (1989), p. 4.

78 Bernard Jacobson, *The Music of Johannes Brahms*, London: The Tantivy Press, 1977, p. 71.

79 N.A. Rimsky-Korsakoff, *My Musical Life*, London: Martin Secker, 1924, p. 129.

80 Léon Vallas, *César Franck*, Westport, CT: Greenwood Press, 1973, p. 232.

81 stephenhough/writings/album-notes/franck-piano-music.

82 Paul Elie, *Reinventing Bach*, London: Union Books, 2013, p. 117.

83 See Thorau, op. cit., p. 176.

84 Elie, op. cit., pp. 411, 478.

85 Walter Frisch, "Reger's Bach and Historicist Modernism", *19th-Century Music*, 25/2–3 (2002), p. 299.

86 Schweitzer, op. cit., vol I., p. 240.

87 Ian Crofton and Donald Fraser, *A Dictionary of Musical Quotations*, London: Croom Helm, 1985, p. 125.

88 Frisch, op. cit., pp. 296–312.

89 Percy Young (ed.), *Letters to Nimrod: Edward Elgar to August Jaeger*, London: Dennis Dobson, 1965, p. 242.

90 William Hoffman, "Bach and Mahler", *Bach Cantatas Website*, 2012, bach-cantatas.com/Articles/Bach/Mahler.

91 Roger Nichols, *The Life of Debussy*, Cambridge: Cambridge University Press, 1998, p. 101.

92 Debussy mentions Goya and refers to his pieces as "Caprices" in a letter to his publisher; see François Lesure and Denis Herlin (eds), *Claude Debussy Correspondence, 1872–1918*, Paris: Gallimard, 2005, p. 1909.

93 Jean-Michel Nectoux (ed.), J. Barrie Jones (trans), *The Correspondence of Camile Saint-Saëns and Gabriel Fauré*, Aldershot: Ashgate, 2004, p. 108.

94 Robert Orledge, *Satie the Composer*, Cambridge: Cambridge University Press, 1990, p. 95.

95 For a discussion of the "Stokowski sound", see Elie, op. cit., p. 130.

96 Stephen Hinton, "Back to Bach: The Conscience of History", American Symphony Orchestra, 2011, americansymphony.org/orchestra-notes/back-to-bach-the-conscience-of-history.

97 Quoted in Keith Waters, *Rhythmic and Contrapuntal Structures in the Music of Arthur Honegger*, Aldershot: Ashgate, 2002, p. 5.

98 Arthur Honegger, Wilson O. Clough (trans.), *I am a Composer*, London: Faber & Faber, 1966, p. 101.

99 collections.vam.ac.uk/item/O18749/les-noces-de-lamour-et-theatre-design-benois-alexandre.

100 Waters, op. cit., p. 128.

101 Interview in the *Daily Mail*, 13 February 1913, quoted in Henseler, op. cit., p. 264.

102 Quoted in French, in Heinemann and Hinrichsen, 2000, op. cit., p. 274.

103 Igor Stravinsky and Robert Craft, *Dialogues and a Diary*, London: Faber & Faber, 1968, p. 40.

104 Quoted in Malcolm MacDonald, *The Master Musicians: Schoenberg*, London: J.M. Dent, 1976, p. 103.

105 In a letter of 5 March to Nikolai Miaskovsky, cited in Harlow Robinson (ed.), *Selected Letters of Sergei Prokofiev*, Boston: Northeastern University Press, 1998, p. 257.

106 Igor Stravinsky and Robert Craft, *Themes and Episodes*, New York: Alfred A. Knopf, 1966, p. 40.

107 In the words of Schweitzer, op. cit., vol. II, pp. 56–7.

108 Lillian Libman, *And Music at the Close: Stravinsky's Last Years, A Personal Memoir*, New York: W.W. Norton, 1972, p. 207.

109 Robert Craft, *Stravinsky: Chronicle of a Friendship*, Nashville: Vanderbilt University Press, 1994, p. 548.

110 Schweitzer, op. cit., vol. I, p. 402.

111 Arnold Schoenberg, "New Music, Outmoded Music", in *Style and Idea*, New York: Philosophical Library, 1950, p. 42.

112 In the words of MacDonald, 1976, op. cit., p. 162.

113 Arnold Schoenberg, Leonard Stein, ed., "Bach" in *Style and Idea: Selected Writings of Arnold Schoenberg*, London: Faber & Faber, 1975, pp. 393–7.

114 "Anton Webern: Passacaglia, op. 1", *Fugue for Thought*, 6 May 2015, fugueforthought.de/2015/05/06/anton-webern-passacaglia-op-1.

115 Thomas Pynchon, *Gravity's Rainbow*, London: Vintage, 1995, p. 440.

116 Quoted in the publisher's note, London: Boosey & Hawkes (HPS 1326), February 1998.

117 From an address that Hindemith delivered at the bicentennial of Bach's death in Hamburg in 1950, published as *Johann Sebastian Bach: Heritage and Obligation*, New Haven: Yale University Press, 1952, p. 43.

118 Passage in Hindemith's *A Composer's World* (1951), quoted in Heinemann and Hinrichsen, 2000, op. cit., p. 222.

119 Geoffrey Skelton, *Paul Hindemith: The Man Behind the Music: A Biography*, London: Victor Gollancz, 1975, p. 159.

120 Crofton and Fraser, op. cit., p. 77.

121 Stephen Hinton, "Hindemith, Bach and the Melancholy of Obligation",

in Michael Marissen (ed.), *Bach Perspectives 3: Creative Responses to Bach from Mozart to Hindemith*, Lincoln, NB: University of Nebraska Press, 1998, pp. 133–55.

122 David Blake (ed.), *Hanns Eisler: A Miscellany*, Edinburgh: Harwood Academic Publishers, 1995, p. 220.

123 Billaudot.com/Charles-koechlin-6.html

124 See Michael Kennedy, *The Dent Master Musicians: Britten*, London, J.M. Dent, 1993, p. 22.

125 D. Rabinovich, *Dmitry Shostakovich, Composer*, London: Lawrence & Wishart, 1959, p. 94.

126 In a letter of July 1960, quoted in Elizabeth Wilson, *Shostakovich: A Life Remembered*, London: Faber & Faber, 1994, p. 380.

127 In the words of Richard Taruskin, *Defining Russia Musically: Historical and Hermeneutical Essays*, Princeton: Princeton University Press, 1997, p. 494.

128 Wilson, op. cit., p. 535.

129 Quoted in Susanne Schaal, "Johann Sebastian Bach im Musikleben Amerikas", in Heinemann and Hinrichsen, 2000, op. cit., p. 238.

130 See Stephen A. Crist, "Bach as Modern Jazz", in Laura Buch (ed.), *Bach Perspectives, Vol. 13, Bach Reworked*, Champaign: University of Illinois Press, 2000, pp. 101–21.

131 See "Eugen Cicero", *AllAboutJazz*, 2021, allaboutjazz.com/musicians/eugen-cicero.

132 Ennio Moricone, *In His Own Words*, Oxford: Oxford University Press, 2019, p. 67.

133 Peter Neal (ed.), *Jimi Hendrix, Starting at Zero, His Own Story*, London: Bloomsbury, 2014, p. 47.

134 Quoted in Otto Deutsch, "Bach and The Beatles", *Medium*, 31 July 2019, medium.com/ottodeutsch/bach-and-the-beatles-6435f2881367.

135 Barry Miles, *Paul McCartney: Many Years From Now*, London: Secker & Warburg, 1997, p. 485.

136 Stuart Maconie, *The People's Songs: The Story of Modern Britain in 50 Records*, London: Ebury Press, 2013, p. 82.

137 Alexis Petridis, "With A Whiter Shade of Pale, Gary Brooker accelerated pop's future at warp-speed", *The Guardian*, 23 February 2022, theguardian.com/music/2022/feb/23/with-a-whiter-shade -of pale-gary-brooker-accelerated-pops-future-at-warp-speed.

138 Interview in *Falk & Sons, Celebrate Bach*, 2011.

139 "Chaconne avec 62 Variations", No. 9 in *Suites de pièces pour le clavicen*, London: John Walsh, 1733.

140 Björn Heile, *The Music of Mauricio Kagel*, Farnham: Ashgate, 2006, p. 144.

141 Elie, op. cit., p. 295.

142 *"Switched-On Bach"*, *Wikipedia*, wikipedia-org/wiki/switched-on_bach.

143 Alex Ross, "Consolations", *The New Yorker*, 24 November 2022, newyorkor.com/magazine/2002/12/02/consolations.

144 Alexander Ivashkin (ed.), *A Schnittke Reader*, Bloomington, IN: Indiana University Press, 2002, p. 17.

145 Heile, op. cit., p. 123.

146 Tom Johnson, "The Minimal Slow-Motion Approach", *Village Voice*, 30 March 1972.

147 Quoted in "Ghost Opera (1994)", *Wise Music Classical*, wisemusicclassical.com/work/33560/Ghost-Opera-Tan-Dun.

148 Stephen Eddins, "Lambarena-Bach to Africa Review", *AllMusic.com*, allmusic.com/album/lambarena-bach-to-africa-mw0001824270.

149 Booklet accompanying the CD of Grabowsky's *Passion*, Melbourne: ABC Classics, 1998.

150 Nicholas Anderson, "Bach: Goldberg Variations", *ClassicalMusic.com*, 20 January 2012, classical-music.com/reviews/bach-65.

151 "Bach Perspectives", *Brentano Quartet*, 11 November 2012, brentanoquartet.com/projects/bach-perspectives.

152 Robin Holloway, "Gilded Goldbergs op. 86 (1992–97)", *Boosey & Hawkes*, 1998, boosey.com/cr/music/Robin-Holloway-Gilded-Goldbergs/4972.

153 Andrew McGregor, "BBC 3 Record Review", 30 March 2024, nikolausmatthes.org/up-content.

154 Helga Thoene, "A Secret Language – Hidden chorale variations in J.S. Bach's 'Sei Solo a Violino'", in *Morimur*, booklet accompanying the ECM record, 2001, pp. 47–57.

155 Patrick Pittman, "Max Richter is a Composer", *Dumbo Feather*, 1 July 2012, dumbofeather.com/conversations/max-richter-is-a-composer.

156 "PENTATONE OXINGALE SERIES Overtures to Bach", pentatonemusic.com/product/pentatone-oxingale-series-overtures-to-bach.

157 William Whitehead (ed.), *The Orgelbüchlein Project: A 21st-century Compilation of Bach's Orgelbüchlein*, vol. 4, London: Peters Edition, 2017, p. v.

158 Sertan Sanderson, "DJ Marc Romboy gives Baroque composer electronic update", *DW*, 12 December 2019, dw.com/en/bach-meets-techno-dj-marc-tomboy-gives-the-baroque-composer-an-electronic-update/a-51199586.

159 saraband.de/Prog_APe.shtml

160 Quoted in Max Graf, *Composer and Critic: Two Hundred Years of Musical Criticism*, London: Chapman & Hall, 1947, p. 297.

161 "La Revue" in *Societé Internationale de Musique*, 1913, quoted in Herbert Kupferberg, *Basically Bach*, London: Robson Books, 1986, p. 8.

162 Haydn heard Handel's oratorios when he first visited London in the early 1790s. They were to inspire choruses in *The Creation* and *The Seasons*, which he wrote in 1798 and 1801.

163 See Young, 1970, op. cit., p. 299.

164 Wilfrid Mellers discusses this Sinfonia in *Bach and the Dance of God*, London: Faber & Faber, 1980, pp. 247–9.

165 For example, Johann Philipp Kirnberger, who in 1774 published his two-volume treatise *The Art of Strict Musical Composition*.

166 As expressed in a letter of 15 January 1801 to his publisher. See Hamburger, op. cit., p. 34.

167 In a letter to Jacques Durand, 3 September 1907; see François Lesure and Roger Nichols (eds), *Debussy Letters*, London: Faber & Faber, 1987, p. 184.

168 Yulia Kreinin, "Choosing an Influence, or Bach the Inexhaustible: The Heterophony of the Voices of Twentieth-Century Composers", *Israel Studies in Musicology*, 13 (2016).

169 Schweitzer, op. cit., vol. I, p. 385.

170 See Young, 1970, op. cit., p. 98.

171 Schweitzer, op. cit., vol. I, p. 269.

172 "Why jazzers love Bach", BBC, 2013, https://www.bbc.co.uk/programmes/articles/1YvyKf5w1QvQDxfDzq6HM06/why-jazzers-love-bach.

173 David Rumsay, "Bach and Numerology: 'dry mathematical stuff'?", *The Sydney Society of Literature and Aesthetics*, 7 (1997), p. 143.

174 Gardiner, op. cit., p. xxxiv.

175 Mellers, op. cit., p. 16.

176 "Coleman Hawkins", *AZquotes*, azquotes.com/quote/693647.

177 Mellers, op. cit., p. 9.

178 Marshall, op. cit., p. 68.

179 Notably Ruth Tatlow in *Bach's Numbers: Compositional Proportion and Significance*, Cambridge: Cambridge University Press, 2015.

180 Discussed by Kenyon, op. cit., p. 319.

181 This planetary interpretation is dismissed by Peter Williams in *Bach: The Goldberg Variations*, Cambridge: Cambridge University Press, 2001, pp. 98–101.

182 Kenyon, op. cit., p. 12.

183 Kenyon, op. cit., p. 179.

184 Herbert Anton Kellner argues for this interpretation in "The Mathematical Architecture of Bach's Goldberg Variations", *English Harpsichord Magazine*, 2/8 (1981).

185 Claire Rubbio, "Bach's Favorite Number", *Veritas Journal*, 15 December 2022, https://veritasjournal.org/2022/12/15/bachs-favorite-number/.

186 R.H. Blyth, *Zen in English Literature and Oriental Classics*, Tokyo: The Hokuseido Press, 1942, pp. 181–3.

187 Schweitzer, op. cit., vol. I, p. 245.

188 J.M. Coetzee, *Diary of a Bad Year*, London: Harvill Secker, 2007, p. 221.

GLOSSARY OF MUSICAL TERMS

adagio, slow

agitato, in an agitated fashion

alla marcia, like a march

allegro, allegretto, fast, moderately fast

allegro molto, very fast

Allemande, German dance

Amapiano, South African musical genre

andante, andantino, moderately slow

antiphonal, alternating singing by two voices or two choirs

appassionato, with passion

aria, song derived from Italian opera, often with a central section and a repeat of the first part

arioso, aria-like composition for voice and/or instrument(s)

arpeggio, chordal notes played in broken succession, often to create rapid cascades

atonal, not in any tone (key)

augmented, augmentation, expanding the theme, usually to double its duration

B-A-C-H, Bach's musical "signature", created from the notes B-flat, A, C and B-natural (B, A, C and H in German notation)

Bachian, in the style of Bach

badinerie, lively French dance

baroque, musical style that reached its culmination in the first half of the eighteenth-century

basso continuo, an essential harmonic support in baroque music provided by a keyboard reinforced with a lower string instrument

bourrée, French dance in double time

bravura, display of technical skill

BWV, *Bach-Werke-Verzeichnis* [*Bach Works Catalogue*], definitive and convenient reference to all of Bach's music

cadence, end of a phrase

cadenza, improvised or written solo passage in an improvisatory style to display the ability of the player

canon, precise imitation, with one voice copied later by another voice to produce an audible overlap

canonic, in the style of a canon

cantabile, song-like

cantata, in Bach, refers to a work written for the Sunday service, often around a biblical text, supplied with recitatives, arias, choruses and chorales

capriccio, a lively piece, free in form

chaconne, dance form in triple time on a repeated chord pattern or bass line

chorale, sung hymn in the German Protestant church; many of Bach's chorales are set to words and music by Martin Luther

chorale prelude, instrumental work, generally for the organ, with the chorale theme elaborated by counterpoint, sometimes derived from the theme itself

chromatic, "colouring" a theme or chordal progression with semitones

classical, musical style developed in the second half of the eighteenth century

clavier, generic German term for a harpsichord, clavichord or organ

coda, passage that ends a movement

con brio, brilliantly

con fuoco, furiously

concerto, work for an instrumental ensemble and one or soloists, with opportunities for artists to display their skills

concerto grosso, "great concerto", featuring interplays between two or more soloists and an instrumental ensemble

continuo, in baroque music a keyboard supported by a bass instrument

contrapunctus, Latin name for counterpoint, used by Bach in *Art of Fugue*

contrapuntal, music built from counterpoint

counterpoint, "one voice against another"; two or more voices sung or played together with independent lines and rhythmic patterns

countertheme; a secondary theme heard together with the principal theme

da capo, instruction to return to the beginning of a piece

diminished seventh, interval spanning three superimposed minor thirds

diminution, theme in compressed form, usually half as long

discordant, not in accordance with the prevailing harmony

dissonant, dissonance, against traditional harmony, often with jarring, adjacent semitones

divertimento, light-hearted piece, generally for a small ensemble, often intended as an entertainment

dominant, fifth note of a scale

double fugue, fugue with two themes, often developed simultaneously

double stop, playing on two strings simultaneously

DSCH, Shostakovich's musical signature, created from the notes D, E-flat, C and B-natural (D, Es, C and H in German notation)

episode, connecting passage, sometimes with new ideas

espressivo, with expression

exposition, first section in a sonata form movement

fantasia, fantasy, freely composed movement, often with contrasting sections

figure, theme (either whole or in part)

forte, fortissimo, loud, very loud

fortepiano, early version of a pianoforte

fugato, limited fugal episode

fughetta, small fugue

fugue, contrapuntal composition in two or more parts or voices entering one after another in imitation, sometimes separated by freer episodes

galant, eighteenth-century musical style with elegant melodies carried on simple harmonies

gavotte, French dance

gigue, lively English dance with a jagged rhythmic pattern in triple time

glissando, a slide upwards or downwards

grave, serious

homophonic, two or more voices in the same harmonic pattern

imitation, strict or approximate copying

intermezzo, intermediate piece or episode

invention, in Bach, a short keyboard piece in two voices

inversion, upside-down form of a theme; a chord beginning on a triad's middle note (first inversion) or top note (second inversion)

invertible counterpoint, multiple voices in different vertical combinations

key, harmonic basis of a musical work; generally referred to as major or minor on one of the twelve semitones of the octave (C, C-sharp, D, etc.)

largo, larghetto, in a broad manner

legato, joined

leitmotif, identifying theme in a Wagner opera

lento, lento assai, slow, very slow

libretto, text of an oratorio, cantata or opera

Lydian mode, ancient musical scale

maestoso, in a dignified, majestic manner

major chord, major triad, the first, third and fifth notes of a major scale

minimalism, musical style built around repeated notes and rhythmic patterns

minor chord, minor triad, the first, third and fifth notes of a minor scale

minor third, third note of a minor scale

minor seventh, interval spanning the first seven notes of a minor scale

minuet, dance form in triple time

mirror fugue, a fugue capable of being played separately upside down

modulation, transition from one key to another

molto agitato, very agitated

molto allegro, very fast

morendo, dying away

motet, sacred work for unaccompanied singers

neoclassical, revival of classical-style musical forms

obligato, ("indispensable") essential musical part

octave, eight-note span of the musical scale

octaves, the same note repeated eight notes above or below

oratorio, sacred work for soloists, chorus and orchestra

oscillation, rotation around a single note

ostinato, ("obstinate") persistent, repeated bass theme

overture, instrumental introduction

palindrome, in music, a piece that can be played both forwards and backwards, sometimes simultaneously

partita, set of contrasting movements

passacaglia, movement based on an ostinato bass theme

Passion oratorio, musical setting of the last days of Jesus commonly performed on Good Friday

perfect cadence, dominant to tonic progression

perfect fifth, "natural" interval, as on a string instrument

piano, pianissimo, soft, very soft

piu lento, very slow

pizzicato, plucked

polyphony, music with two or more independent "voices"

polystylism, eclectic style developed by Alfred Schnittke

prelude, musical movement of diverse form; in Bach, usually precedes a fugue

presto, fast

quodllibet, ("as you please"), light-hearted composition combining popular tunes

recitative, speechlike singing with accompaniment; in Bach's Passion music, sung by a tenor soloist called an Evangelist

related key, with the same number of sharps or flats

retrograde, back-to-front

ricercar, antiquated term used by Bach for a fugue with complicated counterpoint

riff, improvised introduction to a pop work or jazz piece

rondo, musical form with repeated sections

sarabande, stately, Spanish origin dance in triple time; in an instrumental suite, slow movement

scat, lively jazz vocal style with wordless vocables and syllables

scherzo, rapid movement in triple time with sharp rhythms and accents

sempre pianissimo, always softly

serial, serialism, music based on a predetermined series of notes, such as the twelve-tone system advocated by Schoenberg

seventh, interval of seven notes in a scale; varies by a semitone in a major or minor scale

seventh chord, created from the first, third, fifth and seventh notes of the scale

sforzando, sharp accent

siciliano, **sicilienne**, slow, pastorale-like movement in double/triple time

sinfonia, in Bach, an extended instrumental or keyboard introduction

sixth, interval of six notes in a scale

sonata, a work with three or four contrasting movements in quick and slow time

sonata form, in classical music, a movement with three divisions: an exposition with contrasting ideas; a development, in which the ideas are elaborated; and a recapitulation, in which the ideas are repeated

sostenuto, sustained

sprechgesang, vocal style mingling speech with melody

staccato, detached

stretto, episode in a fugue with the theme overlapping against itself in close imitation

suite, group of stylised dance movements

symphony, multi-movement work for orchestra, the first in sonata form

syncopation, irregular rhythmic pattern, often avoiding the first beat of the bar

tempering, tuning the notes of a musical scale

Thema Regium, Bach's term for the theme given to him by Frederick the Great

tintinnabuli, individual style developed by Arvo Pärt

toccata, freely composed movement, often with brilliant passages contrasting with reflective episodes

tonic, first note of a scale; prevailing key of a movement

tranquillo, calmly

transcription, arrangement for instruments and/or voices different to the original

transposition, arrangement in another key other than the original

tremolo, **tremolando**, rapidly repeated notes

triad, chord consisting of the first, third and fifth notes of a scale

trio, work for three players; waltz-like piece between a pair of minuets

triple counterpoint, with three simultaneous voices

tutti, ("all"), to be played by all instruments

vivace, lively

voice, in instrumental music, indicates a particular line

vorspiel, ("prelude") instrumental overture in a Wagner opera

well-tempered, tuning the strings of a keyboard so that music can be played in the keys on all twelve semitones of the octave

FURTHER READING

An ever-growing literature is available on Johann Sebastian Bach's life and music, as well as on the reception of his music after his death and its influence on later composers. Here, I list a selection of published monographs and articles that I found particularly helpful. They are almost all in English, except for the musical and cultural developments surveyed in the four volumes of *Bach und die Nachwelt*, and the indispensable *Bach-Werke-Verzeichnis, Kleine Ausgabe*. Additional references can be found in the Notes.

We live in an age of expanding online information. Most music history entries in Wikipedia are professionally written and underpinned with notes and bibliographies. There is now also a host of internet sites with useful information – foremost among these is Aryeh Oron's comprehensive *Bach Cantatas Website* (https://www.bach-cantatas.com/).

BACH

Boyd, Malcolm, *Bach: The Brandenburg Concertos*, Cambridge: Cambridge University Press, 1993.

(ed.), *Oxford Composer Companions: J.S. Bach*, Oxford: Oxford University Press, 1999.

Butt, John (ed.), *The Cambridge Companion to Bach*, Cambridge: Cambridge University Press, 1997.

David, Hans T. and Arthur Mendel (eds), *The New Bach Reader: A Life of Johann Sebastian Bach in Letters and Documents*, revised and enlarged by Christoph Wolff, New York: W.W. Norton, 1998.

Dreyfus, Lawrence, *Bach and the Patterns of Invention*, Cambridge, MA: Harvard University Press, 1996.

Dürr, Alfred and Yoshitake Kobayashi, *Bach-Werke-Verzeichnis, Kleine Ausgabe*, Wiesbaden: Breitkopf & Härtel, 1998.

Eggebrecht, Hans Heinrich, *J.S. Bach's The Art of Fugue, The Work and its Interpretation*, Ames: Iowa State University Press, 1993.

Gaines, James, *Evening in the Palace of Reason: Bach Meets Frederick the Great in the Age of Enlightenment*, London: Harper Perennial, 2005.

Gardiner, John Eliot, *Music in the Castle of Heaven: A Portrait of Johann Sebastian Bach*, London: Penguin Books, 2014.

Geck, Martin, *Bach*, London: Haus Publishing, 2003.

Geiringer, Karl, *Johann Sebastian Bach: The Culmination of an Era*, London: George Allen & Unwin, 1966.

Jones, Gordon, *Bach's Choral Music: A Listener's Guide*, New York: Amadeus Press, 2009.

Keller, Hermann, *The Well-Tempered Clavier by Johann Sebastian Bach*, London: George Allen & Unwin, 1976.

Kenyon, Nicholas, *The Faber Pocket Guide to Bach*, London: Faber & Faber, 2011.

Leaver, Robin A. (ed.), *The Routledge Research Companion to Johann Sebastian Bach*, London: Routledge, 2017.

Ledbetter, David, *Bach's Well-Tempered Clavier: The 48 Preludes and Fugues*, New Haven: Yale University Press, 2002.

Lederer, Victor, *Bach's Keyboard Music: A Listener's Guide*, New York: Amadeus Press, 2010.

Lester, Joel, *Bach's Works for Solo Violin: Style, Structure, Performance*, New York: Oxford University Press, 1990.

Marshall, Robert L., *The Music of Johann Sebastian Bach: The Sources, the Style, the Significance*, New York: Schirmer Books, 1989.

Mellers, Wilfrid, *Bach and the Dance of God*, London: Faber & Faber, 1980.

Moser, Andreas (ed.), *The Bach Chaconne for Solo Violin: A Collection of Views*, Bloomington, IN: Frangipani Press, 1985.

Rumsey, David, "Bach and Numerology: 'dry mathematical stuff?'", *The Sydney Society of Literature and Aesthetics*, 7 (1997), pp. 143–65.

Schweitzer, Albert, *J.S. Bach*, London: Adam & Charles Black, 1923.

Stinson, Russell, *J.S. Bach and His Royal Instrument: Essays on His Organ Works*, Oxford: Oxford University Press, 2012.

Tatlow, Ruth, *Bach's Numbers: Compositional Proportion and Significance*, Cambridge: Cambridge University Press, 2015.

Williams, Peter, *Bach: The Goldberg Variations*, Cambridge: Cambridge University Press, 2001.
   The Organ Music of J.S. Bach, Cambridge: Cambridge University Press, 2003.

Wolff, Christoph (ed.), *The World of the Bach Cantatas*, New York: W.W. Norton, 1995.
   Johann Sebastian Bach, The Learned Musician, Oxford: Oxford University Press, 2000.

Bach's Musical Universe: The Composer and His Work, New York: W.W. Norton, 2020.

Young, Percy M., *The Bachs, 1500–1800*, London: J.M. Dent & Sons, 1970.

BACH'S INFLUENCE

Applegate, Celia, *Bach in Berlin: Nation and Culture in Mendelssohn's Revival of the St. Matthew Passion*, Ithaca: Cornell University Press, 2005.

Blume, Friedrich, "Bach in the Romantic Era", *The Musical Quarterly*, 50/3 (1964), pp. 290–306.

Brown, Marshall, "Mozart, Bach and Musical Abjection", *The Musical Quarterly*, 83/4 (1999), pp. 509–35.

Buch, Laura (ed.), *Bach Perspectives, Vol. 13: Bach Reworked*, Champagne: University of Illinois Press, 2000.

Dirst, Mathew, *Engaging Bach: The Keyboard Legacy from Marpurg to Mendelssohn*, Cambridge: Cambridge University Press, 2012.

Domling, Wolfgang and Barbara Schwendoweirs (eds), *Bach: Life, Times, Influence,* New Haven: Yale University Press, 1984.

Einstein, Alfred, *Music in the Romantic Era*, New York: W.W. Norton, 1947.

Elie, Paul, *Reinventing Bach*, London: Union Books, 2013.

Elste, Martin, *Meilensteine der Bach-Interpretation 1750–2000*, Stuttgart and Weimar: J.B. Metzler, 2000.

Erickson, Raymond (ed.), *The Worlds of Johann Sebastian Bach*, New York: Amadeus Press, 2009.

Finscher, Ludwig, "Bach in the Eighteenth-Century", in Don O. Franklin (ed.), *Bach Studies*, Cambridge: Cambridge University Press, 1989, pp. 281–96.

Heinemann, Michael and Hans-Joachim Hinrichsen (eds), *Bach und die Nachwelt, Vol. 1, 1750–1850; Vol. 2, 1850–1900; Vol. 3, 1900–1950; Vol. 4, 1950–2000*, Laaber: Laaber Verlag, 1997–2002.

Herz, Gerhard, "Johann Sebastian Bach in the Age of Rationalism and Early

305

Romanticism", in *Essays on J.S. Bach*, Ann Abor: UMI Research Press, 1985.

Hindemith, Paul, *Johann Sebastian Bach: Heritage and Obligation*, New Haven: Yale University Press, 1952.

Hinrichson, Max, "Compositions Based on the Motive B-A-C-H", in *Hinrichson's Musical Yearbook 7*, London: Hinrichson Edition, 1952, pp. 379–81.

Kanwischer, Alfred, *From Bach's Goldberg to Beethoven's Diabelli: Influence and Independence,* Lanham, MD: Rowman & Littlefield, 2014.

Kirkendale, Warren, *Fugue and Fugato in Rococo and Classical Chamber Music*, Durham, NC: Duke University Press, 1979.

Kreinin, Yulia, "Choosing an Influence, or Bach the Inexhaustible: The Heterophony of Twentieth-Century Composers", *Israel Studies in Musicology*, 12 (2016).

Marissen, Michael (ed.), *Bach Perspectives 3: Creative Responses to Bach from Mozart to Hindemith,* Lincoln, NB: University of Nebraska Press, 1998.

Schoenberg, Arnold, *Style and Idea*, New York: Philosophical Library, 1950.

Schultz, Hans-Joachim, "Bach in the Early Twenty-First Century", in Raymond Erickson (ed.), *The Worlds of Johann Sebastian Bach*, New York: Amadeus Press, 2000.

Stinson, Russell, *The Reception of Bach's Organ Works from Mendelssohn to Brahms*, New York: Oxford University Press, 2006. *Bach's Legacy: The Music as Heard by Later Masters*, Oxford: Oxford University Press, 2020.

Tomita, Yo, "Bach Reception in Pre-Classical Vienna: Baron van Swieten's Circle Edits the 'Well-Tempered Clavier' II", *Music and Letters*, 81/3 (2000), pp. 364–91.

COMPOSERS AFTER BACH

Alegant, Brian, *The Twelve-Tone Music of Luigi Dallapiccola*, Rochester, NY: University of Rochester Press, 2010.

Barham, Jeremy (ed)., *The Cambridge Companion to Mahler*, Cambridge: Cambridge University Press, 2007.

Beaumont, Antony, *Busoni the Composer*, London: Faber & Faber, 1985.

Bittmann, Antonius, *Max Reger and Historicist Modernism*, Baden-Baden: Koerner, 2004.

Blockker, Roy, *The Symphonies of Dmitri Shostakovich*, London: The Tantivy Press, 1979.

Boss, J., *Schoenberg's Twelve-Tone Music: Symmetry and the Musical Ideas*: Cambridge: Cambridge University Press, 2014.

Cantoni, Angelo, *La référence à Bach dans les oeuvres néo-classique de Stravinsky*, Hildesheim: Georg Olms, 1998.

Chernaik, Judith, *Schumann, The Faces and the Masks*, New York: Alfred A. Knopf, 2018.

Cooper, Martin, *Beethoven: The Last Decade 1817–1827*, Oxford: Oxford University Press, 1970.

Cross, Jonathan, *The Cambridge Companion to Stravinsky*, Cambridge: Cambridge University Press, 2003.

Dalhaus, Carl, "Wagner und Bach", in *Klassische und Romantische Musikästhetik*, Laaber: Laaber Verlag, 1988, pp. 440–58.

Daverio, John, *Robert Schumann: Herald of a "New Poetic Age"*, New York: Oxford University Press, 1997.

Einstein, Alfred, *Mozart, His Character, His Work*, London: Cassell, 1961.

Evans, Peter, *The Music of Benjamin Britten*, Oxford: Clarendon Press, 1996.

Frisch, Walter, *Brahms: The Four Symphonies*, New York: Schirmer Books, 1996.

Gillies, Malcolm (ed.), *The Bartók Companion*, London: Faber & Faber, 1993.

Gramit, David (ed.), *Beyond the 'Art of Finger Dexterity': Reassessing Carl Czerny*, Rochester, NY: University of Rochester Press, 2008.

Gutman, Robert, W., *Richard Wagner: The Man, His Mind and His Music*, Harmondsworth: Penguin Books, 1971.

Heile, Björn, *The Music of Mauricio Kagel*, Farnham: Ashgate, 2006.

Henderson, Lyn, "Shostakovich and the Passacaglia: Old Grounds or New", *The Musical Times*, 141/1870 (2000), pp. 53–60.

Hillier, Paul, *Arvo Pärt*, Oxford: Oxford University Press, 1997.

Ivashkin, Alexander, *A Schnittke Reader*, Bloomington, IN: Indiana University Press, 2002.

Johnson, Lee, "The 'Haunted' Shostakovich and the Co-Presence of Bach", *Tempo*, 63/249 (July 2009), pp. 41–50.

Johnson, Robert Sherlaw, *Messiaen*, London: Omnibus, 2008.

Kendall, Raymond, "Brahms's Knowledge of Bach's Music", *Papers of the American Musicological Society* (1941), pp. 50–6.

Kerman, Joseph, *The Beethoven Quartets*, London: Oxford University Press, 1975.

King, A. Hyatt, "Mozart's Counterpoint: Its Growth and Significance", *Music & Letters*, 26/1 (1945), pp. 12–20.

Kregor, Jonathan, *Liszt as Transcriber*, Cambridge: Cambridge University Press, 2010.

Lee, Meebae, "Schumann's Romantic Transformation of Fugue: 'Fugegeschichte', the *Well-Tempered Clavier*, and *Vier Fugen* Op. 72", *Acta Musicologica*, 86/1 (2014), pp. 75–99.

Lockwood, Lewis, *Beethoven: The Music and the Life*, New York: W.W. Norton, 2003.

MacDonald, Malcolm, *The Dent Master Musicians, Brahms*, London: J.M. Dent & Sons, 1990.
Schoenberg, the Master Musician Series, Oxford and New York: Oxford University Press, 2009.

Machlis, Joseph, *Introduction to Contemporary Music*, London: J.M. Dent & Sons, 1980.

Marshall, Robert L., *Bach and Mozart: Essays on the Enigma of Genius*, Rochester, NY: Eastman Studies in Music, 2019.

Mazullo, Mark, *Shostakovich's Preludes and Fugues: Context, Style, Performance*, New Haven and London: Yale University Press, 2010.

Minturn, Neil, *The Music of Prokofiev*, New Haven: Yale University Press, 1997.

Near, John Richard, *The Life and Work of Charles-Marie Widor*, Boston: Boston University Press, 1985.

Newman, Ernst, *The Wagner Operas*, New York: Alfred A. Knopf, 1984.

Pople, Anthony, *Berg Violin Concerto*, Cambridge: Cambridge University Press, 1991.

Quinn, Peter, "Out with the Old and in with the New: Arvo Pärt's 'Credo'", *Tempo*, 211 (2000), pp. 16–20.

Raport, Paul (ed.), *Sorabji, A Critical Celebration*, Aldershot: Scolar Press, 1992.

Reed, John, *Schubert: The Final Years*, London: Faber & Faber, 1972.

Samson, Jim, *The Music of Chopin*, London: Routledge & Kegan Paul, 1985.

Solomon, Maynard, *Late Beethoven: Music, Thought, Imagination,* Berkeley: University of California Press, 2003.

Spratt, Geoffrey K., *The Music of Arthur Honegger*, Cork: Cork University Press, 1987.

Tarasti, Eero, *Heitor Villa-Lobos: The Life and Works 1887–1959*, Jefferson, NC: McFarland, 1995.

Todd, R. Larry, *Mendelssohn: A Life in Music*, New York: Oxford University Press, 2003.

Vallas, Léon, *César Franck*, Westport, CT: Greenwood Press, 1973.

Walsh, Stephen, *The Music of Stravinsky*, Oxford: Clarendon Press, 1993.

Watson, Derek, *The Master Musicians: Liszt*, London: J.M. Dent, 1989.

Zenk, Martin, "Tradition as Authority and Provocation: Anton Webern's Confrontation with Johann Sebastian Bach", in Don O. Franklin (ed.), *Bach Studies*, Cambridge: Cambridge University Press, 1989, pp. 297–322.

INDEX OF WORKS BY BACH

ORGAN MUSIC

HARPSICHORD MUSIC

INDEX OF WORKS BY COMPOSERS & MUSICIANS AFTER BACH